CURRENT ISSUES
IN LAW AND RELIGION

EDITOR A. KEITH THOMPSON

SHEPHERD
STREET PRESS

Published in 2021 by Connor Court Publishing Pty Ltd under the imprint Shepherd Street Press.

Shepherd Street Press is an imprint of Connor Court Publishing and The School of Law, The University of Notre Dame Australia, Broadway.

Shepherd Street Press Editorial Executive:

Michael Quinlan
A. Keith Thompson
Iain T. Benson

Connor Court Publishing Pty Ltd
PO Box 7257
Redland Bay QLD 4165
sales@connorcourt.com
www.connorcourtpublishing.com.au
Phone 0497-900-685

Printed in Australia

ISBN: 9781922449450

Front Cover Image: Title: Murder of David van der Leyen and Levina Ghyselins, Ghent, 1554] / I. Luyken Abstract/medium: 1 print : engraving.
Date 1685, Source, Library of Congress: Wikipedia Commons

Peer Review Policy
This book has been prepared in compliance with the Peer Review Policy of the Shepherd Street Press which provides for double blind peer review by at least two expert reviewers.

The editor also wishes to acknowledge the assistance he has received from Alex Du Maurier, a final year Honours student. Among other tasks, Alex has assisted in ensuring compliance with the fourth edition of the Australian Guide to Legal Citation.

TABLE OF CONTENTS

INTRODUCTION

One of our specialisations in the Sydney School of Law at The University of Notre Dame Australia is research into the nature and importance of freedom of conscience and the closely related freedom to manifest one's religious belief in everyday life.

While these freedoms are said to be protected by our common law heritage in Australia, the nature of the freedoms which the common law protects are not always clear even after they have been litigated. Thus, most lovers of liberty have celebrated the additional clarity that has come to law and religion studies since the *Universal Declaration of Human Rights* and its descendent *Covenants* lighted upon the world in 1948 following the end of World War II. But that understanding continues to evolve.

While it has been philosophically arguable that human dignity is predicated upon freedom of thought for more than 2000 years, it is still not clear whether absolute freedom of thought exists only in the mind (the *forum internum*), or whether some manifestations of religious belief are also absolutely protected in law. That question arises because it is said that unfettered freedom of thought is meaningless if thought can never be projected from the mind into real life (the *forum externum*) without legal constraint. Examples which identify this problem quite simply include the Old Testament prophet Daniel's secret prayer that was evidently observed on Babylonian CCTV, and Saint Thomas More's unwillingness to swear allegiance to King Henry VIII's *Act of Succession* passed in 1534.

Though our *Australian Constitution* does not reference the inviolability of human conscience directly, it does recognise that old chestnut implicitly when it provides the constitutional assurance that "no religious test shall be required as a qualification for any office or public trust under the Commonwealth." That much seems to accept that the *Act of Succession* in 1534 presents as an example of legislative overreach. But where should we draw the line between the inviolable commitments human beings make in conscience and the way they live out those commitments in private and public life?

The Royal Commission into Institutional Responses to Child Sexual Abuse has suggested that Religious Confession Privilege can be appropriately abrogated by law passed in accordance with the *International Covenant on Civil and Political Rights 1966* (the *ICCPR*) because that is necessary to protect the fundamental rights and freedoms of children. Laying aside the status of the *ICCPR* in Australian law, and the dubious question of the necessity of such a change in the law — would not a law which intruded into conscience offend the *forum internum* in breach of the very *ICCPR* provisions which the Royal Commission cited in justification? How could the esteemed Commissioner misunderstand that expression of what is at the core of human rights and dignity?

The Covid-19 pandemic has raised many further questions about when it is necessary to limit the free exercise of religion. For example, medical science has been said to justify the limitation of gatherings where the virus might spread in the air when people express themselves with vigour — as for example, when they shout out as fans at sports events or sing with joy in churches. But does approval of social gatherings in bars and clubs show that it is unnecessary to prohibit religious worship when restrictions on singing observed by mask-wearing and socially distanced worshippers could reasonably achieve the medical objectives?

The same-sex marriage plebiscite and subsequent Ruddock Review drew attention to the lack of legal protection for the free exercise of religion in Australia despite the use of those words in the *Australian*

Constitution. But does or should freedom of religion trump other anti-discrimination norms? And if not, how should judges balance rights that appear to compete when the judges are not competent to adjudicate the issues of belief and practice that such conflicts sometimes expose? Should parents be allowed to educate their children in private ethos schools of their choice as 35% of Australian parents choose to do? Or should such ethos schools be forced to avoid all religious teaching and to enrol children whose families want to eliminate all religious expression from the public square?

These and many other contemporary law and religion issues arise in our classes each semester at Notre Dame. It is therefore not surprising that some of our research students choose to write about them when they can select their own research topics. That is the watershed from which these five chapters flow. While they do not develop a single theme, they are all about law and religion issues in 21st century western society.

Alana Rafter has written about the harm principle in modern international jurisprudence. She notes Thomas Jefferson's defence of religious freedom with the aphorism that we ought not prohibit or even regulate that which does not 'pick [our] pocket or break [our] leg'. But as John Stuart Mill predicted 50 years later, western government has not been prepared to accept Jefferson's 'keep out' mandate. Harm has been enlarged, but should it be extended so as to prevent every perceived affront to human dignity?

There is a sense in which Jon Powy's chapter picks up Alana's idea. Should law proscribe religious expression that merely offends the sensibilities of non-believers as Martine Delaney said when she complained about the *Don't Mess with Marriage* booklet which Archbishop Julian Porteous had distributed to all families with children attending Catholic schools in Tasmania? Or should there still be some safe space where religious believers can speak freely without proscription?

Adjunct Senior Lecturer Gil Tabucanon takes us to the international plight of Baha'i believers in Iran where their faith is not one of those recognised in that country's *Constitution*. Is the 'othering' of those believers justified in a nation that ratified the *ICCPR* in 1975 because the new *Constitution* does not recognise the Baha'i faith? Gil does not raise the plight of the Rohinga Muslims in Myanmar, the Jehovah's Witnesses in Russia or the Uighur Muslims in China. But his questions are completely relevant to those believers and to many more — and what of Muslim women in Australia who are regularly vilified and even physically assaulted because they wear their headscarves as an outward manifestation of their covenant to live lives of personal virtue?

Associate Professor Neil Foster from the University of Newcastle is a friend of Notre Dame and takes us on a rather different journey. Outside of his day job, Neil is an unashamedly active evangelical Christian who is often asked how believers should respond when changes in the law and social consciousness seem to unpick Christian expectations about even the fabric of that way of life. Though he normally responds to those questions on his blog (<https://lawandreligionaustralia.blog/about/>), here he walks us through the questions which arise when new gender identity laws seem to conflict with more established freedoms. This paper is a more complete version of an address originally presented at the Holy Cross Church at Templestowe in Melbourne just before the Covid crisis unfolded.

My own piece seems somewhat esoteric by comparison since I have not used flesh and blood examples to illustrate my points. But I may raise some eyebrows when I suggest that religious believers in Australia, Singapore and the United States are treated almost identically despite the failure of all three countries to implement the international law standards of the *ICCPR* into their domestic law. Does that mean that implementing the *ICCPR* would not add value in Australia despite the commitment of our federal government to do so in 1980? Or does it mean that we still have a long way to go until we meet international standards when it comes to religious liberty?

These papers — each of which has been through double blind academic peer review — will not answer all the questions of any reader; indeed, they are more likely to provoke others. But that is the point of this first in what we hope will become a series — a collection of thoughtful inquiries into the nature of contemporary law and whether it responds adequately to questions raised by our human condition as the new millennium begins to unfold.

Professor A. Keith Thompson
Associate Dean, Sydney School of Law
The University of Notre Dame Australia
29-35 Shepherd Street
Chippendale, NSW, 2008
25 October 2020

1

INTANGIBLE HARM AND THE FORUM INTERNUM

ALANA ANNE RAFTER

ABSTRACT

International human rights instruments divide protection of religious liberty into private and public aspects. The protection is non-derogable. Carolyn Evans and Paul M Taylor have pointed out that the existing limits in the *ICCPR* and *Convention* do not acknowledge or respond to the fact that any meaningful non-derogable version of the private component (the *forum internum*) requires that eligible grounds of limitation concerning the public component (the *forum externum*) are suitably confined so as to avoid restriction of any sort upon the *forum internum*.

At an international level, the United Nations Human Rights Committee and the European Court of Human Rights have treated the separation between *forum internum* and *forum externum* as 'self-evident'. However, in practice, the *forum internum* interacts with the *forum externum*. At a domestic level, the non-derogable status of the *forum internum* is tested in the context of discrimination claims on the basis of sexual orientation. This paper considers the example of *Lee v Ashers*, a Christian baker that declined to make a cake supporting gay marriage, and its treatment at first instance through to the Supreme Court of the United Kingdom.

The current guarantee of inviolable protection for the *forum internum* is empty without clearer definition of the scope of recognition, guidelines for responding to claims of violation, and consistency of approach across both international and domestic jurisdictions.

INTRODUCTION

The *International Covenant on Civil and Political Rights* ('*ICCPR*')[1] and the *European Convention on Human Rights* ('*Convention*')[2] divide protection of religious liberty into private and public aspects:

- The private component primarily concerns freedom of thought, conscience and religion (the *forum internum*).[3] It is described as non-derogable and is not subject to express limitation.[4]

- The public component concerns the manifestation of religion or belief (the *forum externum*).[5] The stated limits on the *forum externum* in the *ICCPR* and *Convention* are 'public safety, order, health, or morals or the fundamental rights and freedoms of others'.[6]

---

1   *International Covenant on Civil and Political Rights*, opened for signature 16 December 1966, 999 UNTS 171 (entered into force 23 March 1976) ('*ICCPR*').

2   *European Convention for the Protection of Human Rights and Fundamental Freedoms*, opened for signature 4 November 1950, 213 UNTS 221 (entered into force 3 September 1953) ('*Convention*').

3   Malcolm D Evans, *Manual on the Wearing of Religious Symbols in Public Areas* (Martinus Nijhoff Publishers, 2008) 8–9; *ICCPR* (n 1) art 18(1); *Convention* (n 2) art 9(1). Both the *Convention* and *ICCPR* also recognise the right to manifestation of religion applies to public and private manifestation. The *Convention* states, 'either alone or in community with others and in public or private': at art 9(1). The *ICCPR* states, 'either individually or in community with others and in public or private': at art 18(1). However, the *ICCPR* also recognises the right to freely choose religion and not be subject to coercion: at art 18(3).

4   Carolyn Evans, *Legal Protection of Religious Freedom in Australia* (Federation Press, 2012) 33; Human Rights Committee, *General Comment No 22: Article 18 (Freedom of Thought, Conscience or Religion)*, 48th sess, UN Doc CCPR/C/21/Rev.1/Add.4 (30 July 1993) [1] ('*General Comment 22*').

5   Malcolm D Evans (n 3) 8–9.

6   *ICCPR* (n 1) art 18.

Carolyn Evans and Paul M Taylor have pointed out that the existing limits in the *ICCPR* and *Convention* do not acknowledge or respond to the fact that any meaningful non-derogable version of the *forum internum* requires that eligible grounds of limitation concerning the *forum externum* are suitably confined so as to avoid restriction of any sort upon the *forum internum*.[7] That overlap is what this paper is about.

The United Nations Human Rights Committee (the 'HRC') and the European Court of Human Rights (the 'ECHR') have treated the separation between *forum internum* and *forum externum* as 'self-evident'.[8] This is demonstrated through the repeated justification of state law, which interfered with the manifestation of religion, and the consequential impact upon the *forum internum*, which was treated very lightly, if it was acknowledged at all.[9] The HRC and ECHR have both recognised the importance of the *forum internum* but have failed to define the scope of *forum internum* protection.

This paper considers the protection afforded to the *forum internum* at both international and domestic levels. At an international level,

---

7   Carolyn Evans, *Freedom of Religion under the European Convention on Human Rights* (Oxford University Press, 2001) 67–102, 204–9; Paul M Taylor, *Freedom of Religion: UN and European Human Rights Law and Practice* (Cambridge University Press, 2005) 115–202; Paul M Taylor, *A Commentary on the International Covenant on Civil and Political Rights: The UN Human Rights Committee's Monitoring of ICCPR Rights* (Cambridge University Press, 2020) 505–13, 534–7.

8   Carolyn Evans, *Freedom of Religion under the European Convention on Human Rights* (n 7) 73.

9   See, eg, *Kokkinakis v Greece* (1993) 17 EHRR 397 ('*Kokkinakis*'), the ECHR recognised proselytism as relevant to both belief and manifestation but judicial commentary was brief; *Bhinder v Canada*, 37th sess, UN Doc CCPR/C/37/D/208/1986 (9 November 1989), the HRC debated the right to manifest religion and held no article of the *ICCPR* had been contravened by the State; *SAS v France* (2015) 60 EHRR 11, focused on manifestation of belief but acknowledged that genuineness of belief was an irrelevant consideration. See also, evidence at a domestic level, *Lee v Ashers Baking Co Ltd* [2015] NICty 2 ('*Lee v Ashers [No 1]*'), a reliance upon religious belief was disregarded as an acceptable motivation for conduct; *Elane Photography LLC v Willock*, 309 P.3d 53 (NM 2013) ('*Elane Photography*'), state law did not require accommodation of religious belief within a commercial setting.

the HRC and ECHR decisions in *Bhinder v Canada*[10] and *SAS v France*[11] are assessed. At a domestic level, the Northern Ireland and New Mexico competing rights claims in *Lee v Ashers*[12] and *Elane Photography*[13] are also considered. The contrast within both international and domestic jurisdictions demonstrate the breadth of the problem that stems from an undefined scope of *forum internum* protection. That problem is explored in the following parts.

The first part explores harm. It explains the development of harm from the classic approach of Thomas Jefferson to John Stuart Mill, to the modern approach of Patrick Devlin and Jeremy Waldron. It showcases the diversity of the concept of harm and how it can be used to justify state interference with individual liberty. This part also explains that harm is no longer limited to objectively determinable injury. That is, intangible harms have been found to activate the limitations in the *ICCPR* and *Convention*.

The second part considers harm under the *ICCPR* and *Convention*. It sets out the limitation clauses of both instruments. It explores the nature of harm addressed by the *ICCPR* and *Convention*. It concludes that while no limitation is extended to the *forum internum*, that omission does not ensure that unconditional protection is afforded.

The third part defines the term 'non-derogable' and explores the source of the presumption of non-derogability. It confirms that classifying a liberty as non-derogable provides no guarantee of protection and suggests that although the *forum internum* has been recognised as a fundamental liberty in international human rights instruments, it has been afforded minimal protection in domestic law in practice.

---

10   *Bhinder v Canada* (n 9).
11   (2015) 60 EHRR 11.
12   *Lee v Ashers [No 1]* (n 9); *Lee v Ashers Baking Co Ltd* [2016] NICA 39 ('*Lee v Ashers [No 2]*'); *Lee v Ashers Baking Co Ltd* [2018] UKSC 49 ('*Lee v Ashers [No 3]*'). Collectively, the three decisions shall be referred to as '*Lee v Ashers*'.
13   *Elane Photography* (n 9).

The fourth part challenges the practicality of upholding the non-derogability of the *forum internum*, while allowing justifiable limitations upon the *forum externum*. It showcases the overlap between the two forums, demonstrates a consistent disregard for consideration of the potential derogation of the *forum internum*, particularly in instances of competing individual rights such as sexual orientation and religious belief. This is explored at both international and domestic levels. While the development of law is inconsistent across jurisdictions, the recent decision of the United Kingdom Supreme Court in *Lee v Ashers Baking Co Ltd* ('*Lee v Ashers [No 3]*'),[14] highlights the important role the judiciary plays in the development of this area.

This paper concludes the *forum internum* is susceptible to intangible harm and that the resulting approach at law is presently, for the most part, unsatisfactory. Recognising the right as fundamental and describing the liberty as inviolable or classifying the liberty as non-derogable does not provide protection. It only promotes the ideal that the *forum internum* should not be diluted by the concept of harm. In practice, the *forum internum* interacts with the *forum externum*. Complete protection of the *forum internum* requires that additional protection be provided to the *forum externum* when the two forums overlap. The current guarantee of inviolable protection for the *forum internum* is empty without clearer definition of the scope of recognition, guidelines for responding to claims of violation, and consistency of approach across both international and domestic jurisdictions.

---

14   *Lee v Ashers [No 3]* (n 12).

PART I: WHAT IS THE NATURE OF HARM?

A   *The Classic Approach*

The classic approach to harm concerns the right of citizens to be free from injurious conduct and the limits of state intervention. Thomas Jefferson in *Notes on the State of Virginia* (1781) argued: 'The legitimate powers of government extend to such acts only as are injurious to others. But it does me no injury for my neighbor to say there are twenty Gods, or no God. It neither picks my pocket nor breaks my leg'.[15] His words encapsulate the fundamental liberty of freedom of thought, conscience and religion. The *forum internum* or the personal thought processes of one individual cannot directly injure another. This representation echoes the idiom 'to each his own' – everyone may not agree upon a singular set of beliefs, but everyone is entitled to believe what they believe. This reduction of liberty to an approach to harm was also reflected in the *Declaration of the Rights of Man and Citizen* (France, August 1789):

> Liberty consists in the power to do anything that does not injure others; accordingly, the exercise of the rights of each man has no limits except those that secure the enjoyment of these same rights to the other members of society. These limits can be determined only by law.[16]

The consistent justification for state intervention is injury to another. John Stuart Mill upheld this as the basis for his harm principle in *On Liberty* (1859).[17] He stressed '[t]hat the only purpose for which power can be rightfully exercised over any member of a civilised community, against his will, is to prevent harm to others'.[18] The impetus was self-protection.[19] Despite being influenced by utilitarian theory, Mill rejected consideration of the perceived betterment or happiness of

---

15   Thomas Jefferson, *Notes on the State of Virginia* (J W Randolf, 1853) 170.

16   *Declaration of the Right of Man and Citizen* (France), 26 August 1789, art 4.

17   Simon Shaw-Miller (ed), *On Liberty: John Stuart Mill* (Yale University Press, 2003).

18   Ibid 80.

19   Ibid.

an individual as a justifiable basis for deterring or compelling action. His conception was not dependent upon the enforcement of social good.[20] In contrast, if an individual's actions were demonstrated as 'calculated to produce evil to some one else', only in that instance would the state be justified in acting to prevent harm to another.[21] Mill's conception of harm emphasised the importance of individual liberty; it is absolute to the extent an individual's conduct concerns himself: 'over his own body and mind, the individual is sovereign'.[22]

Mill also argued that a society that did not uphold the individual liberties of conscience, the liberty of 'tastes and pursuits' and the 'freedom to unite' – in circumstances that did not harm or seek to harm others – was not a free society:

> No society in which these liberties are not, on the whole, respected, is free, whatever may be its form of government; and none is completely free in which they do not exist absolute and unqualified ... Mankind are greater gainers by suffering each other to live as seems good to themselves, than by compelling each to live as seems good to the rest.[23]

Despite his emphatic stance on individual liberty, Mill also recognised the necessity and inevitability of state interference: 'every one who receives the protection of society owes a return benefit, and the fact of living in society renders it indispensable that each should be bound to observe a certain line of conduct towards the rest'.[24] However, that recognition was not unqualified. Mill noted a potential for authorities 'to stretch unduly the powers of society over the individual, both by the force of opinion and even by that of legislation'.[25] He also predicted, 'encroachment is not one of the evils which tend spontaneously to disappear, but, on the contrary, to grow more and more formidable'.[26] This paper explores

---

20   Ibid 80–1.
21   Ibid.
22   Ibid.
23   Ibid 83.
24   Ibid 139.
25   Ibid 84.
26   Ibid.

Mill's prediction by challenging the current construction of religious liberty law and its impact upon the *forum internum*.

B   The 20*th* Century Approach

Patrick Devlin, in *The Enforcement of Morals* (1968), criticised the approach of Mill: '[he failed] to distinguish sufficiently between freedom of thought and freedom of action'.[27] Mill focused upon injury that could be seen and quantified, whether it was caused by an act or omission.[28] In the 20th century Devlin broadened the discussion of justifiable state intervention to include tangible and intangible harm. His approach noted the relationship between *forum internum* and *forum externum* but was dependent upon the existence and recognition of human morals. 'Tangible harm' was described as damage caused to society by immoral activity. 'Intangible harm' included 'moral belief'.[29]   Moral belief referred to the individual *forum internum*. Devlin explained that a lack of moral belief could contribute to immoral activity (the *forum externum*). Equally, immoral activity could promote disbelief in the accepted public morality. [30] He identified public morality as 'the common belief in right and wrong'.[31] This 'common belief' was 'the intangible property of society'.[32] He clarified that no intangible harm was inflicted upon belief in the common good of society if the immoral conduct was committed with the knowledge that it is vicious and sinful. However, when an immoral belief was upheld as good, and combined with immoral conduct, it promoted disbelief. He explained it was this disbelief that could lead to a shift in public morality.[33] A modern example of a shift in public morality is the change of approach to

---

27   Patrick Devlin, *The Enforcement of Morals* (Oxford University Press, 1968) 122.
28   See generally Shaw-Miller (n 17) 139–55.
29   Devlin (n 27) 113–4.
30   Ibid.
31   Ibid 114.
32   Ibid.
33   Ibid 113–4.

homosexuality in law over the 20th and 21st century.

Devlin's approach required a determination of the appropriate scope of public morality. For example, if homosexuality fell outside the belief of what was deemed good in a society, it was against the public morality: it was a vice. Hence, Devlin stated that society had a right, and perhaps even a duty, to make laws criminalising homosexual acts. He justified his theory by noting that Mill's harm principle did not adequately describe English law.[34] In contrast, there was evidence that demonstrated the influence of morality upon law making: 'Parliament added incest and homosexual offences to the list of crimes without inquiring what harm they did to the community if they were committed in private; it was enough that they were morally wrong'.[35] He stressed, if the state did not intervene 'society as a whole is impoverished, for such a man puts less than his share into the common well-being'.[36] Although Devlin was able to provide evidence of the influence of morality, HLA Hart in *Law, Liberty and Morality* (1963), argued that there was little evidence to support 'the theory that those who deviate from conventional sexual morality are in other ways hostile to society'.[37] Hart did not deny the relevance and influence of morality on law but he saw no basis for accepting Devlin's unfounded 'assumption' that:

> all morality – sexual morality with the morality that forbids acts injurious to other such as killing, stealing and dishonesty – forms a single seamless web, so that those who deviate from any part are likely or perhaps bound to deviate from the whole.[38]

Hart interpreted Devlin's approach as supporting the 'absurd' conclusion that a change in society's morality 'is tantamount to the

---

34   Ibid 86–7.
35   Ibid.
36   Ibid 104.
37   HLA Hart, 'Law, Liberty, and Morality' in D Don Welch (ed), *Law and Morality* (Fortress Press, 1987) 43, 49.
38   Ibid.

destruction of a society'.[39] He criticised this conclusion as there was no 'evidence that any deviations from a society's shared morality threatens its existence.'[40]

Hart agreed with Mill's 'emphatic' stance on interference with liberty: '[t]hat the only purpose for which power can be rightfully exercised ... is to prevent harm to others'.[41] Laws concerning sexual morality were arbitrarily passed with no evidence of harm to another. Hart did not accept Devlin's argument of intangible harm.[42]

The idea of intangible harm was also impliedly addressed in *Toonen v Australia*.[43] The application challenged ss 122 and 123 of the *Criminal Code Act 1924* (Tas). Section 123 provided: 'Any person who has sexual intercourse with any person against the order of nature ... is guilty of a crime'.[44] That former Tasmanian law represented a departure from the classic approach to harm to the enforcement of public morality. To declare sodomy illegal was to establish a crime based on a perception of public morality (i.e. sodomy was a vice that impoverished society).[45] The applicant claimed that the continued existence of the law had a 'profound and harmful impact on many people in Tasmania, ... [and fuelled the] discrimination and harassment of, and violence against, the homosexual community of Tasmania'.[46] The HRC held that the applicant:

> had made reasonable efforts to demonstrate that the threat of enforcement and the persuasive impact of the continued existence of these provisions on administrative practices and public opinion had affected him and *continued to affect him personally*.[47]

---

39   Ibid.
40   Ibid.
41   Shaw-Miller (n 17) 80.
42   Devlin (n 27) 104–14.
43   *Toonen v Australia*, 50th sess, UN Doc CCPR/C/50/D/488/1992 (31 March 1994).
44   *Criminal Code Act 1924* (Tas) s 123, later repealed by *Criminal Code Amendment Act 1997* (Tas).
45   See Devlin (n 27) 104.
46   *Toonen v Australia* (n 43) [2.7].
47   Ibid [5.1] (emphasis added).

It was sufficient that the applicant demonstrated a strong suggestion of 'unlawful attacks on the honour and the reputation of the individuals concerned'.[48] The HRC found in the applicant's favour despite no evidence of tangible harm.

The approach of the HRC represents a departure from Devlin's theory of sexual morality. However, Devlin's acknowledgment of intangible harm, when considered outside of morality, ironically supports the recognition and the vulnerability of secular individual beliefs (regardless of moral content). Similarly, his stance on public morality can support the removal of laws discriminating against sexual morality – if it is accepted the majority of society now deem such laws immoral.

These examples demonstrate that in the 20th century western society decided that indirect harm should also be an exception to human rights norms. Harm was no longer limited to quantifiable injury. The definition had expanded. However, a problem remained: the need to determine limits upon intangible forms. This difficulty became prominent in the 21st century with discussion surrounding the appropriateness of offence and hate speech laws.

C   The 21st Century Approach

Jeremy Waldron in *The Harm in Hate Speech* built upon the theories of his classic and modern contemporaries and considered the relevance of individual dignity and social standing in defining harm.[49] Waldron observed the increasing encroachment of organised government upon 'dignity and individuality'[50] – a threat predicted by Mill in 1859.[51] However, his focus was upon emphasising the

---

48   Ibid [3.1].
49   Jeremy Waldron, *The Harm in Hate Speech* (UBC Press, 2000) 4–14.
50   Ibid 26.
51   Shaw-Miller (n 17) 84.

intangible harm of hate speech upon individuals.[52] He argued the impact was an assault on individual dignity. Hence, Waldron concluded the aim of any implemented hate speech law should be the protection of dignity.[53] However, he did not support prevention of all forms of intangible harm. He was emphatic that hate speech laws should not incorporate offence: '[p]rotecting people's feelings against offence is not an appropriate objective for the law'.[54] An example of such protection appears in s 18C of Australia's *Racial Discrimination Act 1975* (Cth) ('*RDA*'), which reads:

(1) It is unlawful for a person to do an act, otherwise than in private, if:

   a)   the act is reasonably likely, in all the circumstances, to offend, insult, humiliate or intimidate another person or a group of people; and

   b)   the act is done because of the race, colour or national or ethnic origin of the other person or of some or all of the people in the group.[55]

In 2014, the proposed removal of 'offence' and 'insult' from the *RDA* sparked debate in Australia.[56] Chris Berg[57] recognised freedom of speech to be a 'fundamental liberty'.[58] He was in favour of the amendment and argued, '[b]eing prevented from expressing those [potentially offensive] thoughts is an attack on our individuality'.[59] In contrast, Marie Iskander[60] disagreed with the proposal. She argued, '[s 18C] plays a valuable role in protecting racial and ethnic minority

52   Waldron (n 49) 34–5.
53   Ibid 105.
54   Ibid 106.
55   *Racial Discrimination Act 1975* (Cth) s 18C ('RDA').
56   See Attorney-General's Department, 'Racial Discrimination Act' (Media Release, 25 March 2014), the draft amendments were titled 'Freedom of Speech (Repeal of S. 18C)'.
57   Chris Berg is a Senior Fellow at the Institute of Public Affairs ('IPA') in Melbourne, Australia. His experience with IPA includes being a researcher, writer and policy director. He was also the former editor of the *IPA Review*.
58   Chris Berg, 'Free Speech is Non-negotiable' (2014) 66(2) *IPA Review* 6, 7.
59   Ibid.
60   Marie Iskander was the editor of the Australian Indigenous Law Review ('AILR'), 2013–2015.

groups, such as Indigenous Australians, who are often the target of unnecessary offensive and insulting speech'.[61] The debate demanded the state prioritise either protecting citizens against intangible harm or protecting citizens' freedom of speech. It highlighted the tension that surrounded defining and protecting citizens against intangible harm. The proposal was eventually abandoned and the law remained unchanged.

In the context of religious liberty Waldron maintained that legislation to protect religious believers from offence could not work:

> Especially in a multifaith society, religion is an area where offense is always in the air. Each group's creed seems like an outrage to every other group: Christian trinitarianism seems like an affront to Jewish or Islamic monotheism, while Islam's relegation of Jesus to the status of a mere prophet, and Judaism's characterization of him as a deceiver, seem like affronts in the other direction. Even within faith communities, each person's attempt to grapple with diverse beliefs in the circumstances of modernity is likely to involve their saying things that seem blasphemous, heretical, irreverent, and offensive. I see no way around this. Persons and peoples have to be free to address the deep questions raised by religion the best way they can.[62]

He concluded, '[r]eligious freedom means nothing if it is not freedom to offend'.[63] Waldron's argument differentiating offence from hate speech was indicative of his belief that not all forms of interference with the *forum internum* amount to harm, and that only interference of a certain severity should require justification at law.[64] It can be inferred from Waldron's focus upon 'assault on dignity and the public good of assurance' that he recognised a form of intangible harm that could violate the *forum internum*.[65]

---

61   Marie Iskander, 'Balancing Freedoms and Creating a Fair Marketplace of Ideas: The Value of 18C of the Racial Discrimination Act' (2014) 9(10) *Indigenous Law Bulletin* 19, 19.

62   Waldron (n 51) 127.

63   Ibid 130.

64   Ibid 105–6.

65   Ibid 115.

Harm is a complex concept – academics can reduce it to physical injury or hypothesise about its unquantifiable nature. It is important to recognise that there are different approaches to assessing its nature. It is still developing. Harm is no longer considered limited to tangible and quantifiable injury, but it is still recognised as a basis for intervention by the state. Hence, the part of the *forum internum* the state needs to protect, and the part it can interfere with, needs to be defined. A discussion of the interconnectedness of harm and the *forum internum* must occur. The next part will consider the harm recognised at international law, and the limits it would impose upon state interference with religious liberty.

PART II: WHAT IS THE NATURE OF THE HARMS THAT THE *ICCPR* AND *CONVENTION* RECOGNISE ARE REASONABLE LIMITS ON THE FREEDOM OF MANIFESTATION OF RELIGION OR BELIEF?

A   *The Protection of Religious Liberty*

It is accepted that religious liberty is susceptible to interference by the state and individuals. However, both the *ICCPR* and *Convention* limit permissible state interference to the *forum externum*. State interference is only discussed in connection with freedom of manifestation and the scope of *forum internum* protection has never been confirmed. If the scope of the *forum internum* was confined to the 'right to maintain one's internal beliefs' then it would be difficult to derogate from.[66] Carolyn Evans suggested that ECHR might deem the line between *forum internum* and *forum externum* 'self-evident and needing little in the way of explanation'.[67] She argued that 'a more sophisticated definition of what the *forum internum* is' was required in order 'to explain in greater detail how it can be interfered

---

66   Carolyn Evans, *Freedom of Religion under the European Convention on Human Rights* (n 7) 74–9.
67   Ibid.

with'.[68] This will require recognition that 'there is a point where State coercion to force someone to act in a certain way is so severe that it interferes with belief as well as with manifestations'.[69] In other words, the courts must accept there is an overlap, a potential for 'subtle interference', and determine what impact this should have on application of the limitation upon manifestation.[70]

Both the *ICCPR* and *Convention* distinguish protection of the *forum internum* from the *forum externum*:

- *ICCPR* – art 18(1):

  Everyone shall have the right to freedom of thought, conscience and religion. This right shall include freedom to have or to adopt a religion or belief of his choice, and freedom, either individually or in community with others and in public or private, to manifest his religion or belief in worship, observance, practice and teaching.[71]

- *Convention* – art 9(1):

  Everyone has the right to freedom of thought, conscience and religion; this right includes freedom to change his religion or belief and freedom, either alone or in community with others and in public or private, to manifest his religion or belief, in worship, teaching, practice and observance.[72]

However, distinguishing between the two forums does not automatically represent a distinction between, or recognition of, tangible and intangible harm. Only the physical aspect of religious liberty, the right to manifest, is expressly limited and subject to interference by the state.[73] Carolyn Evans supports the need to recognise the impact of overlap.[74] She stated, 'the crucial question is

---

68   Ibid 205.
69   Ibid.
70   Ibid.
71   *ICCPR* (n 1) art 18(1).
72   *Convention* (n 2) art 9(1).
73   *ICCPR* (n 1) art 18(3); *Convention* (n 2) art 9(2).
74   Carolyn Evans, *Freedom of Religion under the European Convention on Human Rights*

the point at which an action by the State is so intrusive that it is held
to interfere, not merely with a person's right to manifest a religion,
but also with his or her right to have a religion or belief'.[75]

The next section explores the construction of the limitation clauses
in the *ICCPR* and *Convention*.

B   *The Limitation on Religious Liberty*

Both instruments express a limitation in similar terms, which are
extracted below:

- *ICCPR* – art 18(3):

    Freedom to manifest one's religion or beliefs may be subject
    only to such limitations as are prescribed by law and are
    necessary to protect public safety, order, health, or morals or
    the fundamental rights and freedoms of others.[76]

- *Convention* – art 9(2):

    Freedom to manifest one's religion or beliefs shall be subject
    only to such limitations as are prescribed by law and are
    necessary in a democratic society in the interests of public
    safety, for the protection of public order, health or morals,
    or for the protection of the rights and freedoms of others.[77]

The limitation embodies the classical approach to harm: '[the state
can intervene] to prevent harm to others'.[78] It acknowledges the
fact we live in community and that the actions of one individual
could potentially negatively interfere with another. Hence, it is
reasonable that 'each should be bound to observe a certain line of
conduct towards the rest'.[79] However, the breadth of the power to

---

    (n 7) 74–9.

75   Ibid 78.

76   *ICCPR* (n 1) art 18(3).

77   *Convention* (n 2) art 9(2).

78   Shaw-Miller (n 17) 80.

79   Ibid 139.

interfere and to 'legitimately' justify interference with individual liberty demonstrates the threat of encroachment that Mill predicted would only worsen over time.[80] The limitation is triggered by a manifestation that has an impact upon the public. However, the state must also demonstrate that the impact is at odds with the necessary protection of the public. Only then may it validly interfere with an individual's religious liberty.[81]

The HRC and ECHR have failed to explore the impact of this limitation upon the *forum internum* in any depth. The HRC stated that the limitation in art 18(3) does not extend to the *forum internum*.[82] The ECHR provided less commentary on the issue, but recognised the fundamental nature of the *forum internum* to individual liberty.[83] In *Kokkinakis*, the ECHR described 'freedom of thought, conscience and religion' as:

> one of the foundations of a 'democratic society' within the meaning of the *Convention*. It is, in its religious dimension, one of the most vital elements that go to make up the identity of believers and their conception of life, but it is also a precious asset for atheists, agnostics, sceptics and the unconcerned.[84]

Whilst the HRC and ECHR are in agreement that the *forum internum* is an important individual liberty worthy of protection, they have not explained how limitations upon the manifestation of religion, a qualified right subject to interference by the state, should be treated when it is shown that lawful forms of derogation upon the *forum externum* also interfere with the *forum internum,* which is supposed to be absolutely protected.

The realm of discussion is wide as both the *ICCPR* and *Convention* omit express recognition of any form of limitation upon the *forum*

---

80   Ibid 84.
81   *ICCPR* (n 1) art 18(3); *Convention* (n 2) art 9(2).
82   *General Comment 22* (n 4) [3].
83   *Kokkinakis* (n 9) [31].
84   Ibid.

internum. This construction could imply that the *forum internum* is passive and cannot cause interference, so that no limitation is necessary. Alternatively, it could also indicate that because the *forum internum* cannot be interfered with, no express limitation is required. Omitting a limitation does not confirm the inviolable nature of the *forum internum*. It simply leaves the construction of the liberty open for courts to define. But no court has yet recognised the indirect effects that limiting the *forum externum* can have on the *forum internum*, and then acted to protect the *forum internum* from such interference.

1 *Identifying the liberty which is the subject of the forum internum*

As earlier mentioned, the *forum internum* is the internal aspect of individual liberty.[85] It is also the first component of each article: 'the right to freedom of thought, conscience and religion'.[86] Mill identified individual conscience as necessarily 'absolute and unqualified' within a free society.[87] He described it as 'the inward domain of consciousness ... in the most comprehensive sense; liberty of thought and feeling; absolute freedom of opinion and sentiment on all subjects, practical or speculative, scientific, moral, or theological'.[88]

Carolyn Evans described the *forum internum* as the 'right of every person to formulate his or her own internal beliefs'.[89] However, competing arguments exist concerning the meaning of art 18 (*ICCPR*) and art 9 (*Convention*). Carolyn Evans attempted to determine why manifestation of 'thought and conscience' was excluded from the limitation upon 'religion or belief'. She questioned whether 'thought and conscience' were 'distinct in some way from "religion or belief",

---

85   Malcolm D Evans (n 3) 8–9.
86   *ICCPR* (n 1) art 18(1); *Convention* (n 2) art 9(1).
87   Shaw-Miller (n 17) 83.
88   Ibid 82–3.
89   Carolyn Evans, *Legal Protection of Religious Freedom in Australia* (n 4) 25.

as there is a non-derogable obligation to protect the right to freedom of thought and conscience, but there is no right to manifest them'.[90] The argument was not pursued in detail and she concluded, 'the drafters of the *Convention* [in contrast to the *ICCPR*] do not seem to have given the issue much thought'.[91] In the context of art 18 (*ICCPR*), K J Partsch took an alternative approach to construction.[92] He argued that the combination of 'thought, conscience and religion' was 'carefully chosen for the *ICCPR* to mean different things to different people'.[93] He claimed the 'diplomatic wording' of the *ICCPR* was deliberate.[94] Either way, both articles communicate a distinction between holding a belief and manifesting a belief.

Carolyn Evans explained that art 9 (*Convention*) protects the personal sphere, but it 'does not always guarantee the right to behave in the public sphere in a way which is dictated by such belief: for instance by refusing to pay certain taxes because part of the revenue so raised may be applied for military expenditure'.[95] She stressed that 'the protection of religious freedom in international instruments is not an unlimited protection for the right to act on one's conscience'.[96] Her argument referred to a potential overlap between *forum internum* and *forum externum*. It was based on the fact that belief is capable of motivating action. That argument identifies the problem this paper seeks to address. First, if there is even a partial overlap between the *forum externum* and *forum internum*, the limitation upon the *forum externum* must impact upon the *forum internum*. Second, if the limitation impacts upon the *forum internum*, even incidentally, then

---

90   Carolyn Evans, *Freedom of Religion under the European Convention on Human Rights* (n 7) 52.
91   Ibid 51.
92   K J Partsch, 'Freedom of Conscience and Expression and Political Freedoms' in Louis Henkin (ed), *The International Bill Of Human Rights: The Covenant on Civil and Political Rights* (Columbia University Press, 1981) 209.
93   Ibid 211, also cited in Carolyn Evans, *Freedom of Religion under the European Convention on Human Rights* (n 7) 51.
94   Ibid.
95   Carolyn Evans, *Legal Protection of Religious Freedom in Australia* (n 4) 36–7.
96   Ibid.

the issue of intangible harm must be discussed and the presumption of non-derogability revisited. Legitimate non-derogability cannot coincide with any legitimate power of derogation. This is because if it is illegal to derogate from the *forum internum*, then any law which purports to legally derogate from the *forum externum*, must be illegal to the extent that it derogates from the *forum internum* at the same time.

Consider art 18 of the *ICCPR*. The *forum internum* is not subject to any express limitation because neither art 4 nor art 18(3) apply.[97] If a recognised nexus existed between the *forum internum* and *forum externum*, the door would be opened to consider intangible harm to the *forum internum* caused by limitation upon manifestation.[98] In contrast, if the nexus is ignored and the division upheld, the content of the *forum internum* freedom would arguably appear to be minimal. Carolyn Evans explored the consequence of the latter construction:

> At the most basic level, [the *forum* internum] could [then] be considered simply the right to hold opinions silently (on religious or other important issues) without interference by the State. At this level the right is almost impossible for the State to breach, except by use of invasive mind-altering techniques, such as brain-washing or systematic indoctrination.[99]

That overlap and the significance of the non-derogable classification of the *forum internum* are developed in the subsequent chapters. This is necessary, as the only factor that both the HRC and ECHR have expressly addressed is the importance of the *forum internum* as an individual liberty.[100] There is a need for further clarification as to the actual scope and impact of such protection.

---

97   See *ICCPR* (n 1) arts 4(2), 18(1), 18(3).

98   See also Carolyn Evans, *Freedom of Religion under the European Convention on Human* Rights (n 7) 74–9.

99   Ibid 68.

100   See, eg, *General Comment 22* (n 4) [1]; *Kokkinakis* (n 9) [31].

2   *Identifying the liberty which is the subject of the forum externum and the scope of limitations upon that liberty*

The *forum externum* is described as 'the sphere of external manifestation'[101] of thought and religion. In both articles it is described as the right 'to manifest [a person's] religion or belief in worship, observance, practice and teaching'.[102] The manifestation of thought or religion is subject to limitation and can be legitimately interfered with by the state. However, the limitation is not automatically engaged as a result of manifestation. All requirements within the clause must also be present and satisfied. Carolyn Evans noted that '[t]he state must demonstrate that the measures that it has taken to restrict religious freedom are proportionate to the legitimate ends that it seeks to protect'.[103] In order for the state to legitimately limit the manifestation, the following criteria must be present and satisfied:

- the conduct must concern a manifestation of 'religion or beliefs';[104]
- the limitation must be 'prescribed by law';[105]
- the limitation must be 'necessary to protect [one of the specified grounds]';[106] and
- the law must have a legitimate aim 'to protect public safety, order, health, or morals or the fundamental rights and freedoms of others'.[107]

The HRC stated that this limitation does not apply to the *forum internum*.[108] The ECHR has not provided express comment. This section will outline the accepted construction of each criterion.

---

101   Malcolm D Evans (n 3) 9.
102   *ICCPR* (n 1) art 18(1); *Convention* (n 2) art 9(1).
103   Carolyn Evans, *Legal Protection of Religious Freedom in Australia* (n 4) 29.
104   *ICCPR* (n 1) art 18(3); *Convention* (n 2) art 9(2).
105   Ibid.
106   Ibid.
107   Ibid.
108   *General Comment 22* (n 4) [3].

(a)   Manifestation of religion or beliefs

Malcolm D Evans identified the subjectivity of the first criterion as problematic:

> who is to decide whether a form of action is to be understood, in a *prima facie* sense, as a manifestation of a religion or belief at all. If the applicant asserts that something they have done was as a result of their religion or belief, is it open to the Court simply to deny that this is so on the basis of its scrutiny of the facts, or is it bound to accept the applicant's 'subjective' characterisation of their actions?[109]

This difficulty was also addressed in *Valsamis v Greece*.[110] The applicants were parents who alleged that involvement of their child in a parade that commemorated war offended their religious convictions as Jehovah's Witnesses.[111] However, the Court held that there was 'nothing, either in the purpose of the parade or in the arrangements for it, which could offend the applicants' pacifist convictions'.[112] Malcolm D Evans argued that the approach taken by the ECHR in *Valsamis v Greece* was 'problematic'.[113] Manifestation of religion begins with a belief. The judgment separated the belief from the action and made a subjective judgment as to whether or not the action applied to the belief.[114] Thus, whilst the limitation may not expressly apply to the *forum internum*, it unavoidably engages it as a criterion for application: manifestation is based on 'religion or beliefs'.[115]

Interpretations and reactions to recognition of the *forum internum* are diverse, intangible and beyond proof. Waldron alluded to this complexity in his discussion of the impact of hate speech upon minorities:

---

109   Malcolm D Evans (n 3) 12.
110   *Valsamis v Greece* (1997) 24 EHRR 294.
111   Ibid [7]–[11]. The judgment acknowledged that the applicants believed 'pacifism is a fundamental tenet of their religion and forbids any conduct or practice associated with war or violence, even indirectly': at [7].
112   Ibid [31].
113   Malcolm D Evans (n 3) 12, citing *Valsamis v Greece* (n 110).
114   *Valsamis v Greece* (n 110) [34]–[38].
115   *ICCPR* (n 1) art 18(3); *Convention* (n 2) art 9(2).

The phenomenology of the reaction by a minority member to any particular incident of hate speech is likely to be complex and tangled. As a man walking with his family turns a corner and sees a swastika or a burning cross or posters depicting people of his kind as apes, he will experience a plethora of thoughts and emotions. It will not be easy to differentiate terror from outrage, from offense, from insult, from incredulity, from acutely uncomfortable self-consciousness, from the perception of a threat, from humiliation, from rage, from a sense that one's world has been upended, from sickening familiarity ('Here we go again'), from the apprehension of further assaults or worse, and all these from the shame of having to explain to one's children what is going on.[116]

Identifying a belief requires recognition of the *forum internum*. However, neither art 18 (*ICCPR*) nor art 9 (*Convention*) expressly require consideration of any intangible harm to the *forum internum* when a limitation is imposed on the *forum externum*. Application of the limitation clause only requires a connection between belief and action. The ECHR has stated in deciding whether an act is a 'manifestation' of a religious belief, that 'the existence of a sufficiently close and direct nexus between the act and the underlying belief must be determined on the facts of each case'.[117]

Both the HRC and ECHR have recognised the importance of the *forum internum* and either impliedly or directly addressed the presence of a connection to the *forum externum*. The impact of this recognition upon the classification of the *forum internum* as non-derogable is discussed in the next chapter.

(b)   Prescribed by Law

In its *General Comment 22*, the HRC explained:

In interpreting the scope of permissible limitation clauses, state parties should proceed from the need to protect the rights guaranteed under the Covenant ... Limitations imposed must be established by

---

116   Waldron (n 49) 113.
117   *Eweida v UK* (2013) 57 EHRR 8 [82].

law and must not be applied in a manner that would vitiate the rights guaranteed in article 18.[118]

The ECHR also provided a guide for interpretation in *Sunday Times v the United Kingdom [No 1]* ('*Sunday Times*'):

> In the Court's opinion, the following are two of the requirements that flow from the expression 'prescribed by law'. Firstly, the law must be adequately accessible: the citizen must be able to have an indication that is adequate in the circumstances of the legal rules applicable to a given case. Secondly, a norm cannot be regarded as a 'law' unless it is formulated with sufficient precision to enable the citizen to regulate his conduct: he must be able – if need be with appropriate advice – to foresee, to a degree that is reasonable in the circumstances, the consequences which a given action may entail.[119]

The ECHR decision in *Hasan v Bulgaria* provided an example of an art 9 limitation claim that did not satisfy the criterion: 'prescribed by law'.[120] The criterion was not satisfied as the law 'was arbitrary and was based on legal provisions which allowed an unfettered discretion to the executive and did not meet the required standards of clarity and foreseeability'.[121] The decision reinforced the approach taken in *Sunday Times*.[122] The ECHR observed:

> In matters affecting fundamental rights it would be contrary to the rule of law, one of the basic principles of a democratic society enshrined in the *Convention*, for a legal discretion granted to the executive to be expressed in terms of an unfettered power. Consequently, the law must indicate with sufficient clarity the scope of any such discretion conferred on the competent authorities and the manner of its exercise.[123]

To satisfy this criterion a state law must be clear, precise and accessible.

---

118   *General Comment 22* (n 4) [8].
119   *Sunday Times v the United Kingdom [No 1]* (1979-80) 2 EHRR 245 [49] ('*Sunday Times*').
120   *Hasan v Bulgaria* (2002) 34 EHRR 55; *Convention* (n 2) art 9(2).
121   *Hasan v Bulgaria* (n 120) [86].
122   *Sunday Times* (n 119)
123   *Hasan v Bulgaria* (n 120) [84].

(c)   Necessary

For a law to be necessary, consideration of whether it was proportionate to the legitimate aim being pursued is required.[124] The ECHR defined 'necessary' with reference to 'assessment of the reality of the pressing social need implied by the notion of "necessity" in this context'.[125] In *Otto-Preminger Institut v Austria,* the ECHR said 'it is not possible to discern throughout Europe a uniform conception of the significance of religion in society; even within a single country such conceptions may vary'.[126] Malcolm D Evans attributed this perspective to the ECHR practice of granting 'states a relatively broad margin of appreciation'.[127] However, he also stressed, 'this does not give the state an unfettered discretion to determine whether a restriction is proportionate to the aim pursued'.[128] He observed:

> Not only is the national assessment subject to European scrutiny in order to ensure that does indeed meet the requirements of proportionality on the facts of the case, but it is always open to the Court to narrow that margin should a more general consensus on the relationship between the state and the manifestation of religion or belief emerge.[129]

Both the HRC and ECHR invoke notions of proportionality in their analysis of whether a limitation on the *forum externum* is necessary.[130]

(d)   Legitimate Aim

To be a 'legitimate aim' the law 'must be directly related and proportionate to the specific need on which they are predicated'.[131]

---

124   Malcolm D Evans (n 3) 19.
125   *Handyside v United Kingdom* (1979-80) 1 EHRR 737 [48].
126   *Otto-Preminger Institut v Austria* (1994) 19 EHRR 34 [50].
127   Malcolm D Evans (n 3) 21.
128   Ibid.
129   Ibid.
130   See generally M Todd Parker, 'The Freedom to Manifest Religious Belief: An Analysis of the Necessity Clauses of the ICCPR and the ECHR' (2006) 17 *Duke Journal of Comparative & International Law* 91.
131   Carolyn Evans, *Legal Protection of Religious Freedom in Australia* (n 4) 32, citing *Gen-*

Both art 18 (*ICCPR*) and art 9 (*Convention*) provide an undeniably broad list of grounds for the state to legislate upon: 'public safety, order, health, or morals or the fundamental rights and freedoms of others'.[132] However, the HRC have emphasised the exhaustive nature of the list in art 18 and the need to be specific. In its *General Comment* 22, the HRC stated:

> The Committee observes that paragraph 3 of article 18 is to be strictly interpreted: restrictions are not allowed on grounds not specified there, even if they would be allowed as restrictions to other rights protected in the Covenant, such as national security. [133]

In contrast, in the context of art 9 of the *Convention*, Malcolm D Evans argued identification of a legitimate aim in accordance with the specified grounds 'is not a difficult hurdle to surmount'.[134]

Carolyn Evans noted the grounds for limitation do not include 'a public good or convenient idea'.[135] This construction is in line with the classic approach to harm: an individual's 'own good, either physical or moral, is not a sufficient warrant' to interfere with his or her liberty.[136] Hence, a state cannot rely on the perceived benefit of a law. However, while 'mere public good' may not be acceptable,[137] neither article rules out the possibility of legislating upon 'public morality' as suggested by Devlin.[138] One of the legitimate grounds for limiting religious liberty in the context of the *forum externum* is 'public morals'.[139] This inclusion reflects Devlin's argument that the state should have the power to legislate on 'the basis of a common good or public morality'.[140] It also demonstrates that both art 18

---

eral Comment 22 (n 4).

132   *ICCPR* (n 1) art 18(3); *Convention* (n 2) art 9(2).

133   *General Comment 22* (n 4) [8].

134   Malcolm D Evans (n 3) 19.

135   Carolyn Evans, *Legal Protection of Religious Freedom in Australia* (n 4) 29.

136   Shaw-Miller (n 17) 80–1.

137   Carolyn Evans, *Legal Protection of Religious Freedom in Australia* (n 4) 29.

138   Devlin (n 27).

139   *ICCPR* (n 1) art 18(3); *Convention* (n 2) art 9(2).

140   Devlin (n 27) 92.

(*ICCPR*) and art 9 (*Convention*) recognise the potential threat of intangible harm. Theorists have discussed the appropriateness of including 'morals' in law.[141] However, this paper is focused upon exploring derogation from the non-derogable *forum internum*.

The nature of harm is not limited to tangible forms of potential injury. This is evident from consideration of the development of approach to state interference with manifestation of religion. In contrast, despite this development, the approach to the *forum internum* has not undergone significant development. It is a component of religious liberty that is often ignored, as it is not expressly subject to limitation and is described as non-derogable. The next section will explore the impact of classifying a right as non-derogable.

PART III: WHAT DOES NON-DEROGABLE MEAN?

To understand the significance of a 'non-derogable' classification requires an understanding of the state power of derogation. Both the *Convention* and *ICCPR* include an express power of derogation.[142] To 'derogate' from an obligation is to breach the protection promised by an article of the *ICCPR* or the *Convention*. Article 4 of the *ICCPR* sets out an express power of derogation:

> In time of public emergency which threatens the life of the nation and the existence of which is officially proclaimed, the States Parties to the present Covenant may take measures derogating from their obligations under the present Covenant to the extent strictly required by the exigencies of the situation, provided that such measures are not inconsistent with their other obligations under international law and do not involve discrimination solely on the ground of race, colour, sex, language, religion or social origin.[143]

That article 'allows governments to temporarily suspend the

---

141   See, eg, Hart (n 37); Devlin (n 27); James Allan, *A Sceptical Theory of Morality and Law* (Peter Lang, 1998).
142   *ICCPR* (n 1) art 4; *Convention* (n 2) art 15.
143   *ICCPR* (n 1) art 4(1).

application of some rights in the exceptional circumstance of a "state of emergency" and subject to certain conditions, including official notification'.[144] However, the power to derogate is expressly forbidden from application to liberties under arts 6, 7, 8 (paragraphs 1 and 2), 11, 15, 16 and 18.[145] Those liberties are classified as non-derogable.

The *Convention* also has an express power of derogation in art 15:

> In time of war or other public emergency threatening the life of the nation any High Contracting Party may take measures derogating from its obligations under this *Convention* to the extent strictly required by the exigencies of the situation, provided that such measures are not inconsistent with its other obligations under international law.[146]

This clause does not exempt art 9 from derogation in 'time of war or other public emergency'.[147] Malcolm D Evans argued:

> In theory, this could be taken to suggest that in such emergency situations the state might be able to act in a manner which even impinged upon the *'forum internum'* – for example, seeking to persuade or coerce individuals to abandon forms of thinking or of beliefs which were considered inimical to national security. However, given the primarily personal and private scope of the *forum internum*, it is difficult to see how such intrusions could ever be 'strictly required'.[148]

However, he also noted that '[a]rticle 3 of the *Convention* prohibits "inhuman or degrading treatment" in absolute terms and is not subject to the limitations of Article 15'. He concluded that it was 'difficult to see how activities capable of coercing a change in private patterns of

---

144   Attorney-General's Department, *Absolute Rights* <https://www.ag.gov.au/ RightsAndProtections/HumanRights/PublicSectorGuidanceSheets/Pages/ Absoluterights.aspx>, citing Human Rights Committee, *General Comment No 29: Article 4: Derogations during a State of Emergency*, 72nd sess, UN Doc CCPR/C/21/ Rev.1/Add.11 (31 August 2001).
145   *ICCPR* (n 1) art 4(2).
146   *Convention* (n 2) art 15.
147   Ibid.
148   Malcolm D Evans (n 3) 17.

thought would not fall foul of this provision.'[149]

A 'non-derogable' right cannot be subject to the power of derogation, even in a time of 'national emergency'.[150] Although, art 4 does not apply to art 18 (*ICCPR*), protection of religious liberty is not without limitation. Article 18 includes an express limitation upon the right to manifest religion or belief. A state may legitimately interfere when 'necessary to protect public safety, order, health, or morals or the fundamental rights and freedoms of others'.[151] However, this power of derogation is strictly limited to the *forum externum*. It does not extend to the *forum internum*.[152] Hence, the freedom of conscience, thought and religion, a non-derogable right, free from lawful limitation, is an inviolable liberty. It cannot be subject to any justifiable interference in accordance with the *ICCPR*.

A contrary approach to that classification exists. In Victoria, the *forum internum* is recognised in the *Charter of Human Rights and Responsibilities Act 2006* (Vic) (the '*Charter*').[153] The *Charter* does not expressly recognise the non-derogable nature of the *forum internum*. However, it stipulates that interpretation of each right, '[s]o far as it is possible to do so ... must be interpreted in a way that is compatible with human rights'.[154] This includes consideration of 'the nature of the right' before a limitation is accepted.[155]

Rachel Ball, a director of advocacy at the Human Rights Law Centre of Victoria ('HRLC'), claimed that non-derogable rights are not automatically absolute rights. She suggested that a non-derogable

---

149 Ibid.

150 Carolyn Evans, *Legal Protection of Religious Freedom in Australia* (n 4) 33, citing, *General Comment 22* (n 4) [1]; *ICCPR* (n 1) art 4(2).

151 *ICCPR* (n 1) art 18(3).

152 Attorney-General's Department, *Right to Freedom of Thought, Conscience and Religion or Belief* <https://www.ag.gov.au/RightsAndProtections/HumanRights/Public-SectorGuidanceSheets/Pages/Righttofreedomofthoughtconscienceandreligion-orbelief.aspx>.

153 *Charter of Human Rights and Responsibilities Act 2006* (Vic) s 14 (the '*Charter*').

154 Ibid s 32(1).

155 Ibid s 7.

liberty might be limited where 'necessary and proportionate'.[156] Ball opined to be completely free from derogation would require the classification 'absolute'.[157]

An application of Ball's distinction between 'non-derogable' and 'absolute' rights may provide a basis for justifiable interference by the state with part of the *forum internum*. An example of interference, in line with that approach, is prescribed by s 8 of the *Abortion Law Reform Act 2008* (Vic) ('*ALRA*'). Section 8 imposes an obligation upon doctors who have a 'conscientious objection to abortion', namely, the practitioner must 'refer the woman to another registered health practitioner in the same regulated health profession who the practitioner knows does not have a conscientious objection to abortion'.[158]

Frank Brennan argued that s 8 of the *ALRA* was not compatible with the *Charter*.[159] He was also critical of the *Charter* for failing to expressly distinguish, in a manner consistent with the *ICCPR*, between derogable and non-derogable rights.[160]

While Brennan defined a non-derogable right as 'one that the State cannot pare back even during times of national emergency', he did not consider the *forum internum* to be a completely non-derogable right. Brennan identified and separated the *forum internum* into two bundles of rights. The first grouping consisted of the right to be free from 'coercion that would impair his or her freedom to have or to adopt a religion or belief of his or her choice'. It was classified as non-derogable. The second grouping concerned the right to freedom

---

156   Rachel Ball, *Absolute and Non-derogable Rights in International Law* (21 July 2011) <http://www.parliament.vic.gov.au/images/stories/committees/sarc/charter_review/supplementary_info/263_-_Addendum.pdf> 1.

157   Ibid 2.

158   *Abortion Law Reform Act 2008* (Vic) s 8(1)(b) ('*ALRA*').

159   Frank Brennan, 'Human Rights, the Churches, and the Vocation of the Christian Lawyer' (Speech delivered at the Queensland Christian Lawyers Dinner, The Ship Inn, South Bank, 14 July 2011) 15.

160   Ibid 10.

of thought, conscience and belief, and was identified as a 'derogable right'.[161] By that qualification, similar to Ball, Brennan recognised the potential for lawful interference with the *forum internum vis-à-vis* the right to freedom of thought, conscience and belief.

Neither the approach of Ball nor Brennan is supported by the HRC's construction of art 18. In its *General Comment 22*, the HRC stated that art 18 does 'not permit any limitations whatsoever on the freedom of thought and conscience or on the freedom to have or adopt a religion or belief of one's choice'.[162] The article only permits limitations upon the individual right to manifest religion or belief.[163]

Unlike the HRLC, the approach of the Australian Attorney-General's Department ('AGD') is in line with the HRC commentary. Although the AGD classified art 18 as a non-absolute non-derogable right it clarified that the 'right to freedom of religion in article 18 of the *ICCPR* is non-derogable under article 4(2) but may be subject to limitations in accordance with article 18(3)'.[164] In contrast to the HRC, the AGD did not discuss the scope of 18(3).[165]

Although the HRLC approach is at odds with the HRC, it raised two important questions: can the *forum internum* be protected as non-derogable and should the *forum internum* be protected as non-derogable? Freedom of conscience, thought and religion is recognised as a human right.[166] However, this paper focuses upon the need to readdress the traditional approach to the non-derogability of the *forum internum*.[167] This is because of its overlap with the

161 Ibid.
162 *General Comment 22* (n 4) [3].
163 Discussed in previous part, above n Pt II.
164 Attorney-General's Department, *Absolute Rights* (n 144).
165 Ibid. Cf *General Comment 22* (n 4).
166 *Universal Declaration of Human Rights*, GA Res 217A (III), UN GAOR, 3rd sess, 183rd plen mtg, UN Doc A/810 (10 December 1948) ('*UDHR*') art 18; *ICCPR* (n 1) art 18(1); *Convention* (n 2) art 9(1).
167 See *General Comment 22* (n 4) [1]; Human Rights Committee, *General Comment No. 24: Issues Relating to Reservations Made upon Ratification or Accession to the Covenant or the Optional Protocols thereto, or in Relation to Declarations under Article 41 of*

forum externum. The implication this overlap has upon the *forum internum* is yet to be discussed by courts or international tribunals. The two ideas at present, non-derogability of the *forum internum* and justified limitation of the *forum externum,* cannot co-exist.[168] This paper adopts the HRC classification of the *forum internum* as a non-derogable right that is not subject to any permissible form of interference or limitation. The next section explores the correctness of classifying the *forum internum* as non-derogable.

B   *Is the forum internum Really Free from Derogation?*

Carolyn Evans described the right as 'inviolable' and cited *General Comment 22* to describe the non-derogability of the *forum internum*: '[t]he internal aspect of freedom of thought, conscience and religion (the *forum internum*) may never be interfered with by the government, even in times of national emergency'.[169] Taylor described the internal aspect as 'elemental and inviolable' and observed that it is 'susceptible to no restriction at all'.[170]

Documents released by the HRC support the conclusion that the *forum internum* is free from derogation.[171] In its *General Comment 24,* the HRC described 'freedom of thought, conscience and religion'

---

the Covenant, 52nd sess, UN Doc CCPR/C/21/Rev.1/Add.6 (4 November 1994) [8] ('*General Comment 24*').

168   Carolyn Evans, *Freedom of Religion under the European Convention on Human Rights* (n 7) 67–102; 204–9, briefly expands upon this issue. She suggests a need to extend non-derogable protection to part of the *forum externum*. However, to suggest acceptance of the derogation from the *forum internum* and increase the strictness of the limitation upon it is currently opposed by the HRC. In its *General Comment 22* (n 4) [1], [3], the HRC stated that art 18 (*ICCPR*) does not create a limitation, and its decision in *Bhinder v Canada* (n 9), supports the argument that article 18 (*ICCPR*) does not create a positive obligation of reasonable accommodation.

169   Carolyn Evans, *Legal Protection of Religious Freedom in Australia* (n 4) 33, citing *General Comment 22* (n 4) [1]; *ICCPR* (n 1) art 4(2).

170   Taylor, *A Commentary on the International Covenant on Civil and Political Rights: The UN Human Rights Committee's Monitoring of ICCPR Rights* (n 7) 500, 503.

171   *General Comment 22* (n 4) [1], [3]; *General Comment 24* (n 167) [8]; *ICCPR* (n 1) art 4(2).

as 'customary international law... [that] may not be the subject of reservations'.[172] The HRC also expressly emphasised the importance of non-derogable rights, but rejected the suggestion of a hierarchy of human rights.[173] The HRC provide two explanations for classifying a right as non-derogable:

> One reason for certain rights being made non-derogable is because their suspension is irrelevant to the legitimate control of the state of national emergency (for example, no imprisonment for debt, in article 11). Another reason is that derogation may indeed be impossible (as, for example, freedom of conscience).[174]

The conclusion that 'derogation may indeed be impossible' fails to account for the moments of overlap between *forum internum* and *forum externum*.[175] Carolyn Evans and Taylor noted the consistency of courts to ignore both 'subtle interference' with the *forum internum* and frame claims as legitimate limitations upon the *forum externum*.[176] The above HRC commentary supports the conclusion that the *forum internum* is easily upheld as inviolable. The comment ignores the potential for intangible harm. If this interpretation were accepted it would confirm the minimal content of the right.[177] However, in the same year the HRC released its *General Comment 24*, it had recognised intangible harm in *Toonen v Australia*.[178] Despite extensive commentary on the construction of art 18, decisions like *Toonen v Australia* highlight the HRC's inconsistent approach to issues relating to the *forum internum* and

---

172   *General Comment 24* (n 167) [8].
173   Ibid [10]. Cf Koji Teraya, 'Emerging Hierarchy in International Human Rights and Beyond: From the Perspective of Non-derogable Rights' (2001) 12 *European Journal of International Law* 917.
174   *General Comment 24* (n 167) [10].
175   Ibid.
176   Carolyn Evans, *Freedom of Religion under the European Convention on Human Rights* (n 7) 205; Taylor, *Freedom of Religion: UN and European Human Rights Law and Practice* (n 7) 115–202.
177   Carolyn Evans, *Freedom of Religion under the European Convention on Human Rights* (n 7) 68.
178   *Toonen v Australia* (n 43).

intangible harm.[179]

In contrast, the ECHR has provided no commentary on the subject of the non-derogability of the *forum internum*. Taylor argued that the reluctance of the ECHR to expressly recognise that the *forum internum* as a right free from limitation, has undermined the protection that art 9 provides.[180] Despite the omission, the ECHR has implied the *forum internum* is a 'morally essential human right' in its judgments.[181] Furthermore, the construction of art 9(2) makes clear that the limitation only applies to the *forum externum*.[182]

The next part will determine whether or not the classification of non-derogable, implied or express, has had any practical impact upon protection of the *forum internum*.

PART IV: DO THE EXISTING LIMITATIONS IN THE *ICCPR* AND *CONVENTION* PROTECT THE *FORUM INTERNUM*?

This part will consider the protection afforded to the *forum internum* at both international and domestic levels. First, it will analyse the classification in the context of both the *ICCPR* and *Convention*. This analysis will focus upon the protection of the *forum internum* in the context of a human rights claim brought by a citizen against the state. Second, it will analyse the extent of protection available at a domestic level and whether or not the classification is reflected in the approach of courts in different jurisdictions. Both sections analyse cases of the late 20th century and early 21st century and work together to prove that the *forum internum* is not being consistently protected.

---

179   Ibid.
180   Taylor, *Freedom of Religion: UN and European Human Rights Law and Practice* (n 7) 200.
181   Brian D Lepard, *Customary International Law: A New Theory with Practical Applications* (Cambridge University Press, 2010) 356; See, eg, *Kokkinakis* (n 9); *Otto-Preminger Institut v Austria* (n 126).
182   *Convention* (n 2) art 9(2).

A   *Human Rights Claim: Citizen v State*

Taylor argued that despite 'growing recognition of the *forum internum* in a variety of circumstances, particularly at United Nations level, this falls far short of a comprehensive, cohesive pattern of protection'.[183] He observed weaknesses within the approach of the HRC and ECHR to the *forum internum*. First, the ECHR have failed to clarify and confirm the non-derogability of the *forum internum*. Second, the non-derogability of the *forum internum* has not been adequately focused upon in cases anywhere in the world.[184] This section will assess those weaknesses in the context of the HRC decision in *Bhinder v Canada* and the ECHR decision in *SAS v France*.[185]

1   *The HRC Approach to an Article 18 Claim in Bhinder v Canada*[186]

In *Bhinder v Canada* the HRC concluded that no article of the *ICCPR* had been violated under the facts presented.[187] That conclusion was not limited to the scope of art 18. The HRC was adamant that no aspect of the *ICCPR* had been violated.[188]

Mr Bhinder was a maintenance technician for the Canadian National Railway Company ('the CNR'). He was employed for four years before a requirement was put in place that required all employees in the coach yard to wear hard hats.[189] The applicant's complaint to the HRC principally rested upon his commitment to his belief. While the HRC accepted 'it is a fundamental tenet of Sikh religion

---

183   See Taylor, *Freedom of Religion: UN and European Human Rights Law and Practice* (n 7) 200.

184   Ibid 115–202.

185   *Bhinder v Canada* (n 9); *SAS v France* (n 11).

186   *Bhinder v Canada* (n 9).

187   Ibid [7].

188   Ibid [6.2]–[7].

189   Ibid [2.1]–[2.3].

that men's headware should consist exclusively of a turban,'[190] that brief reference to the *forum internum* was only stated by the HRC to communicate understanding as to the reason for the applicant's refusal to wear a hard hat. The statement did not recognise any form of derogation to the *forum internum*. The HRC recognised an art 18 claim but only in connection with manifestation.[191]

In contrast, the dissenting judgment in *Bhinder v Canadian National Railway Co*[192] attempted to communicate the importance of the individual liberty being interfered with. Dickson CJ and Lamer J argued that construction of the *Canadian Human Rights Act* did not require a complete disregard of the evident 'discriminatory impact of an occupational requirement on an individual'.[193] Dickson CJ further criticised the majority's construction of the *Canadian Human Rights Act*. He observed that their construction achieved the complete opposite effect to the overall intention of the Act. He argued, '[s]uch reduction... would require clear and explicit words to that effect.'[194] The 'impact' on the individual, considered by the dissent, was not limited to the right to manifest and appeared to include reference, albeit implied, to the concurrent interference with the *forum internum*. The majority judgment overlooked consideration of the *forum internum* entirely.

The ultimate decision of both the HRC and the majority in the Supreme Court of Canada ignored the intangible harm to Mr Bhinder's *forum internum*. However, the HRC approach revealed greater inconsistency, as the HRC had previously acknowledged the potential for intangible harm in *Toonen v Australia*.[195] Although the Canadian law may not target Sikhs in the specific way that

---

190   Ibid [2.7].
191   Ibid [6.1]–[6.2].
192   [1985] 2 SCR 561.
193   Ibid 563, citing *Ontario Human Rights Commission v Borough of Etobicoke* [1982] 1 SCR 202; *Canadian Human Rights Act*, RSC 1985, c H-6, s 14(a).
194   Ibid 571, citing *Canadian Human Rights Act* (n 192) ss 2, 14(a).
195   *Toonen v Australia* (n 43).

Australian law in Tasmania had targeted homosexuals, a persuasive claim as to violation of the *forum internum* could still be ignored for the same reasons.[196] Mr Bhinder's conduct in wearing a turban was not completely distinct from his acceptance and commitment to a system of beliefs derived from Sikhism. Just as Mr Toonen's conduct, whether it was in private or public, could not be tangibly distinguished from his sexual orientation.

Although Mr Bhinder argued the conduct of his employer unjustifiably impacted upon manifestation of his religious convictions, the impact on his individuality was not discussed. The connection between religious manifestation and religious belief was not a point of focus.

2   *The ECHR Approach to an Article 9 Claim in SAS v France*[197]

In *SAS v France* the ECHR rejected the applicant's appeal 15:2.[198] It was held that a blanket ban on wearing facial coverings in public did not violate the art 9 right of a Muslim woman who wished to wear a niqab.[199] The validity of the law was upheld under the 'legitimate aim' of protecting the 'rights and freedoms of others'.[200] However, no evidence of any actual harm to the public was presented.[201]

The majority stressed that the legitimacy of the aim pursued was made clear in the explanatory memorandum, which stated:

> The voluntary and systematic concealment of the face is problematic because it is quite simply incompatible with the fundamental requirements of 'living together' in French society ... [Furthermore,] [t]he systematic concealment of the face in public places, contrary to

---

196   Ibid [5.1].
197   *SAS v France* (n 11).
198   Ibid [163].
199   Ibid [106]–[159], [163].
200   Ibid [142].
201   See also *Bhinder v Canada* (n 9), an HRC decision where no evidence of actual harm (physical injury) was proved.

the ideal of fraternity, ... falls short of the minimum requirement of civility that is necessary for social interaction.[202]

The explanation by France demonstrated a substantial move away from the state's original approach to individual liberty, formerly articulated in the *Declaration of the Rights of Man and Citizen*: 'Liberty consists in the power to do anything that does not injure others'.[203] The only element of the *Declaration of the Rights of Man and Citizen* that appears to remain is that 'limits can be determined only by law'.[204]

The decision highlights the continued relevance of Devlin's approach to intangible harm. The state did not present evidence of tangible harm. Instead it relied upon the intangible threat to the fabric of French society.[205] This intangible threat was suggested upon multiple art 9(2) grounds.[206] However, only the argument of protecting the 'rights and freedoms of others' was accepted.[207] The law stipulated that face coverings go against 'the minimum requirement of civility that is necessary for social interaction'.[208] Hart's criticism of Devlin is relevant because the ECHR's acceptance of this argument presents as an acceptance of Devlin's idea that society can impose upon the *forum internum* if such interference is deemed necessary to preserve the established morality of society.[209]

The ECHR's finding that wearing a niqab harmed the fabric of French society overrules the Jefferson and Mill idea that society can only claim an interest in regulating religious activity if it causes tangible harm. It accepts Devlin's premise that intangible harm

---

202   *SAS v France* (n 11) [25]–[27], [141].
203   *Declaration of the Right of Man and Citizen* (n 16) art 4.
204   Ibid.
205   *SAS v France* (n 11) [25]–[27], [141].
206   Ibid [137]–[159].
207   Ibid [142].
208   Ibid [141].
209   Hart (n 37) 49.

justifies regulatory control.[210] However, there is no analysis of the impact regulatory control of intangible harm has on the *forum internum*. Without evidence, it is difficult to accept that a minority of individuals wearing a full-face veil could lead to the 'the destruction of [social interaction]'.[211]

The ECHR should give additional explanation when making judgment on intangible harm. Waldron alluded to this need by fleshing out the complex and broad nature of intangible harm. This is evident in his distinction between the duty to legislate against allowing an assault on dignity but not offence.[212] It is objectively easier to assess the severity of tangible harm. However, the challenge for the courts and legislature is to determine a consistent means of assessment for an unquantifiable distinction.

In *SAS v France*, the ECHR simply weighed the preferred values of the majority against those of the minority and deemed the former preferable within a democratic society.[213] The implementation of the blanket ban was not 'necessary' but a 'majority rules' decision founded on a specific construction of *laïcité* values (which could be classified in Devlin terms as the 'public morality' of France).[214] It is also arguable that allowing the state to arbitrarily determine what is necessary to protect 'rights and freedoms' is a limitation based on 'a mere public good or convenient idea'. Carolyn Evans rejected this justification because it offended art 9(1).[215]

---

210   See Devlin (n 27) 86–101, 113–4.

211   See Hart (n 37) 49.

212   Waldron (n 49) 112–30.

213   *SAS v France* (n 11) [OI-8]–[OI-14]. Nußberger and Jäderblom JJ (dissent) recognised: 'While communication is admittedly essential for life in society, the right to respect for private life also comprises the right not to communicate and not to enter into contact with others in public places – the right to be an outsider.': at [OI-8].

214   See *SAS v France* (n 11) [OI-13]–[OI-14] (dissent); Devlin (n 27) 113–4; Cf Hart (n 37) 49. See especially Hart's criticism of Devlin's construction of morality as a 'seamless web': at 49.

215   Carolyn Evans, *Legal Protection of Religious Freedom in Australia* (n 4) 29.

In contrast to the majority, Nußberger and Jäderblom JJ argued that derogation of art 9 rights had occurred:

> It sacrifices concrete individual rights guaranteed by the *Convention* to abstract principles. It is doubtful that the blanket ban on wearing a full-face veil in public pursues a legitimate aim ... In any event, such a far-reaching prohibition, touching upon the right to one's own cultural and religious identity, is not necessary in a democratic society ... Therefore we come to the conclusion that there has been a violation of arts 8 and 9 of the *Convention*.[216]

The dissenting judgment also highlighted the potential unfairness arising from this subjective construction. Nußberger and Jäderblom JJ observed that the majority could have relied on *laïcité* values to support the applicant's argument of religious liberty:

> all those values could be regarded as justifying not only a blanket ban on wearing a full-face veil, but also, on the contrary, the acceptance of such a religious dress-code and the adoption of an integrationist approach. In our view, the applicant is right to claim that the French legislature has restricted pluralism, since the measure prevents certain women from expressing their personality and their beliefs by wearing the full-face veil in public.[217]

They identified the duty of the state is 'not to remove the cause of tension by eliminating pluralism, but to ensure that the competing groups tolerate each other'. Nußberger and Jäderblom JJ concluded:

> By banning the full-face veil, the French legislature has done the opposite [of its state duty to citizens]. It has not sought to ensure tolerance between the vast majority and the small minority, but has prohibited what is seen as a cause of tension.[218]

In other words, the law could be interpreted as failing to embrace liberty, equality and fraternity.

By limiting the claim to a discussion based on manifestation, the

---

216   *SAS v France* (n 11) [OI-2].
217   Ibid [OI-13]–[OI-14].
218   Ibid [OI-14].

Court was able to ignore the implications of valid derogation from *forum externum* upon the assumed non-derogable *forum internum*. The ECHR's finding in *SAS v France* thus follows Devlin in finding that it is legitimate for the state to impose a majoritarian view of public morality upon the whole of society even when minority practice does not cause that society any tangible harm.[219] The dissenting judgment concluded that the law was not made to 'to ensure tolerance between the vast majority and the small minority'. It was a paternalistic measure to ban what it deemed to be 'a cause of tension'.[220] This was a departure from France's previously acknowledged 'duty to ensure mutual tolerance between opposing groups'.[221] Instead, a blanket ban of the full-face veil increased tension.

3   *The ECHR Wide Margin of Appreciation in SAS v France*[222]

The success of France in *SAS v France* cannot be discussed without consideration of the exceptionally 'broad margin of appreciation' that was applied by the majority.[223] Taylor listed the margin of appreciation as a significant distinction between the HRC and ECHR standards 'in the area of discrimination'.[224] This is because the *ICCPR* has no counterpart.[225] He criticised the device for 'allow[ing] States wide discretion, even in the case of interference with one of the most fundamental unrestricted rights'.[226] In *SAS v France*, Nußberger and

---

219   *SAS v France* (n 11). See generally Devlin (n 27) 86–123.
220   *SAS v France* (n 11) [OI-14] (Nußberger and Jäderblom JJ).
221   Ibid [OI-14].
222   *SAS v France* (n 11).
223   Ibid [OI-16].
224   Taylor, *Freedom of Religion: UN and European Human Rights Law and Practice* (n 7) 198.
225   Ibid.
226   Ibid. See also Steven Greer, 'The Margin of Appreciation: Interpretation and Discretion Under the European Convention on Human Rights' (Human Rights Files No 17, Council of Europe, July 2000) 5 <http://www.echr.coe.int/Library-Docs/DG2/HRFILES/DG2-EN-HRFILES-17(2000).pdf>. Greer's article explores the ECHR application of the margin of appreciation and also explores the argument for its removal from practice.

Jäderblom JJ were in dissent and disagreed with the wide margin of appreciation applied by the majority. They did not accept 'that the respondent State [France] should be accorded a broad margin of appreciation'.[227] Despite this criticism they did not dispute the necessary application of the margin.[228]

Both Nußberger and Jäderblom JJ recognised the need to apply 'special weight' to different states as 'matters of general policy ... can differ widely between states'.[229] However, they did not elaborate or provide guidance for determining appropriate weighting. In contrast, the majority judgment provided an explanation for their lenient approach:

> The national authorities have direct democratic legitimation and are, as the Court has held on many occasions, in principle better placed than an international court to evaluate local needs and conditions. In matters of general policy, on which opinions within a democratic society may reasonably differ widely, the role of the domestic policy-maker should be given special weight.[230]

The majority judgment emphasised the authoritative position of the state to determine the secular needs within the state. This approach was also supported by the ECHR's comments in *Şahin v Turkey* where it was said that 'the choice of the extent and form such regulations should take must inevitably be left up to a point to the state concerned, as it will depend on the domestic context'.[231] Despite this available discretion, the dissenting judgment in *SAS v France* maintained that 'it still remains the task of the Court to protect small minorities against disproportionate interferences'.[232] Malcolm D Evans has also emphasised the role and discretionary power of the ECHR. He stated, 'it is ... always open to the Court to narrow that

---

227   *SAS v France* (n 11) [OI-16].
228   Ibid.
229   Ibid.
230   Ibid [129].
231   *Şahin v Turkey* (2007) 44 EHRR 5 [109].
232   *SAS v France* (n 11) [OI-20] (Nußberger and Jäderblom JJ).

margin should a more general consensus on the relationship between the state and the manifestation of religion or belief emerge'.[233]

The decision in *SAS v France* allowed for a law that oppressed a minority to be upheld.[234] It limited interpretation of a claim to manifestation and triggered discussion of whether or not several secular needs could satisfy the limitation clause.[235]

The next section considers the judicial approach to the *forum internum* at a domestic level. It contrasts protection of sexual orientation as a *forum internum* right with religious liberty.

B   *Competing Rights: Citizen v Citizen*

Carolyn Evans suggested that meaningful protection of the *forum internum* requires that the state not merely refrain from interference, pursuant to the *ICCPR* and *Convention*, but that it must also protect citizens against *forum internum* violations by their peers.[236] This section will consider two controversial contemporary matters from two different common law jurisdictions, *Lee v Ashers* and *Elane Photography*, to identify the compromises to *forum internum* liberties that can arise when law seeks to impose a majoritarian morality.[237]

The *forum internum* in the context of sexual orientation has received consistent recognition concerning its protected status since the late 20th century.[238] The judgments in *Lee v Ashers Baking*

---

233   Malcolm D Evans (n 3) 21.

234   *SAS v France* (n 11).

235   Ibid [137]–[159].

236   Carolyn Evans, *Freedom of Religion under the European Convention on Human Rights* (n 7) 67–102, 204–9.

237   *Lee v Ashers [No 1]* (n 9); *Lee v Ashers [No 2]* (n 12); *Lee v Ashers [No 3]* (n 12); *Elane Photography* (n 9).

238   See, eg, *Toonen v Australia* (n 43); *Ladele v London Borough of Islington* [2009] EWCA Civ 1357; *McFarlane v Relate Avon Ltd* [2010] EWCA Civ 880; *Elane Photography* (n 9); *Bull v Hall* [2012] EWCA Civ 83; *Christian Youth Camps Limited v Cobaw Community Health Service Limited* [2014] VSCA 75; *Lee v Ashers [No 1]* (n 9); *Lee v Ashers*

Co Ltd (County Court) (*'Lee v Ashers [No 1]'*),[239] *Lee v Ashers Baking Co Ltd* (Court of Appeal) (*'Lee v Ashers [No 2]'*)[240] and *Elane Photography*[241] reveal the reluctance of the courts to seek an alternative interpretive approach that accommodates two competing *forum internum* liberties without sending one side a message of 'otherness'.[242] However, *Lee v Ashers [No 3]* (Supreme Court), which overturned both *Lee v Ashers [No 1]* and *Lee v Ashers [No 2]*, represents a shift in judicial approach towards the reconciliation of competing *forum internum* liberties.[243]

1   *Lee v Ashers*

The factual background to *Lee v Ashers* may be briefly stated. The plaintiff went into the defendants' shop and placed an order for a cake to be iced with his design, which included the headline 'Support Gay Marriage'. While initially accepting the order, the defendants ultimately declined to complete the order. The defendants informed the plaintiff that the order could not be fulfilled because they were a Christian business and could not print the slogan requested. The plaintiff was provided a full refund. The proceedings in *Lee v Ashers* concern a claim of unlawful discrimination brought by the plaintiff against the defendants.

The judgment in *Lee v Ashers [No 1]* made a point of emphasising the intrinsic connection between conduct and identity.[244] The *Equality Act (Sexual Orientation) Regulations (Northern Ireland)*

[No 2] (n 12). See generally *Obergefell v Hodges*, 576 US 644 (2015).

239   *Lee v Ashers [No 1]* (n 9).

240   *Lee v Ashers [No 2]* (n 12).

241   *Elane Photography* (n 9).

242   See also *SAS v France* (n 11) [OI-8]. Nußberger and Jäderblom JJ (dissent) recognised: 'While communication is admittedly essential for life in society, the right to respect for private life also comprises the right not to communicate and not to enter into contact with others in public places – the right to be an outsider': at [OI-8].

243   *Lee v Ashers [No 3]* (n 12).

244   *Lee v Ashers [No 1]* (n 9) [43]. See also *Elane Photography* (n 9) [16].

2006 (the '*2006 Regulations*') protected sexual orientation against discrimination.[245] The defendants, at first instance, unsuccessfully attempted to rely on the distinction between sexual orientation and sexual conduct.[246] District Judge Brownlie observed that '[s]ame sex marriage is inextricably linked to sexual relations between same sex couples which is a union of persons having a particular sexual orientation'.[247] However, this same intrinsic relationship between identity and conduct was not recognised in relation to the defendants' religious liberty. The religious belief that motivated the defendants' conduct was given minimal consideration.[248]

The nexus between the defendants' conscience and action was pivotal to understanding why they felt obliged to decline to complete the order. One of the defendants provided a description of that connection to the Court:

> [w]e consider that it is necessary as Christians to have a clear conscience before God. This means that we must live out our faith in our words and deeds and that it would be sinful to act or speak contrary to God's law ... We could not promote same-sex marriage because it is against God's word ... I wish to emphasize that this is in no way related to Mr Lee's sexual orientation.[249]

In *Lee v Ashers [No 1]*, judicial recognition of the defendants' *forum internum* was restricted to a statement recognising they had 'genuine and deeply held religious beliefs'.[250] By not considering the impact upon the *forum internum*, from the perspective of the defendants, the Court was able to conclude 'what the Defendants were asked to do did not require them to support, promote or endorse any viewpoint'.[251]

---

245   *Equality Act (Sexual Orientation) Regulations (Northern Ireland) 2006* (UK) (the '*2006 Regulations*').
246   *Lee v Ashers [No 1]* (n 9) [30]. See also *Elane Photography* (n 9) [16].
247   *Lee v Ashers [No 1]* (n 9) [43].
248   Ibid [95].
249   Ibid [14].
250   Ibid [27].
251   Ibid [95].

In *Lee v Ashers [No 2]*, the Court of Appeal expressly recognised that '[the] right in play is *the right to freedom of thought, conscience and religion* and the qualified right to manifestation of those beliefs protected by Article 9 ECHR'.[252] In that respect, the Court observed:

> The striking of the balance between the prohibition of discrimination on the grounds of sexual orientation in the provision of goods, facilities and services and the protection of religion, belief and conscience was considered in *Bull v Hall*. It was accepted in that case that the policy of refusing a double bedroom to unmarried couples was a manifestation of the hoteliers' religious beliefs. The importance to be attached to that right in a democratic society was acknowledged by the Supreme Court relying on the following passage in *Bayatyan v Armenia* (2011) 54 EHRR 467:
>
> > "The Court reiterates that, as enshrined in article 9, freedom of thought, conscience and religion is one of the foundations of a 'democratic society' within the meaning of the Convention. This freedom is, in its religious dimension, one of the most vital elements that go to make up the identity of believers and their conception of life, but it is also a precious asset for atheists, agnostics, sceptics and the unconcerned. The pluralism indissociable from a democratic society, which has been dearly won over the centuries, depends on it. That freedom entails, inter alia, freedom to hold or not to hold religious beliefs and to practise or not to practise a religion."
>
> As in *Bull v Hall* it is clear that the limitation on the Article 9 rights of the appellants is in accordance with law and pursues a legitimate aim being the rights of the respondent under the *2006 Regulations*. The issue is whether there is a reasonable relationship of proportionality between the means employed and the aim sought to be achieved.[253]

---

252   *Lee v Ashers [No 2]* (n 12) [61] (emphasis added).
253   Ibid [61]-[62].

In applying that authority, the Court of Appeal held:

> To prohibit the provision of a message on a cake supportive of gay marriage on the basis of religious belief is to permit direct discrimination. If businesses were free to choose what services to provide to the gay community on the basis of religious belief the potential for arbitrary abuse would be substantial.[254]

In the Court below, Brownlie J justified her conclusion in accordance with the acclaimed equality of the law. She explained, '[t]his is not a law which is for one belief only but is equal to and for all', and supported her argument with an analogy:

> If the Plaintiff was a gay man who ran a bakery business and the Defendants as Christians wanted him to bake a cake with the words 'support heterosexual marriage' the Plaintiff would be required to do so as, otherwise; he would, according to the law be discriminating against the Defendants. This is not a law which is for one belief only but is equal to and for all.[255]

A similar analogy was adopted by the Court of Appeal. The Court observed:

> The benefit from the message or slogan on the cake could only accrue to gay or bisexual people. The appellants would not have objected to a cake carrying the message 'Support Heterosexual Marriage' or indeed 'Support Marriage'. We accept that it was the use of the word 'Gay' in the context of the message which prevented the order from being fulfilled. The reason that the order was cancelled was that the appellants would not provide a cake with a message supporting a right to marry for those of a particular sexual orientation. That was the answer to the 'reason why question' that *Shamoon* said should be asked. There was an exact correspondence between those of the particular sexual orientation and those in respect of whom the message supported the right to marry. This was a case of association with the gay and bisexual community and the protected personal characteristic was the sexual orientation of that community. Accordingly this was

---

254   Ibid [64].
255   *Lee v Ashers [No 1]* (n 9) [93].

direct discrimination.[256]

That analogy, combined with the above analysis by the Court of Appeal, demonstrates the failure of the courts to adequately recognise two competing *forum internum* rights. The focus is upon the impact of the defendants' actions upon the *forum internum* of Mr Lee, when considered in the light of the applicable domestic legislation. The unequal recognition of the *forum internum* is further emphasised by the failure of the courts to consider the possibility of accommodating both competing *forum internum* rights. For example, a solution that avoids derogation to either liberty is to suggest the purchaser go elsewhere.

Malcolm D Evans justified a court's focus upon the *forum externum* due to the unquantifiable nature of the *forum internum*. He said that 'it is only possible to discern its scope by examining what falls within the ambit of the so called *"forum externum"*'.[257] He also observed the practice of the court in disregarding religious liberty infringement claims if 'a person's inability to manifest their religion or belief ... is largely attributable to choices which those individuals have freely made for themselves'.[258] This is supported by the judgment of Lady Rafferty J in *Bull v Hall* (considered in both *Lee v Ashers [No 1]* and *Lee v Ashers [No 2]*).[259] She said, 'I do not consider that the Appellants face any difficulty in manifesting their religious beliefs, they are merely prohibited from so doing in the commercial context they have chosen'.[260] This construction allows for extensive unacknowledged derogation from the *forum internum*. This is because the act of manifesting religion is a choice intrinsically connected to an adopted (or handed down) faith. An approach to freedom of choice that excludes the importance of connection could support the assumption:

256   *Lee v Ashers [No 2]* (n 12) [58].
257   Malcolm D Evans (n 3) 8–9.
258   Ibid 15.
259   *Bull v Hall* (n 239).
260   Ibid [56].

> The solution to their [religious believers] difficulties lay in their own hands. If they wished to prioritise their religious observance above their contractual [or commercial] commitments as employees, they could do so by changing the nature of their employment.[261]

If that were accepted, the courts could persuasively argue 'there was no [invalid] interference with their freedom to manifest their religion'.[262] The argument removes the claim of derogation from the *forum internum* by stipulating the violation does not count as interference as it involved an avoidable choice by the individual.

The approach of the court in both *Lee v Ashers [No 1]* and *Lee v Ashers [No 2]* reveals a preference in law, at times, for recognising the secular right of those with a same sex sexual orientation to obtain services from their choice of supplier over the religious right to freely believe in public or private.[263] That preference appears to reflect a secular interpretation of Devlin's majority rules approach. Except now 'public morality' deems the manifestation of religious belief in a commercial setting to be a vice.[264] Ironically, the approach of Mill, Hart and Jefferson now serves the argument of the religious believer to maintain his or her freedom of religion (*forum internum*). This is because to decline to complete a cake order does no injury to the plaintiff (or respondent) – it does not pick his pocket nor break his leg.[265]

In 2018, the United Kingdom Supreme Court decision in *Lee v Ashers [No 3]* reversed the decisions of Brownlie J and the Court of Appeal. The Supreme Court held:

> [T]here was no discrimination on grounds of sexual orientation in

---

261   Malcolm D Evans (n 3) 15, citing *Kottinen v Finland* (Application No 24949/94, 3 December 1996); *Stedman v the United Kingdom* (Application No 29107/95, 9 April 1997).

262   Ibid.

263   *Lee v Ashers [No 1]* (n 9); *Lee v Ashers [No 2]* (n 12).

264   Cf Devlin (n 27) 92. See, eg, *Elane Photography* (n 9); *Bull v Hall* (n 239); *Christian Youth Camps Limited v Cobaw Community Health Service Limited* (n 239); *Lee v Ashers [No 1]* (n 9).

265   Jefferson (n 15) 170. See also Shaw-Miller (n 17) 80.

this case ... It is deeply humiliating, and an affront to human dignity, to deny someone a service because of that person's race, gender, disability, sexual orientation or any of the other protected personal characteristics. But that is not what happened in this case and *it does the project of equal treatment no favours to seek to extend it beyond its proper scope*.[266]

The judgment provides a subtle criticism of the inconsistent treatment of the *forum internum* by the lower courts with the observation 'it does the project of equal treatment no favours to seek to extend it beyond its proper scope'. The '*it*' being a reference to the application of domestic law aimed at protecting certain 'personal characteristics' such as sexual orientation.

Turning to the reasoning of Brownlie J and the Court of Appeal, the Supreme Court observed:

The District Judge did not accept that the defendants were being required to promote and support a campaign for a change in the law to enable same sex marriage (paras 40 and 62). The Court of Appeal, while not deciding the point, appears to have agreed with this: 'the fact that a baker provides a cake for a particular team or portrays witches on a Halloween cake does not indicate any support for either' (para 67). These are, in fact, two separate matters: being required to promote a campaign and being associated with it. As to the first, the bakery was required, on pain of liability in damages, to supply a product which actively promoted the cause, a cause in which many believe, but a cause in which the owners most definitely and sincerely did not. As to the second, there is no requirement that the person who is compelled to speak can only complain if he is thought by others to support the message. Mrs McArthur may have been worried that others would see the Ashers logo on the cake box and think that they supported the campaign. *But that is by the way: what matters is that by being required to produce the cake they were being required to express a message with which they deeply disagreed.*[267]

---

266   *Lee v Ashers [No 3]* (n 12) [35] (emphasis added).
267   Ibid [54] (emphasis added).

Next, the Supreme Court addressed how the decisions of the two courts incorrectly permitted interference with the *forum internum*. The Court observed:

> Articles 9 and 10 are, of course, qualified rights which may be limited or restricted in accordance with the law and insofar as this is necessary in a democratic society in pursuit of a legitimate aim. It is, of course, the case that businesses offering services to the public are not entitled to discriminate on certain grounds. The bakery could not refuse to provide a cake – or any other of their products - to Mr Lee because he was a gay man or because he supported gay marriage. *But that important fact does not amount to a justification for something completely different - obliging them to supply a cake iced with a message with which they profoundly disagreed. In my view they would be entitled to refuse to do that whatever the message conveyed by the icing on the cake - support for living in sin, support for a particular political party, support for a particular religious denomination.* The fact that this particular message had to do with sexual orientation is irrelevant to the *FETO* claim.[268]

While describing art 9 rights as 'qualified', the Supreme Court shifted the emphasis away from the capacity to make a different choice but returned to the individual basis and motivation for the same. The majority judgment cited the decision of *Buscarini v San Marino*,[269] which decision held that obliging a person to manifest a belief which they do not hold has been held to be a limitation on their art 9(1) rights.[270] In that decision, the Court reiterated that freedom of thought, conscience and religion 'entails, *inter alia*, freedom to hold or not to hold religious beliefs and to practise or not to practise a religion'.[271] The Supreme Court also made observations as to the authorities relevant to the intersection with *Convention* rights.[272]

The judgment in *Lee v Ashers [No 3]* provides express guidance as

---

268   Ibid [55] (emphasis added).
269   (1999) 30 EHRR 208.
270   *Lee v Ashers [No 3]* (n 12) [50].
271   *Buscarini v San Marino* (n 270) [34].
272   See *Lee v Ashers [No 3]* (n 12) [49]-[59].

to the appropriate approach to be taken by courts in the resolution of complaints involving competing individual rights, in particular, in circumstances where the complainant is recognised as part of a protected class and the respondent relies upon *forum internum* rights. The Supreme Court held that an individual that offers a service, such as cake decoration, should not be obligated to provide such a service, notwithstanding the fact the customer belongs to a protected class, when it concerns a message with which they profoundly disagree. By that decision, the Supreme Court highlighted the caution to be taken when making findings of fact with respect to an alleged act of discrimination, namely, while the presence of a protected class to a complaint may be relevant, it does not negate the requirement to consider the basis for a respondent's refusal of service within the specific circumstances of the dispute.

2   *Elane Photography*[273]

The approach of the New Mexico Supreme Court in *Elane Photography* mirrored that of *Lee v Ashers [No 1]*.[274] The appellant was a company that declined to provide its service for a same-sex committal ceremony.[275] The reason was based on the owners' Christian beliefs. It was an act based on conscience. The owners also argued that their conduct 'did not discriminate on the basis of sexual orientation'.[276] Despite this, the New Mexico Supreme Court was reluctant to explore the *forum internum* of the owners, and focused upon the connection between the *forum internum* and the *forum externum* of the respondent:

The difficulty in distinguishing between status and conduct in the

---

273   *Elane Photography* (n 9).

274   Ibid. See also *Willock v Elane Photography LLC* (New Mexico Human Rights Commission, HRD No 06-12-20-0686, 9 April 2008). The New Mexico Human Rights Commission found Ms Willock, the complainant, proved her discrimination claim based on sexual orientation.

275   Ibid [7]–[9].

276   Ibid [11], [14].

context of sexual orientation discrimination is that people may base their judgment about an individual's sexual orientation on the individual's conduct. To allow discrimination based on conduct so closely correlated with sexual orientation would severely undermine the purpose of the [law].[277]

The secular version of Devlin's approach appears again. The connection between the forums and law echoes the 'seamless web' of public and private morality.[278] Hence, harm to the *forum internum* is recognised as harm to the *forum externum* – and vice versa. Edward L Chávez J supported this analogy by stating that 'when a law prohibits discrimination on the basis of sexual orientation, that law similarly protects conduct that is inextricably tied to sexual orientation'.[279] He concluded that there was 'no basis for distinguishing between discrimination based on sexual orientation and discrimination based on someone's conduct of publicly committing to a person of the same sex'.[280] The judgment supported recognition of an overlap between private-public spheres but only in the context of the protected liberty of sexual orientation.[281]

Unlike *Lee v Ashers*, it may be noted, the matter did not progress through the appellate courts.[282]

---

277 Ibid [16].
278 Hart (n 37) 49; Devlin (n 27) 113–4.
279 *Elane Photography* (n 9) [17].
280 Ibid [18].
281 See also, Tim Wilson, 'Religious Freedom isn't a Trump Card, but it Does Need to be a Part of Marriage Equality and Rights Debate', *Sydney Morning Herald* (Sydney) 21 October 2015 <http://www.smh.com.au/comment/religious-freedom-isnt-a-trump-card-but-it-does-need-to-be-a-part-of-marriage-equality-debate-20151020-gkecyn.html>. Wilson explores the 'attitudinal shift' in Australia in connection to same-sex marriage and its impact on religious institutions. He concludes both secular and religious arguments must be engaged, '[r]eligious freedom doesn't trump the rights and freedoms of others, but it is something to be accommodated in the rights and freedoms of all'.
282 The US Supreme Court declined to hear the appeal, without comment, on April 7, 2014: Order of US Supreme Court in *Elane Photography LLC v Willock* (No 13-585, 7 April 2014).

3   *The Power of Domestic Legislation to Protect Individual Rights*

The decisions in *Lee v Ashers [No 1]*, *Lee v Ashers [No 2]* and *Elane Photography* justified interference with religious liberty on the basis of domestic legislation protecting sexual orientation.[283] Northern Ireland provided express protection of sexual orientation in the *2006 Regulations* and *Fair Employment and Treatment Order 1998* (*'FETO'*).[284] New Mexico recognised similar protection set out in the *New Mexico Human Rights Act* (*'HRA'*).[285] Although, both the *FETO* and *HRA* also included reference to religion, protection was only provided to the person seeking a service, not to the provider.[286]

Although the judgment in *Lee v Ashers [No 1]* briefly considered the *Convention*, Brownlie J limited consideration of the defendants' right to 'manifest their religion without *unjustified* limitation'.[287] Her Honour said:

> in relation to the requirement to balance competing interests, I find that the extent to which the *2006 Regulations* and/or the *1998 Order* limit the manifestation of the Defendants' religious beliefs, those limitations are necessary in a democratic society and are a proportionate means of achieving the legitimate aim which is the protection of the rights and freedoms of the Plaintiff. I am satisfied that this does not give rise to any incompatibility between the rights of the Defendants under Article 9 and the rights of the Plaintiff under the *2006 Regulations* and/or the *1998 Order.* To do otherwise would be to allow a religious belief to dictate what the law is.[288]

By framing the defendants' argument in terms of manifestation, the interference with the *forum internum* was disregarded, and valid

---

283   *Lee v Ashers [No 1]* (n 9); *Lee v Ashers [No 2]* (n 12); *Elane Photography* (n 9).

284   *2006 Regulations* (n 244); *Fair Employment and Treatment (Northern Ireland) Order 1998* (UK) s 3 ('FETO'). The *FETO* protects sexual orientation under the broad category of 'discrimination by way of victimisation': at s 3(1)(b).

285   *New Mexico Human Rights Act*, ch 28, NM Laws (2006) § 28-1-7 ('HRA').

286   FETO (n 285) s 3; HRA (n 286) § 28-1-7 (F).

287   *Lee v Ashers [No 1]* (n 9) [81] (emphasis added).

288   Ibid [91].

restriction of the *forum externum* was the primary focus. Brownlie J focused on the *forum externum* rights of the defendants, recognised in international law, and the competing *forum internum* rights of the plaintiff. She found that '[the law] must protect the rights of the Defendants to have and to manifest their religious beliefs but it also recognizes... the rights of the Plaintiff not to be discriminated because of his sexual orientation'.[289]

In *Lee v Ashers [No 2]*, the appellants submitted that in circumstances where ECHR rights are at issue, the function of the courts is to strike the balance between competing rights paying due respect to the legislature.[290] While the Court of Appeal expressly recognised the engagement of art 9(1) and cited authority as to its significance, the Court of Appeal observed:

> The proportionality assessment in this case points firmly to the conclusion that the *2006 Regulations* should be interpreted in accordance with their natural meaning. The structure of the Regulations, the need to protect against arbitrary discrimination, the ability to alter the offer and the lack of any association of the appellants with the message all point that way.[291]

Further, notwithstanding the appellants' contention that 'the legislation discriminates against the appellants and against that class of persons who subscribe to their religious belief concerning the sinful nature of homosexual activity and their political opinion that opposes same sex marriage', the Court of Appeal held:

> How does the legislation treat a person who holds the contrary religious belief and political opinion to that of the appellants in the same circumstances? Those who refuse goods and services to those who accept same sex relations and support same sex marriage are treated *by the legislation* in the same manner as the appellants have been treated. They may not be treated the same by those holding

---

289   Ibid [93]–[94].
290   *Lee v Ashers [No 2]* (n 12) [38].
291   Ibid [72].

opposing religious beliefs or political opinions but *the legislation* treats them all the same.

Neither the *1998 Order* nor the *2006 Regulations* treat the appellants less favourably. The legislation prohibits the provision of discriminatory services on the ground of sexual orientation. The appellants are caught by the legislation because they are providing such discriminatory services. Anyone who applies a religious aspect or a political aspect to the provision of services may be caught by equality legislation, not because the legislation treats their religious belief or political opinion less favourably but because that person seeks to distinguish, on a basis that is prohibited, between those who will receive their service and those who will not. The answer is not to have the legislation changed and thereby remove the equality protection concerned. The answer is for the supplier of services to cease distinguishing, on prohibited grounds, between those who may or may not receive the service. Thus the supplier may provide the particular service to all or to none but not to a selection of customers based on prohibited grounds. In the present case the appellants might elect not to provide a service that involves any religious or political message. What they may not do is provide a service that only reflects their own political or religious belief in relation to sexual orientation.[292]

Thus, the Court of Appeal found against the appellants: '[i]t was not necessary to read down or disapply the provisions of the *2006 Regulations*'.[293]

In contrast to Northern Ireland, New Mexico had enacted the *New Mexico Religious Freedom Restoration Act* ('*RFRA*').[294] The appellants in *Elane Photography* attempted to challenge the provision in the *HRA* by arguing it conflicted with the *RFRA*.[295] The argument was unsuccessful as the *RFRA* was only enforceable against government agencies; it did not apply to the respondent.[296]

---

292   Ibid [99]-[100] (original emphasis).
293   Ibid [105].
294   *New Mexico Religious Freedom Restoration Act*, ch 17, NM Laws (2000) ('*RFRA*').
295   *Elane Photography* (n 9); *HRA* (n 285) § 28-1-7 (F); *RFRA* (n 295) § 28-22-3.
296   *Elane Photography* (n 9) [78]; *RFRA* (n 295) § 28-22-3.

Neither jurisdiction had implemented legislation to specifically protect religious freedom. The law only recognised the right of the customer's individual liberty to be respected.

The respondent was successful in *Elane Photography* due to the express protection of their internal rights being solidified in the *HRA*:[297]

> It is an unlawful discriminatory practice for: ... any person in any public accommodation to make a distinction, directly or indirectly, in offering or refusing to offer its services, facilities, accommodations or goods to any person because of race, religion, color, national origin, ancestry, sex, *sexual orientation*, gender identity.[298]

The Court accepted the application of the *HRA*. Furthermore, it rejected each alternative claim of the applicant, which included appealing to the first amendment rights of free speech and free exercise.[299]

By its decision in *Lee v Ashers [No 3]*, the Supreme Court held that domestic law with respect to the protection of one person's sexual orientation against discrimination need not come at the cost of the art 9 rights of another. However, following the decision of the New Mexico Supreme Court in *Elane Photography*, the domestic legislation of New Mexico encourages an inconsistent approach to protection of the *forum internum*. The latter case limits protection in commercial settings and does not fully acknowledge the impact of the limitation upon the *forum internum*.

Taylor observed, in the context of art 18, 'precision [is] required in domestic law, particularly in confining suitably the eligible grounds of limitation, avoiding any possible restriction on absolute protection and avoiding derogation of any sort'.[300] Precision is also required in

---

297   *Elane Photography* (n 9).
298   *HRA* (n 286) § 28-1-7 (F) (emphasis added).
299   *Elane Photography* (n 9) [79]; *United States Constitution* amend I.
300   Taylor, *A Commentary on the International Covenant on Civil and Political Rights: The*

the approach of the courts. Whilst *Lee v Ashers [No 3]* is an example of a higher court squarely recognising the importance of *forum internum* rights and, by extension, the significance of intangible harm, the impact of that decision must await further consideration following its application in subsequent decisions.

The contrast between the two jurisdictions, considered in this part, highlights the important position of the judiciary in developing clearer understanding of the dichotomy between belief and manifestation of the belief as well as the appropriate approach to resolution of competing individual rights claims.

CONCLUSION

International human rights instruments prepared in the 20th century state that freedom of thought, conscience and religion is a fundamental right. However, neither international customary law nor the *ICCPR* or *Convention* have developed jurisprudence detailed enough to protect the *forum internum* from interference. Both the HRC and ECHR consistently restrict construction of religious liberty claims to the *forum externum* and any consequential interference with the *forum internum* is then either ignored or given minimal attention. If the non-derogable classification of the *forum internum*, in the absence of any permissible grounds of limitation, is said to create an inviolable right and provide absolute protection – in practice, that is not the case.

The first part of this paper explored the nature of harm. It demonstrated that the need to protect citizens from direct physical harm is considered the primary justification for state interference with individual liberty. This part showed that more recent theorists have suggested that the state is justified in restricting liberty when only indirect harm is threatened. However, modern courts have

---

UN Human Rights Committee's Monitoring of ICCPR Rights (n 7) 536.

struggled to consistently explain why intangible harm justifies state intervention which intrudes upon the *forum internum.*

The second part identified the nature of harm addressed in the *ICCPR* and *Convention.* This part explained that the valid grounds for limitation of the *forum externum* under art 18 (*ICCPR*) and art 9 (*Convention*) address the capacity for tangible and intangible harm. Only the HRC has expressly rejected all forms of interference with the *forum internum* on the grounds that it is a truly inviolable right or an absolute human right. The discrepancy between modern justifications for state legislation which interferes with the *forum internum* and the HRC's insistence that the *forum internum* is or should be inviolable ought to be resolved.

The third part explored what 'non-derogable' means. This part concluded that language extolling the non-derogable importance of the *forum internum*, in particular in the absence of any eligible grounds of limitation, which supports a conclusion that the *forum internum* is also inviolable, is meaningless unless it is protected.

The fourth part explained that intervention by the state to prevent intangible harm has become a modern norm. Despite historical insistence by the HRC and ECHR that only tangible harm can justify state intervention which interferes with freedom of conscience, both institutions have upheld state practices that intervened to prevent intangible harm as defined by majoritarian interests. Both the HRC and ECHR have upheld limitations upon religious manifestation that were deemed threatening. In the case of the ECHR, that result was facilitated by their use of their concepts of 'margin of appreciation', 'necessity' and 'proportionality'. A similar departure from Millian principles was continued in contemporary cases at the domestic level. This part identified two competing individual rights claims and demonstrated that, for the most part, only the majoritarian interest was protected. However, the decision of the Supreme Court of the United Kingdom in *Lee v Ashers [No 3]* represents a distinct shift in the approach of the judiciary in the context of competing individual rights claims in the context of an allegation of discrimination. In that decision, domestic legislation protecting sexual orientation rights and the protection that should be afforded to the right of religious belief under international instruments were considered together.

If the *forum internum* is an absolute and inviolable right, the international jurisprudence which concerns it must be clarified. The 21st century approach of states, courts and tribunals has solidified to recognise the existence of intangible harm. Moving forward, the courts and tribunals that consider the *forum internum* need to expressly identify when it arises in a particular complaint. Many *forum externum* claims raise issues of intangible harm under the *forum internum*. It is submitted that such judicial analysis will require future courts to determine whether the *forum internum* should be protected where there is no tangible harm. When the *forum internum* implications of a case have been identified, courts will be better able to decide their proportionality questions. However, modern jurisprudence and theory fails to provide a compelling and clear explanation as to whether state intervention to prevent intangible harm is consistent with an inviolable *forum internum*. Future judicial analysis will have to work out what it means to say that the *forum internum* is inviolable, particularly when that issue arises in a case where the *forum internum* issues that arise suggest only intangible harm. The recent decision in *Lee v Ashers [No 3]* is a turning point in recognising competing claims of intangible harm, but further analysis by the judiciary is required to enable the creation of such a framework.

BIBLIOGRAPHY

Articles

Chris Berg, 'Free Speech is Non-negotiable' (2014) 66(2) *IPA Review* 6

Peter W Edge, 'Religion and Law: An Introduction' (2008) 10(1) *Ecclesiastical Law Journal* 121

Marie Iskander, 'Balancing Freedoms and Creating a Fair Marketplace of Ideas: The Value of 18C of the Racial Discrimination Act' (2014) 9(10) *Indigenous Law Bulletin* 19

M. Todd Parker, 'The Freedom to Manifest Religious Belief: An Analysis of the Necessity Clauses of the ICCPR and the ECHR' (2006) 17 *Duke Journal of Comparative & International Law* 91

Peter Petkoff, 'Forum Internum and Forum Externum in Canon Law and Public International Law with a Particular Reference to the Jurisprudence of the European Court of Human Rights' [2012] 7 *Religion and Human Rights* 183

Koji Teraya, 'Emerging Hierarchy in International Human Rights and Beyond: From the Perspective of Non-derogable Rights' (2001) 12 *European Journal of International Law* 917

Books

James Allan, *A Sceptical Theory of Morality and Law* (Peter Lang, 1998)

Patrick Devlin, *The Enforcement of Morals* (Oxford University Press, 1968)

Carolyn Evans, *Freedom of Religion under the European Convention on Human Rights* (Oxford University Press, 2001)

Carolyn Evans, *Legal Protection of Religious Freedom in Australia* (Federation Press, 2012)

Malcolm D. Evans, *Manual on the Wearing of Religious Symbols in Public Areas* (Martinus Nijoff Publishers, 2008)

Louis Henkin, (ed), *The International Bill of Human Rights: The Covenant on Civil and Political Rights* (Columbia University Press, 1981)

Thomas Jefferson, *Notes on the State of Virginia* (J W Randolf, 1853)

Brian D. Lepard, *Customary International Law: A New Theory with Practical Applications* (Cambridge University Press, 2010)

Simon Shaw-Miller, (ed), *On Liberty: John Stuart Mill* (Yale University Press, 2003)

Paul M. Taylor, *A Commentary on the International Covenant on Civil and Political Rights: The UN Human Rights Committee's Monitoring of ICCPR Rights* (Cambridge University Press, 2020)

Paul M. Taylor, *Freedom of Religion: UN and European Human Rights Law and Practice* (Cambridge University Press, 2005)

Jeremy Waldron, *The Harm in Hate Speech* (UBC Press, 2000)

D. Don Welch, (ed), *Law and Morality* (Fortress Press, 1987)

Cases

Australia

Christian Youth Camps Limited v Cobaw Community Health Service Limited [2014] VSCA 75

Europe

Buscarini v San Marino (1999) 30 EHRR 208

Eweida v UK (2013) 57 EHRR 8

Handyside v United Kingdom (1979-80) 1 EHRR 737

Hasan v Bulgaria (2002) 34 EHRR 55

Kokkinakis v Greece (1993) 17 EHRR 397

Kottinen v Finland (Application No 24949/94, 3 December 1996)

Otto-Preminger Institut v Austria (1994) 19 EHRR 34

Şahin v Turkey (2007) 44 EHRR 5

SAS v France (2015) 60 EHRR 11

Stedman v the United Kingdom (Application No 29107/95, 9 April 1997)

Sunday Times v the United Kingdom [no. 1] (1979-80) 2 EHRR 245

Valsamis v Greece (1997) 24 EHRR 294

United Kingdom

Bull v Hall [2012] EWCA Civ 83

Lee v Ashers Baking Co Ltd [2015] NICty 2

Lee v Ashers Baking Co Ltd [2016] NICA 39

Lee v Ashers Baking Co Ltd [2018] UKSC 49

McFarlane v Relate Avon Ltd [2010] EWCA Civ 880

United States

Bhinder v Canadian National Railway Co [1985] 2 SCR 561

Elane Photography LLC v Willock, 309 P.3d 53 (NM 2013)

Obergefell v Hodges, 576 US 644 (2015)

Ontario Human Rights Commission v Borough of Etobicoke [1982] 1 SCR 202

Willock v Elane Photography LLC (New Mexico Human Rights Commission, HRD No 06-12-20-0686, 9 April 2008)

Legislation

Abortion Law Reform Act 2008 (Vic)

Canada Act 1982 (UK)

Canadian Human Rights Act, RSC 1985, c H-6

Criminal Code *Act 1924* (Tas)

Criminal Code Amendment Act 1997 (Tas)

Equality Act (Sexual Orientation) Regulations (Northern Ireland) 2006 (UK)

Fair Employment and Treatment (Northern Ireland) Order 1998 (UK)

New Mexico Human Rights Act, ch 28, NM Laws (2006)

New Mexico Religious Freedom Restoration Act, ch 17, NM Laws (2000)

Racial Discrimination Act 1975 (Cth)

United States Constitution

Declaration of the Right of Man and Citizen (France)

Treaties

European Convention for the Protection of Human Rights and Fundamental Freedoms, opened for signature 4 November 1950, 213 UNTS 221

(entered into force 3 September 1953)

International Covenant on Civil and Political Rights, opened for signature 16 December 1966, 999 UNTS 171 (entered into force 23 March 1976)

United Nations Documents

Bhinder v Canada, 37th sess, UN Doc CCPR/C/37/D/208/1986 (9 November 1989)

Human Rights Committee, *General Comment No 24: Issues Relating to Reservations Made upon Ratification or Accession to the Covenant or the Optional Protocols thereto, or in Relation to Declarations under Article 41 of the Covenant*, 52nd sess, UN Doc CCPR/C/21/Rev.1/Add.6 (4 November 1994)

Human Rights Committee, *General Comment No 29: Article 4: Derogations during a State of Emergency*, 72nd sess, UN Doc CCPR/C/21/Rev.1/Add.11 (31 August 2001)

Human Rights Committee, *General Comment No 22: Article 18 (Freedom of Thought, Conscience or Religion)*, 48th sess, UN Doc CCPR/C/21/Rev.1/Add.4 (30 July 1993)

Toonen v Australia, 50th sess, UN Doc CCPR/C/50/D/488/1992 (31 March 1994)

Universal Declaration of Human Rights, GA Res 217A (III), UN GAOR, 3rd sess, 183rd plen mtg, UN Doc A/810 (10 December 1948)

Speeches

Brennan, Frank, 'Human Rights, the Churches, and the Vocation of the Christian Lawyer' (Speech delivered at the Queensland Christian Lawyers Dinner, The Ship Inn, South Bank, 14 July 2011)

Websites

Attorney-General's Department, *Absolute Rights* <https://www.ag.gov.au/RightsAndProtections/HumanRights/PublicSectorGuidanceSheets/Pages/Absoluterights.aspx>

Attorney-General's Department, *Right to freedom of thought, conscience and religion or belief* <https://www.ag.gov.au/RightsAndProtections/HumanRights/PublicSectorGuidanceSheets/Pages/

Righttofreedomofthoughtconscienceandreligionorbelief.aspx>

Ball, Rachel, *Absolute and Non-derogable Rights in International Law* (21 July 2011) <http://www.parliament.vic.gov.au/images/stories/committees/ sarc/charter_review/supplementary_info/263_-_Addendum.pdf>

Other

Attorney-General's Department, 'Racial Discrimination Act' (Media Release, 25 March 2014)

Greer, Steven, 'The Margin of Appreciation: Interpretation and Discretion Under the European Convention on Human Rights' (Human Rights Files No 17, Council of Europe, July 2000)

Order of US Supreme Court in *Elane Photography LLC v Willock* (No 13-585, 7 April 2014)

Wilson, Tim, 'Religious Freedom isn't a Trump Card, but it Does Need to be a Part of Marriage Equality and Rights Debate', *Sydney Morning Herald* (Sydney) 21 October 2015

2

ACCOMMODATING RELIGIOUS EXPRESSION IN A SECULAR AGE

JONATHAN POWYS

ABSTRACT

There is currently an ideological battle underway regarding the future of religious practice within Australia. At the center of the conflict is the challenge to religious free expression by the emerging anti-discrimination norm, which has arisen due to a proliferation of emergent rights that often intersect with religious autonomy. This chapter examines the emerging conflict and suggests that the full spectrum of traditional theological concepts can no longer be taught without the risk of anti-discrimination litigation. This is a state of affairs that must be reevaluated in order to preserve authentic pluralism.

The chapter focuses on laws that prohibit discrimination based on sexual orientation, which is the area where traditional religionists are most vulnerable to prosecution due to the divergence between their beliefs and contemporary culture.

Questioning the correct balance between religious freedom and the causing of offense is both difficult and controversial for a variety of reasons. Potential answers are paradoxical, since the laws introduced to protect the rights and dignity of one group may simultaneously restrict the rights of others. Notwithstanding the challenge, legislators must seek tailored solutions that respect all the traditions and beliefs involved. This chapter explores a framework for doing so.

INTRODUCTION

In early 2005, Robin Fletcher, a prisoner in the Victorian prison system attended a religious course offered at the facility in which he was held. The course was known as the Alpha program and introduced participants to the precepts of the Christian faith. After attending the Alpha program Mr. Fletcher, who claimed to practice Wicca (a neo-pagan religion), made a complaint to the Victorian Equal Opportunity Commission pursuant to the *Racial and Religious Tolerance Act 2001* (Vic) on the grounds that several disparaging remarks were made during a discussion about 'witches' and 'astrologers and occultists'. More specifically, issue was taken with the use of certain Old Testament Bible verses.[1] It was claimed this expressed hatred to Wiccans and amounted to religious vilification. As President of the Victorian Civil and Administrative Tribunal, Justice Stuart Morris summarily dismissed Fletcher's appeal after a member of the Commission had refused to entertain it.[2]

Despite the swift dismissal of both of Mr Fletcher's attempts to use the Victorian legislation, those attempts illustrate a troubling aspect of anti-discrimination laws as they presently stand. For the threat of such claims may be enough to stifle some religious teaching.[3]

---

1   The passage of scripture complained of was Deuteronomy ch 18: 10 -12 (King James Version): There shall not be found among you anyone who maketh his son or his daughter to pass through the fire, or that useth divination, or an observer of times, or an enchanter, or a witch, or a charmer, or a consulter with familiar spirits, or a wizard or a necromancer. For all that do these things are an abomination unto the Lord: and because of these abominations the Lord thy God drove them out from before thee.

2   See *Fletcher v Salvation Army* [2005] VCAT 1523, [1]-[4].

3   For example, concerning the circumstances attached to *Fletcher v Salvation Army* [2005] VCAT 1523, Parkinson has observed that even though Justice Morris summarily dismissed the application and regarded the complaint as 'quite hope-

Other cases have seen similar complaints progress much further.[4] Because the affirmative use of anti-discrimination against religious teaching and expression is likely to chill the practice of religion and the free expression of religious beliefs, this chapter raises questions about the reach and impact of anti-discrimination law on religious practice and expression.

This chapter therefore examines the emerging conflict between religious freedom and anti discrimination norms in Australia, suggesting that the full spectrum of traditional theological concepts can no longer be taught without the risk of anti-discrimination litigation. This state of affairs needs to be reevaluated. An analysis of all of the laws able to restrict religious freedom are too many to be covered in the limited space available and so I have focused on the way laws that outlaw discrimination based on sexual orientation impact religious teaching and expression. This is an area where traditional religionists are most vulnerable to becoming the targets of complaints and prosecutions due to the growing divergence of opinion held between them and mainstream consensus.

---

less', it took a hearing to determine this. To arrive at this determination required the respondent to appear in person (by video link from jail), two different barristers to be instructed by the two defendants and a third who appeared for Corrections Victoria. The costs that would accompany such procedures would not be small and are sufficient to cause many to become apprehensive when making statements able to trigger anti-discrimination provisions: see Patrick Parkinson, 'Religious Vilification, Anti Discrimination Laws and Religious Minorities in Australia: The Freedom to be Different' (Legal Studies Research Paper No 08/59, University of Sydney, June 2008) 8 ('Religious Vilification').

4   Once such example is found by way of the circumstances concerning Catch the Fire Ministries, an evangelical Christian group who, on 9 March 2002, hosted a seminar in Melbourne concerning Islam. Members of the Islamic community attended the seminar and latter launched legal action pursuant to the *Racial and Religious Tolerance Act 2001* (Vic), alleging that the discussion, which took place during the seminar, vilified Muslims. The ramifications of that accusation led to years of litigation, extensive media exposure and, according to one report, 'more than $500,000' being spent on defending charges that were later overturned. For an extended discussion of these circumstances and the problems highlighted by the law that enabled them, see Rex Ahdar, 'Religious Vilification: Confused Policy, Unsound Principle and Unfortunate Law' (2007) 26 *University of Queensland Law Review* 293 ('Religious Vilification').

The first part of this chapter argues why the current approach to anti-discrimination laws needs to be reconsidered and is followed by examination of the social changes that have seen anti-discrimination statutes develop. Sketching out these developments provides context for the challenges present to religious liberties. This sketch also raises questions as to whether anti-discrimination laws are the best way to provide effective solutions when there are incommensurable differences that exist between individuals and groups. The incommensurability of the differences between some religious expression and gender orientation is illustrated by consideration of the dispute between Archbishop Julian Porteous and Martine Delaney in 2015 in Tasmania. After that discussion, potential solutions are contemplated.

The impact of Australian law on religious expression in Australia is the primary focus of this chapter. But reference is made to overseas circumstances when they offer useful insights into how we might respond to future problems in Australia.

Questioning the balance needed between religious freedom and the causing of offense on the basis of a person's sexuality is both difficult and controversial for a variety of reasons. Perhaps the foremost is that any potential answers are paradoxical since the laws introduced to protect the rights and dignity of one group would simultaneously restrict the rights of others. Discovering a framework that could work for all of the parties involved is therefore far from straightforward. Notwithstanding the challenge, legislators must seek more carefully tailored solutions that respect all the traditions and beliefs involved.

THE IMPORTANCE OF RELIGIOUS EXPRESSION

Both in Australia and abroad, there are numerous high profile challenges before the courts concerning the free expression of religious concepts. These challenges have arisen in large part due to a proliferation of emergent rights, which frequently intersect with religious autonomy. There is little likelihood that this trend will dissipate.[5] This increasing tension has raised the question why we need religious freedom and religious expression, and why freedom of conscience and religion is seen as a fundamental right.

Covering the full spectrum of reasons as to why religious liberty requires respect is beyond the scope of the present discussion. I therefore focus on key reasons why individuals and organisations should be free to communicate the religiously inspired values to which they hold. Also covered are the risks posed by the close regulation of religious free speech[6] to the broader society and the many benefits enjoyed as a result of religious observance.

Taking Pluralism and the Freedom to be Different Seriously

Modern day Australia is a nation of migrants. Although during its formative years, Australia possessed a dominant Christian value system, it no longer retains a central culture to which minority religious groups need to conform.

Regarding the most apt characterisation of modern Australia, Joel Harrison and Patrick Parkinson writing in the Monash University Law Review have said that:

> It is better to understand Australia as a federation of cultures in which there are different values and beliefs, all of which deserve to be respected and, wherever possible, accommodated.[7]

Given this diversity, and the need for different groups to have a

---

5   For articles that adopt a multi-national perspective upon challenges to religious liberties, see Rex Tauati Ahdar, 'The Vulnerability of Religious Liberty in Liberal States' (2009) 4 *Religion and Human Rights* 177; Iain Benson, 'The attack on Western Religions by Western Law: Re-Framing Pluralism, Liberalism and Diversity' (2013) 6 *International Journal of Religious Freedom* 111.

6   For further reading on this topic, see Ivan Hare and James Weinstein, *Extreme Speech and Democracy* (Oxford University Press, 2009) pt IV.

7   Joel Harrison and Patrick Parkinson, 'Freedom Beyond the Commons: Managing the Tension between Faith and Equality in a Multicultural Society' (2014) 40 *Monash University Law Review* 414, 417 ('Freedom Beyond the Commons').

right to make a distinctive offering, a tolerant pluralism is called for. Respect for another person's religious beliefs has been described by the High Court of Australia as 'the essence of a free society'[8] and both state and federal governments have sought to implement policies to foster this type of pluralism.[9]

A society that aspires to embrace pluralism assumes that the culture at large benefits from a diversity of belief systems. By extension, this requires the freedom for communities to communicate and practice the values which distinguish them from others. Absent a high degree of religious free speech these distinctions are unlikely to be maintained. Legal academic Cole Durham Jr has noted that the aim of government towards the fostering of a healthy pluralism should be 'not to repress differences but rather the enablement of peaceful, *yet authentic*, forms of expression'.[10]

Building and Maintaining Effective Institutions

The value of religious expression is also to be found within the communities and institutions formed around religious belief. Human nature causes people to seek out communities of common purpose. Offering a set of shared beliefs, religion has and remains a catalyst for building various types of institutions that bind people together in common purpose. Very often these communities act as a source of immense benefit for the society at large.[11]

---

8   *Church of the New Faith v Commissioner for Payroll Tax* (Vic) (1983) 154 CLR 120, 130 (Mason ACJ and Brennan J). For further high-level judicial comments concerning the importance of religious liberty to Australia, see *Christian Youth Camps Limited v Cowbaw Community Health Service Limited* [2014] VSCA 75, [560] (Redlich AJ).

9   See National Multicultural Advisory Council, Parliament of Australia, *Australian Multiculturalism for a New Century: Towards Inclusiveness* (1999).

10   Cole Durham Jr, 'Religious Freedom in a Worldwide Setting: Comparative Reflections' in Mary Ann Glendon and Hans F Zacher (eds), *Universal Rights in a World of Diversity: The Case of Religious Freedom* (The Pontifical Academy of Social Sciences Acta 17, 2012) 365 (emphasis added) ('Religious Freedom in a Worldwide Setting').

11   Ryan Messmore, 'Why Religious Liberty is Important for Institutions', *The Daily Signal* (Online, 26 March 2012) <http://dailysignal.com/2012/03/26/why-religious-liberty-is-important-for-institutions/>.

Roy Williams says that understanding the importance of religion in society is more than simple head counting. He has asserted that any assessment of religion in Australia should extend to an analysis of the impact of institutions as well as individual believers on the course of Australian history and the character of the society.[12] While a holistic appraisal regarding the value that religion has had to Australia is a contested issue,[13] a simple measurement is found in the contribution of religious organisations to the nation's wellbeing, both in the past and present. For example, religious education institutions have brought people together to engage in teaching and learning as well as providing a source of employment. Many hospitals with a religious genesis have attracted people around the purposes of healing and health. Religiously motivated charities undertake activities toward a common productive goal and churches bind members together in worship and provide a source of community and belonging.

These and many others institutions owe a debt to religious autonomy, without which the ability to create a shared culture or identity would have been denied. The formation of a shared identity flows from an organisation's ability to define a specific mission and a freedom to determine the framework by which the mission is carried out.[14]

This leads to the conclusion that there is a societal need to be mindful of corporate religious autonomy and respecting the right of organisations to align their policies and behaviours with religious precepts.[15]

---

12   Roy Williams, *Post God Nation* (Harper Collins, 2015) 13.

13   Ibid. This text is a good summary of the benefits provided by religion (mostly focused upon Christianity) while also acknowledging the problematic sectarian divisions that it has facilitated.

14   Craig B Mousin, 'State Constitutions within The United States and The Autonomy of Religious Institutions' in Gerhard Robbers (ed), *Church Autonomy: A Comparative Survey* (Peter Lang, 2001) 401. The words of Patrick Parkinson regarding this issue are also worth noting: '[s]hared religious belief might not be necessary to help clean the gutters of elderly people or provide support to needy families. But the shared motivation may be what brings the people together and inspires their commitment to community service': Parkinson, 'Religious Vilification' (n 3) 14.

15   Ian Leigh and Rex Ahdar, *Religious Freedom in the Liberal State* (Oxford University Press, 2nd ed, 2013) 157. There, the authors provide a useful summary of the

An Argument in Favour of Controversial Doctrines

When communicating religiously inspired ideals the potential for conflict over anti-discrimination norms in respect of same sex attraction is easily apparent. Many faith systems have prohibitions against homosexual practice. Locating scripture able to offend modern sensibilities is therefore not difficult. Such passages and the teachings that flow from them are not an exclusive feature of any mainstream or minority religious faith found in Australia. The discussion above covered reasons why religious liberty and expression need to be respected. Yet, it is difficult to imagine that any of the reasons listed would be severely undermined if the law was used to deter a Rabbi from classifying homosexuality as a sin or caused a Pastor to avoid certain topics when delivering a Sunday sermon. Hence, some may argue that is reasonable and not overly prohibitive to prescribe a limited set of restrictions in relation to this aspect of religious teaching.

Religious teachings cover many areas including compassion, morality, ethics and history. Human sexuality is a very small part of most doctrines and on account of this smallness an important question arises. Why should the law not be free to restrict religious expression that may offend or emotionally wound while allowing practitioners to continue unhindered in all other parts of their faith?

---

width of activities to which religious belief may extend:

The broad right to 'practice' or 'manifest' (to use the wording of the European Convention on Human Rights) one's religion or belief would seem to embrace a huge variety of activity if one takes the view — as many religions do — that all life is inspired by or generated by faith and belief. The most mundane of human behaviours can be 'spiritualized' and take on a religious connotation. One is practising one's religion when one eats, drinks, works, plays and gardens, as much as when one reads scripture, prays or meditates. In Christianity, 'the righteous will live by faith', 'everything that does not come from faith is sin', and 'whether you eat or drink or whatever you do, do it for the glory of God'. On this view there is no activity which is not generated by one's obedience (or disobedience) to God. Countless schools, hospitals, orphanages and shelters have been run by religious organizations as part of their religious mission. Running a café, gymnasium or bookshop could equally be part of one's religious calling.

This passage was cited in *Christian Youth Camps Limited v Cowbaw Community Health Service Limited* [2014] VSCA 75, [560] (Redlich AJ).

Arguing that religious expression should be restricted is underpinned by Australian case law where there is a history of curbing select aspects of religious expression to service what the High Court has regarded as the greater good.[16]

On the other hand, if the law is allowed to stifle religious expression in any part, including reference to sexual behaviour, it facilitates a significant undermining and dilution of religious free practice. The freedom to discriminate between right and wrong, according to the precepts of the religion, is fundamental to the cohesiveness of religion. Legislative intrusion into this area is therefore no small matter. For many, religion is a monumental part of life[17] and for this reason religious liberty has been characterised not as a freedom to do what one wants, but as a freedom to do what one must.[18] This dynamic was expressed remarkably well by Albi Sachs, a now retired judge of the South African Constitutional Court, who wrote:

> For many believers, their relationship with God or creation is central to all their activities. It concerns their capacity to relate in

---

16   Numerous high profile High Court decisions have validated the need to curb religious practice in service of a greater good. An important is example is found by way of *Krygger v Williams* (1912) 15 CLR 366. The facts concerned an adherent of the Jehovah's Witness faith, who was convicted of failing to report for military training and sentenced to temporary custody pursuant to pt XII of the *Defence Act 1903* (Cth). He appealed to the High Court, claiming that the law was an interference with the free exercise of his religion. The Court denied his appeal, finding that although the law imposed an inconvenience upon the way he practiced his religion, he could still comply with the law and continue in his faith to a great extent. Hence there was no undue infringement. Judgements such as *Krygger* signal that Australian jurisprudence is content to relegate religious belief to the world of the private. Note the strong words of Barton J (at 372-3):
[T]he Defence Act is not a law prohibiting the free exercise of the appellant's religion, nor is there any attempt to show anything so absurd as that the appellant could not exercise his religion freely if he did the necessary drill. I think this objection is as thin as anything of the kind that has come before us.

17   Lawrence McNamara, 'Salvation and the State: Religious Vilification Laws and Religious Speech' in Katherine Gelber and Adrienne Stone (eds), *Hate Speech and Freedom of Speech in Australia* (The Federation Press, 2007) 151.

18   Yuval Levin, 'The Perils of Religious Liberty', *First Things* (Web Page, February 2016) <https://www.firstthings.com/article/2016/02/the-perils-of-religious-liberty>.

an intensely meaningful fashion to their sense of themselves, their community and their universe. For millions in all walks of life, religion provides support and nurture and a framework for individual and social stability and growth. Religious belief has the capacity to awaken concepts of self-worth and human dignity which form the cornerstone of human rights. It affects the believer's view of society and founds the distinction between right and wrong.[19]

It is religion's power that makes restrictions placed upon religious speech such an emotive subject and has made the burden of complying with anti-discrimination laws a primary concern of many believers.[20] Religion calls people to live out their deepest convictions. Laws requiring people to deviate from these convictions are therefore often viewed as painful intrusions.

The essential point here is that religion engages deep convictions that are not easily displaced. Given the sensitivities involved, it is practical to suggest that proponents on both sides, as well as those required to adjudicate, approach disputes regarding religious expression with an appropriate degree of sensitivity. The consequences of failing to respect such sensitivities extend well beyond the hypothetical. Recent times provide numerous instances of communities being deprived of the beneficial outworkings of

---

19   *Christian Education South Africa v Minister of Education* 2000 (4) SA 757 (CC), [36] (Albie Sachs J).

20   See generally Ian Leigh, 'Homophobic Speech, Equality Denial, and Religious Expression' in Ivan Hare and James Weinstein (eds), *Extreme Speech and Democracy* (Oxford, 2009) 375 ('Homophobic Speech, Equality Denial, and Religious Expression'). Also on this point, recent times have seen little shortage of horror stories collected by religious believers and used to argue that rights are being irreparably damaged. There has been a proliferation of publications, especially within the United States, seeking to address the threat of legislative overreach upon the rights of religious believers. See, eg, Erick Erickson and Bill Blankschaen, *You will be Made to Care: The War on Faith, Family and you Freedom to Believe* (Regnery Publishing, 2016) ('You will be Made to Care'); Mary Eberstadt, *It's Dangerous to Belief: Religious Freedom and it's Enemies* (HarperCollins, 2016); Alan Sears and Craig Osten, *The Homosexual Agenda, Exposing the Principle Threat to Religious Freedom Today* (B & H Publishing Group, 2003); David Limbaugh, *Persecution: How Liberals are Waging War Against Christianity* (Regnery Publishing, 2003); Matt Barber, *Hating Jesus: The American Left's War on Christianity* (Barbwire Books, 2016).

institutions due to conflict over anti-discrimination provisions. For example, in the United States, Catholic Charities of Boston, the State of Massachusetts' largest adoption provider, was forced to halt their provision of adoption services because the organisation refused to abandon certain tenets of the Catholic faith and place children into the care of same sex couples.[21] This was mirrored several years later in the UK when Catholic Care, the nation's only Catholic adoption agency, was denied the right to continue a policy of offering adoptions only to married heterosexual couples, which led to their eventual closure.[22]

Finally, in a multi-faith society such as Australia, a strong likelihood exists that distasteful ideas will be found across the community. The stifling of religious expression by legal means is not the best way to counter such ideas. Even if the opinion held and being expressed is distasteful and goes against popular sentiment, it is only possible to discern this if persons feel free enough to propose such ideas in the first place. Also, if an offended party wishes to counter the ideas that have been put forward, this too requires the freedom to make statements without fear of religious vilification provisions being triggered against them.[23] Given the binding traction of religious

---

21   Maggie Gaelleger, 'Banned in Boston', *The Weekly Standard* (Online, 15 May 2006) <http://www.weeklystandard.com/banned-in-boston/article/13329>.

22   See *Catholic Care (Diocese of Leeds) v Charity Commission for England and Wales* (Charity Tribunal, McKenna J, Member Carter and Member Hyde, 26 April 2011) 19 [52]; see also Martin Beckford, 'Last Catholic Adoption Agency Faces Closure After Charity Commission Ruling', *The Telegraph* (Online, 19 August 2010) <http://www.telegraph.co.uk/news/religion/7952526/Last-Catholic-adoption-agency-faces-closure-after-Charity-Commission-ruling.html>.

23   For an important news article that details the detriment caused to inter-faith relationships in Victoria, subsequent to the introduction of the *Racial and Religious Tolerance Act 2001* (Vic), a law intended to prevent vilification on account of a person's religion, see Amir Butler, 'Why I've Changed My Mind on Vilification Laws', *The Age* (Online, 4 June 2004) <http://www.theage.com.au/articles/2004/06/03/1086203561682.html>. Butler argues that the idea that criticism of another religion, irrespective of how offensive it might appear, must be banned to protect religious sensibilities is ridiculous and counterproductive. Incitement to commit violence was already illegal and existing legal instruments already covered slander. Therefore, there is no need to add to the laws already

conviction it is unlikely that beliefs will be relinquished because of a parliamentarian's drafting. The two examples cited above, concerning the refusal of adoption agencies located in separate nations that chose closure over departure from their spiritual convictions, testifies to this fact. On account of such convictions, a society *cannot* have freedom of religion without the right to offend.

Even Jeremy Waldron, a contemporary defendant of the need for non-discrimination laws, recognises that '[n]either in its public expression nor in an individual's grappling aloud with these matters can religion be defanged of this potential for offence'.[24] Social cohesion is therefore better served by allowing groups to both express and challenge difficult ideas. As Patrick Parkinson has noted concerning this topic:

> The vigorous proclamation of truth need not lead to disharmony in the community ... In democracies, there is a long tradition of people holding, expressing and passionately debating their views of what is true and right.[25]

In contrast, ideas that are repressed tend to simmer and find their eventual expression via unhealthy methods,[26] or as the English philosopher John Gray warns:

> suppressing religion does not mean it ceases to control thinking and behaviour. Like repressed sexual desire, faith returns, often in grotesque forms, to govern the lives of those who deny it.[27]

---

available. The key point here is that anti-discrimination provisions will often do more to enhance inter-community tensions rather than subdue them.

24   Jeremy Waldron, *The Harm in Hate Speech* (Harvard University Press, 2012) 129, cited in Gospel Society and Culture, *Religion and Anti-Vilification Laws* (2016) <http://www.gsandc.org.au/wp-content/uploads/2016/09/Religion-and-Anti-Vilification-Laws.pdf>.

25   Parkinson, 'Religious Vilification' (n 3) 13-14.

26   Durham Jr, 'Religious Freedom in a Worldwide Setting' (n 10) 361-2.

27   John Gray, *Black Mass: Apocalyptic Religion and the Death of Utopia* (Farrar, Straus and Girroux, 2007) 365.

HISTORICAL DEVELOPMENTS AND THE CHALLENGE TO RELIGIOUS EXPRESSION

American theologian Albert Mohler contends that 'every society has a structure of systems that either influences or coerces behaviour'.[28] Eventually, he concludes: 'societies move to legislate and regulate behaviour in order to align the society with what is commonly, or at least largely, considered morally right and wrong'.[29] Until recently, such an alignment was not threatening for the most part to religious believers in Australia. This has changed as religion has come to take up less space in the national psyche and religious communities have found themselves increasingly on the wrong side of accepted social morality.[30] The reduced importance of religion within the national mindset has been matched by a growth in secularisation, whereby societies have moved away from the binding force of religious belief.[31]

There can be little doubt that secularisation has permeated much of the national consciousness, leading to a repudiation of previously held viewpoints on a wide range of issues. Greater acceptance of various lifestyle choices has led to amendments to the criminal law, widespread dislike for discriminatory behaviour and past social prohibitions being eased.

Perhaps the one historical development that has most influenced society's acceptance of laws that impinge upon the right to communicate religious ideals is in regard to sexual identity. As previously noted, an ever-widening divergence of opinion is emerging in this area between faith-based groups and the secular mainstream. This divergence is not surprising because faith communities tend to

---

28   R Albert Mohler Jr, *We Must Not Be Silent* (Nelson Books, 2015) 119 ('We Must Not Be Silent').
29   Ibid 119.
30   For an extended discussion of this dynamic from a Christian perspective, see Rex Ahdar, *Worlds Colliding: Conservative Christians and the Law* (Ashgate Dartmouth, 2001) ('Worlds Colliding').
31   Mohler Jr, 'We Must Not Be Silent' (n 28) 5.

approach social change more cautiously, weighing the change against their established beliefs, and all of the world's major religious faiths are inherently traditional.[32] Though religious attitudes vary markedly within faiths, because each of the Abrahamic religions feature scriptural prohibitions on homosexual practice, it is reasonable to assert that religious traditionalists generally disapprove of homosexual expression and that opponents of social acceptance of homosexuality often premise their arguments on religious texts.[33] In contrast, acceptance of homosexual expression as a lifestyle choice has become a majority position within Australia and a widespread distaste is evident for discriminatory practices based on a person's sexuality.

The list of controversies, both in Australia and throughout the Western world illustrative of the religious and secular divide concerning this issue, is vast. Australian examples are discussed later, however to better appreciate the scope of the divide, it is helpful to take note of external circumstances. Recently in the United States, a major city Fire Chief was suspended from his position without pay because it was discovered he had written a book teaching that same sex relationships should be avoided.[34] Also in the United States, an Orthodox Jewish counselling agency, Jews Offering New Alternatives for Healing (JONAH), was prosecuted for teaching that counselling could bring 'healing' to men wanting to overcome same sex attraction.[35] A Christian baker in the state of Colorado has faced repeated lawsuits[36]

---

32   Writing in the Monash University Law Review, legal academics Joel Harrison and Patrick Parkinson make this point and note that one reason why religious faith has such a stabilising role in the lives of both individuals and communities is because of this reticence towards social change: see Harrison and Parkinson, 'Freedom Beyond the Commons' (n 7) 426.

33   Patrick Parkinson, 'Accommodating Religious Belief in a Secular Age' (2011) 34(1) UNSW Law Journal 281, 283 ('Accommodating Religious Belief in a Secular Age').

34   Erickson and Blankschaen, 'You will be Made to Care' (n 20) 20.

35   Ibid 25. Interestingly, JONAH was not charged pursuant to the US equivalents of the Racial and Religious Tolerance Act 2001 (Vic), rather they were found guilty of Consumer Fraud pursuant to New Jersey consumer protection laws.

36   Masterpiece Cakeshop et al v Colorado Civil Rights Commission, 584 US ____ (2018).

in relation to his refusal to create cakes that conveyed a message in support of same sex relationships. Similarly, in Northern Ireland, two Christian cake shop owners chose on religious grounds not to supply a cake, the sole purpose of which was to express a message that they disagreed with.[37] They were held by the Court of Appeal to have breached the *Equality Act (Sexual Orientation) Regulations 2006* (NI).[38] The Court of Appeal's decision was later overturned, however, the owners were required to litigate the matter over a period of approximately 4 years.[39] In Sweden, a Christian pastor of a small congregation was sentenced to prison (later overturned) for inciting hatred against people of homosexual orientation on account of statements made during a Sunday sermon. This was despite the nation's Supreme Court finding that the pastor was 'acting out of his Christian conviction to improve the situation of his fellow man' and 'what he considered to be his duty as a pastor'.[40]

These examples indicate that religious objection to homosexual practice is a sensitive and difficult issue. Presently, there is a declining tolerance for those who find it difficult to give same-sex

---

37   The refusal of service based on religious belief is an important contemporary feature of the challenge to religious expression. In a recent decision of the Victorian Court of Appeal, a Christian youth camping organisation, and one of its officers, was fined for declining a booking from a homosexual support group: see *Christian Youth Camps Limited & Ors v Cobaw Community Health Services Limited & Ors* [2014] VSCA 75. Decisions such as this are troubling because they signal a willingness by the courts to require businesses established for a religious purpose to aid the promotion of ideas to which they conscientiously object irrespective of the fact that the complainants could easily obtain the services elsewhere. For further commentary of the *Cobaw* decision, see: Neil J Foster, 'Christian Youth Camp liable for declining booking from homosexual support group' (Unpublished Paper, 21 April 2014) <http://works.bepress.com/neil_foster/78/>.

38   *Lee v McArthur, McArthur & Ashers Baking Co Ltd* [2016] NICA 39. For a useful summary and analysis of the judgment, as well as other UK decisions that concern similar themes, see Neil Foster, 'The Ashers Gay Cake Appeal - One of These Things is not Like the Others', *Law and Religion Australia* (Web Page, 25 October 2016) <https://lawandreligionaustralia.wordpress.com/2016/10/25/the-ashers-gay-cake-appeal-one-of-these-things-is-not-like-the-others/>.

39   *Lee v Ashers Baking Company Ltd and others* [2018] UKSC 49.

40   *Prosecutor General v Ake Ingemar Teodor Green* No.B 1050 – 05 (The Supreme Court of Sweden), cited in Leigh, 'Homophobic Speech, Equality Denial, and Religious Expression' (n 20) 393.

relationships unqualified acceptance[41] driven by an increasingly determined effort to cast those who oppose acceptance as on the wrong side of morality. As British theologian Theo Hobson explains:

> The case for homosexual equality takes the form of a moral crusade. Those who want to uphold the old attitude are not just dated moralists (as is the case with those who want to uphold the old attitude to pre-marital sex or illegitimacy). They are accused of moral deficiency. The old taboo surrounding this practice does not disappear but "bounces back" at those who seek to uphold it. Such a sharp turn-around is, I think, without parallel in moral history.[42]

An outcome of the 'moral crusade' cited by Hobson is the proliferation of anti-discrimination laws. Understandably, such laws are often met with easy acceptance in the wider community because statutes that challenge discrimination represent the values and beliefs ascribed to by most Australians.

Simultaneously, these laws also facilitate circumstances where traditional religionists are becoming the targets of complaints and prosecutions wherever their opinion diverges from mainstream consensus. Anti-discrimination laws concerned with sexual orientation seek to firm up the rights of some while placing restrictions on others. This opens up questions about the kind of tolerance that governments should be seeking to promote and whether freedom of religion should allow someone who holds to religious precepts to state openly that certain forms of sexual behaviour are counter to their personal value system. The drive towards a more tolerant society can easily turn into intolerance of a different kind if the new consensus does not offer respect to those who hold opposing points of view.[43]

---

41   Parkinson, 'Accommodating Religious Belief in a Secular Age' (n 33) 282.

42   Theo Hobson, 'A Pink Reformation', *The Guardian* (Online, 5 February 2007) <https://www.theguardian.com/commentisfree/2007/feb/05/apinkreformation>, cited in Mohler Jr, 'We Must Not Be Silent' (n 28) 3.

43   Parkinson, 'Accommodating Religious Belief in a Secular Age' (n 33) 295.

LAWS THAT RESTRICT RELIGIOUS EXPRESSION

Anti-discrimination legislation established as a means to fight discrimination contains provisions that make religiously motivated speech critical of same-sex behaviour potentially liable. Examples include the:

1   *Discrimination Act 1991* (ACT) s 7;

2   *Anti-Discrimination Act 1991* (Qld) s 124A;

3   *Anti-Discrimination Act 1998* (Tas) s 17; and

4   *Anti Discrimination Act 1977* (NSW) s 49ZT.

Each of these laws vary in the way an offense is identified. The broadest is s 17 of the *Anti Discrimination Act 1998* (Tas) ("ADAT"), which makes it unlawful to engage in conduct which 'offends, humiliates, intimidates, insults or ridicules another person' on the basis of their sexuality. The only qualification being that the conduct must have been carried out:

> in circumstances in which a ***reasonable person***,[44] having regard to all the circumstances, would have anticipated that the other person would be offended, humiliated, intimidated, insulted or ridiculed.[45]

---

44   Academics Joshua Forrester, Augusto Zimmerman and Lorraine Finlay have noted that the requirement for reasonableness, especially in the context of assigning fault under anti-discrimination laws, is deeply problematic as there is no straightforward means by which to determine what constitutes 'reasonableness'. For example, in the decision of *Bropho v Human Rights and Equal Opportunity Commission* [2004] FCAFC 16; (2004) 204 ALR 761, the Court found that 'reasonably' means an objective assessment of whether the act bears a 'rational relationship' to a protected activity and whether the act is 'not disproportionate' to what is necessary to carry out the activity: at 782. In contrast, in *Islamic Council of Victoria v Catch the Fire Ministries Inc* (2006) 15 VR 207, Nettle JA took a different approach, stating that what is reasonable 'must be decided according to whether it would be so regarded by reasonable person in general judged by the standards of an open and just multicultural society': at 241. It is therefore apparent that reasonable minds will differ significantly, even when the reasonable person test is applied: see Joshua Forrester, Augusto Zimmerman and Lorraine Finlay, 'An Opportunity Missed? A Constitutional Analysis of Proposed Reforms to Tasmania's "Hate Speech" Laws' (2016) 7 *The West Australian Jurist* 275, 337-341 ('An Opportunity Missed?').

45   *Anti-Discrimination Act 1998* (Tas) s 17(1) (emphasis added).

At the other end of the spectrum, s 49ZT of the *Anti Discrimination Act 1977* (NSW) sets a far higher bar and requires the incitement of hatred, serious contempt or severe ridicule of same sex attracted persons before the offence is proven.

Religious motivation is a defence able to be claimed against some of these provisions, but not all.[46] Nevertheless, even with exceptions in place, these laws remain problematic. A law's impact is not necessarily what is intended by parliaments or even how the courts interpret it. In the broader context, what matters is how the greater public perceives the law.[47] One way in which a person may defend against such charges is by claiming freedom of religious speech. However, numerous stories of people being brought before tribunals and courts in order to defend their reputation encourages self-censorship which serves to restrict free speech as effectively as explicit legislation. More detailed comment is provided below regarding the practical consequences of reliance upon exemptions to anti-discrimination laws. At present, it is sufficient to note that the same historical pressures that drive the enactment of anti-discrimination norms will eventually call for the narrowing and perhaps removal of religious exemptions altogether. There will also likely be calls for more stringent provisions with a lower threshold of offence.

Recent case law has shown that anti-discrimination provisions

---

46   For example, the *Anti Discrimination Act* (NSW) s 49ZT (2)(C) provides a defense for: a public act, done reasonably and in good faith, for academic, artistic, *religious instruction,* scientific or research purposes or for other purposes in the public interest, including discussion or debate about and expositions of any act or matter (emphasis added).
This type of drafting suggests that a calm and reasoned explanation of religious teaching towards sexuality could easily fall within it. Moreover, in relation to the ADAT, there is currently a proposed reform being but forward which seeks to, amongst other things, amend the Act so that it includes a 'religious purposes' exemption under s 55. Presently, s 55 exempts public acts done for 'academic, artistic, scientific or research purposes'.

47   Parkinson, 'Religious Vilification' (n 3) 9, cited in Neil Foster, 'Defamation and Vilification: Rights to Reputation, Free Speech and Freedom of Religion at Common Law and Under Human Rights Law' in Paul Babie and Neville Rochow (eds), *Freedom of Religion under Bills of Rights* (University of Adelaide Press, 2012) 69.

can be used against persons who have made statements in other jurisdictions. For example, in *Corbett v Burns*[48] the NSW Civil and Administrative Tribunal ("NCAT") considered complaints made against a candidate for the federal seat of Wannon in the 2013 federal election under the *Anti Discrimination Act 1977* (NSW), even though the comments were made in Victoria where she lived. This was because the remarks could be read online in NSW. Though the NSW Court of Appeal[49] later overturned the NCAT decisions and the High Court subsequently affirmed that state and territory tribunals have no jurisdiction to impose penalties on residents of other Australian jurisdictions,[50] this use of anti-discrimination legislation will have a chilling effect on the legitimate expression of persons who wish to express their religious views in public.

Recent circumstances also illustrate that even moderate speech can trigger certain provisions. This low threshold is no small matter. The ability to instil a sense of hesitation accompanies many laws; however, anti-discrimination provisions carry with them a disproportionate impact due to the social stigma attached to contravention.[51] There is also the issue of cost. Finding and funding an appropriately qualified legal team is beyond the resources of everyday citizens.[52] This alone is sufficient for such laws to stifle free speech.[53]

For many persons of faith, speaking about their religious belief and its teachings is an explicit duty. If the law can compel religiously minded persons to refrain from engaging in mild forms of discussion

---

48   [2014] NSWCATAP 42.

49   *Burns v Corbett* (2017) 96 NSWLR 247.

50   *Burns v Corbett* (2018) 353 ALR 386.

51   For a discussion as to how social stigma can stifle authentic speech, see Erving Goffman, *Stigma: Notes on the Management of Spoiled Identity* (Simon and Schuster, 1963).

52   Parkinson, 'Religious Vilification' (n 3) 8.

53   There are many circumstances able to evidence the high costs that accompany the use of anti-discrimination laws and it is worth noting again the prominent example of the use of the *Racial and Religious Tolerance Act 2001* (Vic) against Catch the Fire Ministries, see Ahdar, 'Religious Vilification' (n 4).

due to fears of costly and invasive legal intervention, an important liberty has been suppressed. Archbishop Porteous' case in Tasmania brings this dynamic into focus.

The Archbishop Porteous Saga

In November 2015, the Australian Catholic Bishops Conference ("ACBC") issued a booklet entitled '*Don't Mess With Marriage*'.[54] It was circulated throughout the Tasmanian Catholic school system and given to students who were requested to take it home to their parents.

The booklet was a nine-page pastoral letter addressed to all Australians and intended to express the Catholic Church's position on marriage. It discussed topics such as the importance of family,[55] the complementarity that men and women each bring to relationships[56] and the potential consequences of redefining the legal definition of marriage.[57] None of the content deviated from traditional Catholic teachings on the institution of marriage, which holds it to be the exclusive union of a man and a woman.[58]

Subsequent to the booklet being distributed, Martine Delaney, a transgender federal electoral candidate for the Australian Greens Party, lodged a complaint with the office of the Tasmanian Anti-Discrimination Commissioner. According to media reports, Ms Delaney alleged that she felt humiliated by the marriage booklet.[59]

54　A Pastoral Letter from the Catholic Bishops of Australia to all Australians on the 'Same-sex Marriage' Debate, 2015 <https://www.sydneycatholic.org/pdf/dmm-booklet_web.pdf> ('A Pastoral Letter from the Catholic Bishops of Australia').

55　Ibid 7.

56　Ibid 13.

57　Ibid 12.

58　'Catechism of the Catholic Church', *Vatican* (Web Page, 4 November 2003) [7], [1601], [1602], [1604], [1605] <http://www.vatican.va/archive/ENG0015/_IN-DEX.HTM>.

59　Denis Shanahan, 'Anti-Discrimination Test Over Catholic Church's Marriage Booklet', *The Australian* (Online, 30 September 2015) <http://www.theaustra-

More specifically, it was claimed that the language of *Don't Mess With Marriage* implied criminal activity.[60] This was due to language used in sections of the text. One part provided: 'messing with marriage therefore is also messing with kids' which Ms Delaney asserted linked homosexual activity to pedophilia.[61]

The complaint was made against both the ACBC and the Catholic Archbishop of Tasmania, Julian Porteous.   Also relevant is the timing of the booklet's publication and distribution, which occurred when there was significant public discourse taking place in regards to the issue of same sex marriage.

Following the complaint, both the ACBC and the Archbishop Porteous were notified by the Anti-Discrimination Commission that it believed the booklet caused a potential breach of anti-discrimination legislation.

Facilitating a complaint in accordance with the provision required an assessment of the circumstances and consideration of whether or not the complaint could be dealt with under the ADAT. This entailed considering whether or not the distribution of the booklet could be classified as conduct that is offensive, intimidating, insulting or ridiculing to same-sex attracted people as a class. The ADAT provided the Commissioner with 6 months to complete an investigation. At the end of the six months the complaint could be either dismissed, conciliation between the parties recommended or

---

lian.com.au/national-affairs/antidiscrimination-test-over-catholic-churchs-marriage-booklet/news-story/ea8aaee464a1a65c32db6552117fad5f>.

60   Robert Hiini, 'Anti-Discrimination Commissioner Notifies Archbishop of Possible Breach of the Law', *The Catholic Weekly* (Online, 13 November 2015) <https://www.catholicweekly.com.au/anti-discrimination-commissioner-reportedly-finds-archbishop-julian-porteous-in-possible-breach-of-act/>.

61   It was also alleged that statements advocating that same sex couples were not 'whole' human beings were deeply offensive, see Mathew Denholm, 'Don't Silence us Over Anti Gay Booklet: Catholic Church', *The Australian* (Online, 14 November 2014) <http://www.theaustralian.com.au/national-affairs/policy/dont-silence-us-over-antigay-booklet-catholic-church/news-story/ed46495e013a5058d17612b7fa6901bd>.

the complaint could be referred to the Anti-Discrimination Tribunal for investigation.

If a complaint was referred on to the Anti-Discrimination Tribunal, then the tribunal had the authority to enlist the parties in conciliation conferences that are used to ensure that the parties were ready to proceed to hearing. Alternatively, the parties could be sent directly to a hearing or to a hearing after having first attended conferences.

The party who brought the complaint had the burden of proving it. In normal circumstances, the complainant's case would proceed first and at any stage during the hearing the Tribunal was free to refer a complaint to further conciliation, thus allowing the parties involved to regain the ability to reach an agreement.[62]

Several months after the Anti-Discrimination Commission's decision to investigate the matter, it was reported that proceedings were to advance towards conciliation between the parties.[63] This turned out to be unnecessary as Ms Delaney entered a voluntary withdrawal of her complaint in early 2016. According to media reports, Ms Delaney felt the tribunal's processes were taking too long and that during the time it would take to resolve the matter the booklet and its message would continue to be circulated.[64]

The original decision to proceed with the complaint attracted considerable media attention. This is unsurprising given the legal significance of the circumstances.

---

62   *Alternative Dispute Resolution Act 2001* (Tas). Other anti-discrimination statutes mirror this process of administering complaints across the nation. For a discussion of the complaint processes used pursuant to other anti-discrimination provisions, see Katherine Gelber and Adrienne Stone (eds), *Hate Speech and Freedom of Speech in Australia* (The Federation Press, 2007) 9.

63   'Bishop Porteous Claim Heading to Conciliation', *Catholic Communications Sydney* (Online, 19 November 2015) <https://www.sydneycatholic.org/news/latest_news/2015/20151119_1454.shtml>.

64   Andrew Drummond, 'Same Sex Marriage Discrimination Case Ends', *News.com.au* (Online, 5 May 2016) <http://www.news.com.au/national/breaking-news/antigay-marriage-book-complaint-withdrawn/news-story/d57663aa660f-fab8a0c65f90d19c2590>.

While it is difficult to provide an assessment of what will cause offence, an examination of the *'Don't Mess with Marriage'* booklet makes it difficult to conclude that there was an *intention* to cause offense. For example, there was no reference to homosexuality being a sin[65] and the reader did not need to look past the second paragraph to find an explicit call to treat same-sex attracted persons with respect, compassion and sensitivity.[66]

In light of the tone adopted by the ACBC when writing the booklet, the complaint suggests that mainstream religious teaching will not be able to avoid offence under anti-discrimination norms in the future. Section 17 of the *Anti-Discrimination Act 1998* (Tas) makes it an offence to engage in conduct which *offends, humiliates* or *insults* someone on the basis of their sexual orientation if it is reasonable to anticipate that person might be offended, humiliated or insulted. Intention is not relevant to the law, nor is the reasonableness of a person taking offense. The only requirement for reasonableness is whether it would be reasonable to anticipate that a person could be offended.[67]

It appears that what triggered the claim was the suggestion that same sex couples were not 'whole' human beings. The booklet provided:

> On this traditional view what allows for this special kind of union between a man and a woman in marriage is precisely their difference and complementarity. Their physical, spiritual, psychological and sexual differences show they are meant for each other, their union makes them *whole*, and through their union 'in one flesh' they

---

65   The classification of homosexuality as a sin is an issue that drives much of the debate concerning religious liberty. Increasingly, there is a push, from both within religious communities and from without, to re-think this approach. For an example of the commentary regarding this issue, see Frank Bruni, 'Bigotry, the Bible and the Lessons of Indiana', *New York Times* (Online, 3 April 2015) <http://www.nytimes.com/2015/04/05/opinion/sunday/frank-bruni-same-sex-sinners.html>.

66   'A Pastoral Letter from the Catholic Bishops of Australia' (n 54) 2.

67   'Discrimination Case Against Archbishops Withdrawn', *Catholic Communications Sydney* (Online, 6 May 2016) <https://www.sydneycatholic.org/news/latest_news/2016/201656_413.shtml>.

together beget children who are 'flesh of their flesh'. They share the sameness of humanity but enjoy the difference of their masculinity and femininity, being husband and wife, paternity and maternity.[68]

The inverted commas encompassing the words 'in one flesh' signal that the concept adverted to by the text is the New Testament teachings of Jesus on marriage. In the book of Matthew, it is taught: '[f]or this reason a man will leave his father and mother and be united to his wife, and the two will become *one flesh*';[69] the inference being that the joining of the two persons is what makes them a single whole.

What was communicated was a straightforward Christian precept, presented in moderate terms and offered as a contribution to public debate. Irrespective of the well-recognised ubiquity of this Christian teaching, the ADAT provided a legal mechanism to challenge the legality of such teaching.[70]

At this point, it is also worth noting that the drafting of certain parts of the ADAT is such that a credible argument exists in favour of parts of the legislation (including s 17) being found to be constitutionally invalid. This is because portions of the law may impermissibly infringe upon the implied freedom of political communication.[71]

While it is beyond the scope of this chapter to consider in detail the constitutional issues associated with anti-discrimination legislation, an important ancillary comment regarding anti-discrimination provisions is that when legislation is so restrictive that it limits discussion of politically associated ideas and concepts, then the law may be susceptible to a challenge on constitutional grounds.[72] But once again, defensive litigation premised in an appeal to the implied freedom of political communication under the *Constitution*

---

68   'A Pastoral Letter from the Catholic Bishops of Australia' (n 54) 7 (emphasis added).

69   Matthew 19:5 (New King James Version) (emphasis added).

70   Peter Smith, 'Bashing Bishops and Free Speech too', *Quadrant* (Online, 15 November 2015) <https://quadrant.org.au/opinion/qed/2015/11/bashing-bishops-free-speech/>.

71   See *Lange v Australian Broadcasting Corporation* (1997) 189 CLR 520; [1997] HCA 25.

72   See Forrester, Zimmerman and Finlay, 'An Opportunity Missed?' (n 44).

involves recourse to a legal remedy that is beyond the resources of everyday citizens and raises the question when a legislature should act to criminalise otherwise legitimate human expression. However, it is submitted that an anti-discrimination law that allows central teaching of the nation's largest church to be challenged in a tribunal has gone too far.

Given the relative ease with which anti-discrimination provisions can now be passed and enforced, a chief danger is that there will be a chilling effect on legitimate religious activity. This may occur irrespective of whether or not a complaint is eventually found to be lawful. In a legal context, a chilling effect is the inhibition or discouragement of the legitimate exercise of rights due to the threat of legal sanction. Hence, the punishment imposed by anti-discrimination laws does not lie only in the penalties attached to the legislation, but also in the necessity to defend oneself.[73] It has been noted several times that anti-discrimination provisions carry with them a disproportionate impact due to both social stigma and cost. Regarding this topic Patrick Parkinson, writing in the *Australian Law Journal*, notes:

> A religious organisation or community may be put to considerable expense even if the claim is utterly unmeritorious and is summarily dismissed. A gun does not have to be loaded to be terrifying. It is enough that a person towards whom the gun is pointed believes that it is loaded.[74]

Parkinson goes on to observe that further reasons why anti-discrimination provisions are harmful to religious expressions are because the best way to avoid crossing a boundary is to go nowhere near it.[75] By this it is meant that anti-discrimination provisions create cultures where citizens are afraid to engage in lawful behaviour due to the risk of being in breach of an excessive law. Thus, laws are

---

73   Parkinson, 'Religious Vilification' (n 3) 8.
74   Ibid.
75   Ibid 10.

given an expansionary scope and the chilling effect enhanced. He states: '[l]awyers are interested in defining carefully the boundaries of laws, in order to determine the scope of their application. Managers of organizations are likely to have a different focus'.[76] Easily included with or instead of managers in such a statement could be pastors, priests, imams or rabbis. Often clergy will have other pressing issues to concern them and so may seek to avoid teaching passages of scripture likely to trigger anti-discrimination provisions. On account of this threat, the more prudent course is to exercise self-censorship or alter a message so that it does not offend, or perhaps abandon it altogether.[77] Consider for example the significant exposure and the drawn out investigatory process that accompanied the complaint made against Archbishop Porteous and the ACBC. Given such pressures, would other religious bodies not feel apprehensive about making their views known on similar subjects? More pointedly, could other organisations or individuals fund a legal defence to the extent that the Catholic Church would be able to?

The essential point here is that anti-discrimination provisions, as they currently stand, are able to compel religious teachers to avoid or water down their own doctrine. The substance of the complaint is *not* the principal threat; rather it is simply the risk of *any* complaint being made. This constitutes a dangerous weapon in the hands of those who seek to silence opinions that they find distasteful and will likely result in a form of decaffeinated religion, devoid of potency on account of laws that curb the right to express a counter-cultural narrative.

---

76   Ibid.
77   Ahdar, 'Worlds Colliding' (n 30) 298.

TOLERANT PLURALISM

Thus far, this chapter has presented reasons why religious expression should be afforded legislative respect and examined the statutes that hinder this free expression. It was shown that laws hindering free expression are detrimental to institutions that provide social goods and Australia's commitment to pluralism, as well as imposing a chilling effect upon the communication of religious precepts.

Those in favour of discrimination laws argue that some form of regulation is needed to restrict speech where social conditions marginalise certain groups. On the other hand, opponents argue that non-discrimination provisions single out certain forms of speech simply because they are unpopular.[78] In this regard, the nation is made up of communities that possess deep and perhaps irresolvable differences and the ongoing tension between advocates of religious free speech and non-discrimination norms represent a profound social divide.

What then are appropriate solutions to the identified problems? Is it possible to allow for religious communities and individuals to continue to communicate and teach deeply held beliefs while simultaneously protecting social cohesion and guarding the homosexual community from discrimination and offense? The answer is simply no. Australia is not an assimilative or homogenous society but a pluralistic one in which citizens must be willing to abide distasteful ideas, just as they themselves will pose ideas that place similar demands upon others.[79] Policy initiatives that ignore this reality are short-sighted. Professor Iain Benson from the University of Notre Dame Australia has argued: 'just as the state cannot properly coerce

---

78   Leigh, 'Homophobic Speech, Equality Denial, and Religious Expression' (n 20) 377-8.

79   This is a paraphrasing of an argument made by Brennan J (dissenting) in the United States' case of *Michael H v Gerald D*, (1989) 491 US 110, 141, cited in John D Inazu, 'A Confident Pluralism' (2015) 88 *Southern California Law Review* 587, 598.

religion, it should not coerce sexual practice acceptance'.[80] Indeed, religious identity to one person will oftentimes be as important as sexual identity is to another, and state overreach into this area will do little to promote either acceptance or equality over the long term. Oxford University's Joseph Raz has grappled with this issue by arguing that:

> a government dedicated to pluralism and autonomy cannot make people good. To be autonomous they have to choose their own lives for themselves. Governments and other people generally, can help people flourish, but only by creating the conditions for autonomous life, primarily by guaranteeing that an adequate range of diverse and valuable options shall be available to all. Beyond that they must leave individuals free to make of their lives what they will.[81]

Given this dynamic, what is required is a policy framework that aims towards a 'tolerant pluralism'.[82] Tolerance in this sense does not require a person to embrace the beliefs of others. This simply is not achievable within a polarised society such as Australia. However, it does necessitate a willingness to endure the ideas of other people.

To implement tolerant pluralism, courts and anti-discrimination tribunals need clearer legislative direction to turn away efforts to prosecute religious speech that offends contemporary sensibilities and legislatures need to repeal laws that are overly restrictive. With this challenge squarely in mind, in the following section the question

---

80   Iain Benson, 'A Civil Argument About Dignity, Beliefs and Marriage' Being a Brief for an Appearance Before the Special Legislative Committee of the House of Commons on Bill C-38, <http://www.culturalrenewal.ca/downloads/sb_culturalrenewal/BriefBillC38.pdf>.

81   Joseph Raz, *Ethics in the Public Domain: Essays in the Morality of Law and Politics* (Oxford: Clarendon Press, 1994), 120.

82   The term 'Tolerant Pluralism' is a modification of the term 'Confident Pluralism' used by John D. Inazu, Associate Professor of Law and Political Science at Washington University in St Louis. Professor Inazu has written extensively on how the law can be used to help overcome differences within societies and his work has been deeply influential upon this work. However, as is likely apparent, the author is more sceptical in regards to the type of pluralism that can ultimately be achieved. Hence, opting for tolerance over confidence. See: John D. Inazu, *Confident Pluralism: Surviving and Thriving Through Deep Difference* (University of Chicago Press, 2016).

is raised as to how tolerant pluralism can realistically be achieved. Also considered are the challenges that its implementation will face and the historical realities that policy makers must acknowledge.

Incorporate the International Covenant on Civil and Political Rights

Australia has undertaken to be bound by the *International Covenant on Civil and Political Rights* ("*ICCPR*"),[83] which includes a broad right to religious liberty. Article 18 of the *ICCPR* provides:

1. Everyone shall have the right to freedom of thought, conscience and religion. This right shall include freedom to have or to adopt a religion or belief of his choice, and freedom, either individually or in community with others and in public or private, to manifest his religion or belief in worship, observance, practice and teaching.

2. No one shall be subject to coercion, which would impair his freedom to have or to adopt a religion or belief of his choice.

3. Freedom to manifest one's religion or belief may be subject only to such limitations as are prescribed by law and are necessary to protect public safety, order, health or morals or the fundamental rights and freedoms of others.[84]

The *ICCPR* has not been 'incorporated' into Australian law. To incorporate the *ICCPR* into Australian law, Australian state and federal parliaments need to take a further step and pass statutes that officially enact the Covenant. Absent this extra step, the *ICCPR* is not as forceful, although there still exists an implied requirement to interpret legislative provisions in a manner that ensures, as far as possible, that they are consistent with Australia's international obligations.[85] So far, no law has been found sufficiently unclear in

---

83 *International Covenant on Civil and Political Rights*, opened for signature 19 December 1996, 999 UNTS 171 (entered into force 23 March 1976).

84 Ibid art 18.

85 *Minister of State for Immigration and Ethnic Affairs v Teoh* (1995) 183 CLR 273, 287 (Mason CJ and Deane J). In this decision, the High Court confirmed that stat-

the area of religious freedom for this principle to be applied[86] and international treaties such as the *ICCPR* remain for the most part merely persuasive authority.[87] It is therefore recommended that to better foster tolerant pluralism, the *ICCPR* should be incorporated at the federal level. Doing so will put in place a federal statute that can be used to overrule all inconsistent state laws.[88]

Relevant case law suggests that reference to even unincorporated versions of Australia's international obligations offer solid grounding for the overturn of legislation that infringes too heavily upon free expression. For example, in *Evans v NSW*[89] ("*Evans*") the Federal Court struck down regulations that had prohibited the 'annoying' Catholic World Youth Day participants. In doing so, reference was made to, inter alia, the value of religious expression by acknowledging art 18 of the *ICCPR*.[90]

Branson and Stone JJ commented:

> In the context of World Youth Day it is necessary to acknowledge that another important freedom generally accepted in Australian society

---

utes should be interpreted in a manner that, as much as possible, ensures consistency with international obligations set out in international instruments (such as treaties) ratified by Australia. The High Court also held that ratification of an international instrument raised a 'legitimate expectation' that an executive decision maker would act consistently with the instrument's terms when applying an Australian statute, notwithstanding that the international instrument has not been validly incorporated into the nation's laws. This 'legitimate expectation' principle was overturned by a subsequent High Court decision in *Re Minister for Immigration and Multicultural Affairs; ex parte Lam* [2003] HCA 6; 77 AWR 699, [105] (McHugh and Gummow JJ), however, it remains the case that an international instrument does not form part of Australian law unless its provisions have been validly incorporated into the nation's statutory framework.

86   Neil Foster, 'Religious Freedom in Australia' (Conference Paper, Asia Pacific JR-CLS Conference 2015, 29 May 2015-31 May 2015) 13 ('Religious Freedom in Australia').

87   Ibid.

88   *Commonwealth of Australia Constitution Act 1900* (Cth) s 109. This section of the Constitution provides that when 'a law of a State is inconsistent with a law of the Commonwealth, the latter shall prevail, and the former shall to the extent of the inconsistency, be invalid'.

89   (2008) 250 ALR 33.

90   Foster, 'Religious Freedom in Australia' (n 86) 13.

is freedom of religious belief and expression ... This freedom is recognized in the *Universal Declaration of Human Rights and in the International Covenant on Civil and Political Rights.*[91]

Evans provides useful context in respect of tolerant pluralism. It emphasises that within pluralistic society, freedom to offend religious sensibilities also needs protection from legislative overreach. The facts concerned the complainant (Evans), as well as other members of the public who sought to demonstrate against the Catholic Church during World Youth Day Events which were held in Sydney in 2008. The regulations considered by the Court, which were eventually overturned, restricted their right to protest by requiring them not to 'annoy' World Youth Day participants.[92] The Court held that the law should be struck down on account of the fact that the legislation should not be interpreted as allowing regulations that interfered with the fundamental right of free expression.

Should the *ICCPR* be incorporated, it would *enliven* its scope within Australian law and invite (and require) further deliberations such as in *Evans* that are sensitive to free speech concerns. It will also foster tolerant pluralism on several other fronts, including by providing a mechanism by which to strike down laws that are:

1. overly broad and impinge upon free expression, because courts and discrimination tribunals would be obliged to read legislation in light of art 18; and

2. inconsistent (in relation to state laws) with their federal counterpart.[93]

Throughout this chapter, mention has been made of the difficulty of

---

91   *Evans v NSW* (2008) 250 ALR 33, [79] (emphasis added).

92   Under s 46 of the *World Youth Day Act 2006* (NSW), persons were prohibited from selling or distributing prescribed articles in specified areas of the city between 1 July 2008 and 31 July 2008.

93   *Commonwealth of Australia Constitution Act 1900* (Cth) s 109. Importantly, there are numerous state based anti-discrimination laws that cause religiously motivated speech critical of same-sex behaviour to invite litigation (such as those canvassed above). Accordingly, there is significant utility associated with the implementation of a federal protection able to overrule state laws that are overly restrictive.

arriving at a solution able to satisfy the differing parties affected by non-discrimination laws. Tolerant pluralism does not seek to satisfy everyone, but rather, requires a judicial framework that enables different concepts to inhabit the same public space. Incorporating the *ICCPR* moves towards this by ascribing a more equitable balance. Circumstances such as *Evans* signify that just as religious traditionalists will require such a framework to communicate deeply held convictions, so too will their opponents. Ultimately, an overly litigious society is more of a hindrance than a help to both the religious and the secular.

The English Divisional Court's response to a contest between worldviews in *Redmond-Bate v Director of Public Prosecutions*[94] (*"Redmond-Bate"*) suggests how the implementation of the *ICCPR* at a federal level in Australia could enable courts to find solutions that enhance tolerant pluralism. In *Redmond-Bate*, the Police had arrested three evangelical preachers to quell a pending breach of the peace rather than the small group of protesters who were threatening violence. The Divisional Court suggested arts 9 and 10 of the ECHR provided the tools that could enable the English legislature to avoid a binary result. Sedley LJ's comments are indicative of the type of judicial mindset (and precedent)[95] required to foster tolerant pluralism:

> Free speech includes not only the inoffensive but the irritating, the contentious, the eccentric, the heretical, the unwelcome and the provocative provided it does not tend to provoke violence ... From the condemnation of Socrates to the persecution of modern writers and journalists, our world has seen too many examples of State control of unofficial ideas. A central purpose of the European Convention on Human Rights has been to set close limits to any such assumed

---

94   [1999] EWHC Admin 733.

95   Kevin Boreham from the Australian National University has argued that free-dom of religious belief and expression is now a fundamental right recognised by Australian common law due to the influence of internal law on the Federal Court's decision in *Evans*. See generally Kevin Boreham, '*Evans v NSW South Wales*' (2008) 19 *Public Law Review* 271.

power.[96]

A further benefit attached to the incorporation of the *ICCPR* is the potential influence upon future legislation. Comment was made above regarding the historical developments that have been the driving force behind anti-discrimination provisions. These developments have led to frequent cases where religious expression gave way to societal pressure to enforce non-discrimination norms. Such pressures will not pass away soon. Given this reality there is a need to protect religious expression into the future by providing a legislative bulwark against social trends.[97]

The Problem with Exemption Clauses

Previously it was noted that religious expression is sometimes protected by partial exemption clauses that allow for religious organisations or individuals to be relieved of the requirement to obey particular provisions. These exemptions signal a degree of leniency and even a sense of privilege to believers in spite of contemporary challenges. They also provide a helpful compromise to many of the issues that have been raised. Religious persons are afforded the right to communicate certain ideas if it can be sufficiently evidenced that those ideas were inspired by religious precepts. At the same time, laws that are intended to protect the dignity of same-sex attracted persons are kept in place. They are also able to introduce much-

---

96   *Redmond-Bate v Director of Public Prosecutions* [1999] EWHC Admin 733, [20].

97   Given this need to provide a bulwark against social trends, a potential means of safeguarding religious expression that arises is the implementation of a charter of rights into Australian law. The adoption of a charter of rights has not been explored in this chapter because the author has sought to consider solutions that are practical and mindful of the historic realities concerning this topic. Implementing a charter of rights would have many benefits but it is not something that would be welcomed by most religious bodies and therefore is likely to not be an effective solution able to best meet the concerns of religious adherents. For further commentary regarding this issue, see Patrick Parkinson, 'Christian Concerns about an Australian Charter of Rights' (2010) 15(2) *Australian Journal of Human Rights* 83.

needed contextual nuance when contemplating the harm caused by religious speech.[98] Accordingly, when seeking to develop solutions to the challenges posed to religious free speech, religious exemptions to anti-discrimination laws are often seen as a credible answer and some may suggest that there is no need to look beyond such an approach. However, those who are concerned with the long-term maintenance of religious free speech must be cognisant of the dangers attached to exemption clauses. These dangers are canvassed below.

Simply put, the same historical pressures that have facilitated the contemporary anti-discrimination norms that impinge upon religious expression will also see the eventual removal of exemption clauses themselves. Indicative of this is the high profile debate that took place in California in 2016 regarding an attempt to remove exemption clauses used by faith-based education providers. Academic institutions in the United States are (presently) overseen by Title IX, which is a legislative portion of the *United States Education Amendments of 1972*. It states that:

> No person in the United States shall, on the basis of sex, be excluded from participation in, be denied benefits of, or be subjected to discrimination under any education program or activity receiving Federal financial assistance.[99]

Such a provision poses a challenge to faith-based education providers as the religions that they seek to teach will often hold to principles prohibited by Title IX. As a means of protecting the free practice of religion, religious exemptions under the law allow religious colleges and universities to operate in accordance with their beliefs.[100] In 2016, a proposed legislative amendment (SB-

---

98   See generally Neil Foster, 'Freedom of Religion and Balancing Clauses in Discrimination Legislation' (Conference Paper, Magna Carta and Freedom of Religion or Belief Conference 2015, 21 June 2015-24 June 2015).

99   *United States Education Amendments of 1972* § 901(a).

100 Pursuant Title IX's implementing regulation 34 CFR § 106.12(a), the legislation does not apply to an educational institution that is controlled by a religious organisation to the extent that application of Title IX would be inconsistent with

1146) sought to dramatically limit the exemptions that institutions use for hiring instructors, teaching classes and conducting student services in line with their faith.

If passed, the impact of this amendment is difficult to overstate, as it would have *functionally eliminated* the ability of all California faith-based universities to integrate spiritual life into a broader educational experience.[101] The challenge would of course be generated from the threat of lawsuits on account of the fact that if any program were to teach theory that differed from contemporary moral orthodoxy, then students would be granted standing to bring discrimination proceedings. Although the effort to enact SB-1146 was withdrawn after intense opposition,[102] the Senator who originally sponsored the bill subsequently stated that he intended to bring the same issue to the State legislature the following year.[103] SB-1146's proximity to being made into law and the immediate effort to re-raise the issue highlights the transient nature of religious exemption clauses and the risks posed towards those reliant upon them for protection.

Given the momentum in favour of reducing or removing exemption clauses, long-term solutions must be found elsewhere. Incorporation of the *ICCPR* provides a bulwark against rapid social change by introducing an overarching legislative guideline that historical trends can less easily do away with.

Of course, the incorporation of the *ICCPR* is far from a complete defence of religious expression. The drafting of art 18(3) stipulates

---

the religious tenets of the organisation.

101 Holly Scheer, 'California Bill Would Ultimately Erase Religious Schools', *The Federalist* (Online, 21 June 2016) <http://thefederalist.com/2016/06/21/california-bill-would-ultimately-erase-religious-schools/>.

102 Patrick McGreevy, 'State Senator Drops Proposal that Angered Religious Universities in California' *LA Times* (Online, 1 September 2016) <http://www.latimes.com/politics/essential/la-pol-sac-essential-politics-updates-senator-drops-proposal-that-had-angered-1470853912-htmlstory.html>.

103 Andrew T Walker, 'SB 1146 and Institutional Religious Liberty: The Good the Bad and the Ugly' on *Religious Freedom Institute Cornerstone Blog* (Blog, 14 September 2016) <http://www.religiousfreedominstitute.org/cornerstone/2016/9/14/sb-1146-and-institutional-religious-liberty-the-good-the-bad-and-the-ugly?rq=anti%20discrimination>.

that the freedom to manifest one's beliefs may be subject to the limitations prescribed by law and are necessary to protect public safety, order, health or morals or the fundamental freedoms of others. Such wording invites judges unsympathetic to the need for religious expression to determine that restrictive anti-discrimination legislation should stand in order to service community cohesion. Moreover, if the *ICCPR's* incorporation did prove to be a useful tool for defending religious free speech, then the same historical pressures already discussed throughout this chapter may also call for the convention's removal as an official part of Australian law. It should also be noted that, contrary to the handful of European decisions outlined above that saw the use of international covenants to produce judgments amenable to the right to religious expression, there is a collection of other cases where the same right has been downplayed despite the covenants being in place.[104]

An appropriate response to this challenge is to recognise that no single legislative step can guarantee religious free speech within Australian. Given the times, the challenges listed throughout this chapter will not cease. What is needed is a legislative mechanism that facilitates open debate through which to meet these challenges and strike down the laws that seek to deny it.

CONCLUSION

This chapter has considered the conflict between religious freedom and emergent anti-discrimination norms. In contemporary society, the full spectrum of theological concepts can no longer be taught due to the threat of legal proceedings. This is a deeply problematic set of affairs and has a chilling effect on religious speech as well as the benefits derived from religious expression.

Recent historical developments have therefore brought about the

---

104   See, eg, *Hammond v DPP* [2004] EWHC 69 (Admin).

need for a firmer legislative basis for the protection of religious liberty. A practical, yet limited means by which to assist would be to implement the *ICCPR*, which currently holds only a persuasive authority. The implementation of the *ICCPR* at a federal level would allow the overrule of legislation that infringes too heavily upon free expression, because it would introduce a federal statute able to supersede state based laws that face no constitutional challenge. It would also provide a firmer and positive basis from which to argue that true freedom of religion cannot be detached from the right to express countercultural narratives. Ultimately, the long-term safeguarding of religious liberty is contingent upon numerous cultural and political factors. However, the right for a religious person to say what is offensive, irritating and unwelcome will continue to be the demand of a truly pluralistic society. With this in mind, discovering a framework able to uphold the right of the religious to express ideals that they consider sacred, and that others consider abhorrent, has never been more difficult, yet, never more important.

BIBLIOGRAPHY

Articles

Rex Tauati Ahdar, 'Religious Vilification: Confused Policy, Unsound Principle and Unfortunate Law' (2007), 26 *University of Queensland Law Review* 293.

Rex Tauati Ahdar, 'The Vulnerability of Religious Liberty in Liberal States' (2009), 4 *Religion and Human Rights* 177.

Iain Benson, 'The attack on Western religions by Western law: re-framing pluralism, liberalism and diversity' (2013), 6 *International Journal of Religious Freedom* 111.

Joshua Forrester, Lorraine Finlay and Augusto Zimmermann, 'An Opportunity Missed? A Constitutional Analysis of Proposed Reforms to Tasmania's "Hate Speech" Laws' (2016), 7 *The West Australian Jurist* 275

Mary Ann Glendon and Hans F. Zacher, 'Pontifical Academy of Social

Sciences, Universal Rights in a World of Diversity: The Case for Religious Freedom, Acta 17, Proceedings of the 17th Session, 29 April – 3 May 2011'. (Pontifical Academy of Social Sciences, Vatican City: 2012).

Joel Harrison and Patrick Parkinson, 'Freedom Beyond the Commons: Managing the Tension Between Faith and Equality in a Multicultural Society' (2014), 40 *Monash University Law Review* 414.

John D. Inazu, 'A Confident Pluralism' (2015), 88 *Southern California Law Review* 587.

Patrick Parkinson, 'Religious Vilification Paper, Anti Discrimination Laws and Religious Minorities in Australia: The Freedom to be Different' (2007), 81 *Australian Law Journal* 954.

Patrick Parkinson, 'Accommodating Religious Belief in a Secular Age: The Issue of Conscientious Objection in the Workplace' (2011), 34(1) *UNSW Law Journal* 282.

Patrick Parkinson, 'Christian Concerns about an Australian Charter of Rights' (2010), 15(2) *Australian Journal of Human Rights* 83.

Books

Rex Tauati Ahdar and Ian Leigh, *Religious Freedom in the Liberal State* (Oxford University Press, 2013).

Rex Tauati Ahdar, *Worlds Colliding: Conservative Christians and the Law* (Ashgate Dartmouth, 2001).

Matt Barber, *Hating Jesus: The American Left's War on Christianity* (Barbwire Books, 2016).

W. Cole Durham Jr. and Brett G Sharffs, *Law and Religion: National, International and Comparative Perspectives* (Aspen Publishers, 2010).

W. Cole Durham Jr., 'Religious Freedom in a Worldwide Setting: Comparative Reflections' in Mary Ann Glendon and Hans F. Zacher (eds), *Universal Rights in a World of Diversity – The Case of Religious Freedom* (The Pontifical Academy of Social Sciences Acta 17, 2012).

Mary Eberstadt, *It's Dangerous to Belief: Religious Freedom and it's Enemies* (HarperCollins, 2016).

Erick Erickson and Bill Blankschaen, *You Will be Made to Care: The War on Faith, Family and you Freedom to Believe* (Regnery Publishing, 2016).

Neil Foster, 'Defamation and Vilification: Rights to Reputation, Free Speech and Freedom of Religion at Common Law and Under Human Rights Law' in Paul Babie and Neville Rochow (eds), *Freedom of Religion under Bills of Rights* (University of Adelaide Press, 2012).

Joshua Forrester, Lorraine Finlay and Augusto Zimmermann, *No Offence Intended: Why 18C is Wrong* (Connor Court, 2016).

Katherine Gelber, 'Hate Speech and the Australian Legal Landscape' in Katherine Gelber and Adrienne Stone (eds), *Hate Speech and Freedom of Speech in Australia* (Federation Press, 2007).

Erving Goffman, *Stigma: Notes on the Management of Spoiled Identity* (New York: Simon and Schuster, 1963).

Ivan Hare and James Weinstein, *Extreme Speech and Democracy* (Oxford University Press, 2009).

John D. Inazu, *Confident Pluralism: Surviving and Thriving Through Deep Difference* (University of Chicago Press, 2016).

Ian Leigh, 'Homophobic Speech, Equality Denial, and Religious Expression' in Ivan Hare and James Weinstein (eds), *Extreme Speech and Democracy* (Oxford, 2009).

David Limbaugh, *Persecution: How Liberals are Waging War Against Christianity* (Regnery Publishing, 2003).

Lawrence McNamara, 'Salvation and the State: Religious Vilification Laws and Religious Speech' in Katherine Gelber and Adrienne Stone (eds), *Hate Speech and Freedom of Speech in Australia* (The Federation Press, 2007).

R. Albert Mohler, Jr., *We Must Not Be Silent* (Nelson Books, 2015).

Craig B Mousin, 'State Constitutions within The United States and The Autonomy of Religious Institutions' in Gerhard Robbers (ed), *Church Autonomy: A Comparative Survey* (Peter Lang, 2001).

Joseph Raz, *Ethics in the Public Domain: Essays in the Morality of Law and Politics* (Oxford: Clarendon Press, 1994).

Alan Sears and Craig Osten, *The Homosexual Agenda, Exposing the Principle Threat to Religious Freedom Today* (B & H Publishing Group, 2003).

Jeremy Waldron, *The Harm in Hate Speech* (Harvard University Press, 2012).

Roy, Williams *Post God Nation* (Harper Collins, 2015).

Bryan Wilson, '"Secularization": Religion in the Modern World', in Stewart Sutherland, Leslie Houlden, Peter Clarke and Friedhelm Hardy (eds) '*The World's Religions*', (London: Routledge, 1988).

Cases

Australia

Burns v Corbett (2017) 96 NSWLR 247.

Burns v Corbett (2018) 353 ALR 386.

Church of the New Faith v Commissioner for Pay-Roll Tax (1983) 154 CLR 120.

Christian Youth Camps Limited v Cobaw Community Health Service Limited [2014] VSCA 75.

Evans v NSW [2008] FCAFC 130.

Fletcher v Salvation Army [2005] VCAT 1523.

Krygger v Williams (1912) 15 CLR 366.

Minister for Immigration and Ethnic Affairs v Teoh (1995) 183 CLR 273.

Europe

Hammond v DPP [2004] EWHC 69 (Admin).

Prosecutor General v. Ake Ingemar Teodor Green, The Supreme Court of Sweden, Case No.B 1050 – 05.

United Kingdom

Catholic Care (Diocese of Leeds) v Charity Commission for England and Wales (Unreported).

Lee v McArthur, McArthur & Ashers Baking Co Ltd NICA.

Lee v Ashers Baking Company Ltd and others [2018] UKSC 49.

Redmond-Bate v Director of Public Prosecutions [1999] EWHC Admin 733.

United States

Michael H. v. Gerald D. (1989) 491 U.S 110.

Legislation

Alternative Dispute Resolution Act 2001 (Tas).

Anti-Discrimination Act 1977 (NSW)

Anti-Discrimination Act 1991 (Qld).

Anti-Discrimination Act 1998 (Tas).

Commonwealth of Australia Constitution Act 1900 (Cth).

Discrimination Act 1991 (ACT).

Payroll Tax Act 1971 (Vic).

Racial and Religious Tolerance Act 2001 (Vic).

World Youth Day Act 2006 (NSW).

Other

Australian Catholic Bishops Conference Pastoral Research Office, *Social Profile of the Catholic Community in Australia based on the 2011 Census Data* (2015).

Martin Beckford, 'Last Catholic Adoption Agency Faces Closure After Charity Commission Ruling', The Telegraph (Online) 19 August 2010 <http://www.telegraph.co.uk/news/religion/7952526/Last-Catholic-adoption-agency-faces-closure-after-Charity-Commission-ruling.html>.

Iain Benson, 'A Civil Argument About Dignity, Beliefs and Marriage' Being a Brief for an Appearance Before the Special Legislative Committee of the House of Commons on Bill C-38, *The Civil Marriage Act*, <http://www.culturalrenewal.ca/downloads/sb_culturalrenewal/BriefBillC38.pdf>.

Frank Bruni, 'Bigotry, the Bible and the Lessons of Indiana', *New York Times* (Online), 3 April 2015, <http://www.nytimes.com/2015/04/05/opinion/sunday/frank-bruni-same-sex-sinners.html>.

Amir Butler, 'Why I've Changed My Mind on Vilification Laws', *The Age* (Online), 4 June 2004, <http://www.theage.com.au/articles/2004/06/03/1086203561682.html>.

Catholic Bishops of Australia, *Don't Mess with Marriage* (2015) <https://www.sydneycatholic.org/pdf/dmm-booklet_web.pdf>.

Mathew Denholm, 'Don't Silence us Over Anti Gay Booklet: Catholic Church',

The Australian (Online), 14 November 2014, <http://www.theaustralian. com.au/national-affairs/policy/dont-silence-us-over-antigay-booklet-catholic-church/news-story/ed46495e013a5058d17612b7fa6901bd>.

Andrew Drummond, 'Same Sex Marriage Discrimination Case Ends', *News. com.au* (Online), 5 May 2016, <http://www.news.com.au/national/breaking-news/antigay-marriage-book-complaint-withdrawn/news-story/d57663aa660ffab8a0c65f90d19c2590>.

Neil Foster, 'Freedom of Religion and Balancing Clauses in Discrimination Legislation' (Paper Presented at the Magna Carta and Freedom of Religion or Belief Conference 2015, Oxford United Kingdom, 2015, 21 – 24 June 2015).

Neil Foster, 'The Ashers Gay Cake Appeal – One of These Things is not Like the Others' on *Law and Religion Australia* (October 25 2016) <https://lawandreligionaustralia.wordpress.com/2016/10/25/the-ashers-gay-cake-appeal-one-of-these-things-is-not-like-the-others/>.

Neil Foster, 'Christian Youth Camp liable for declining booking from homosexual support group' (2014), 21 April 2014, (Unpublished) Available at: <http://works.bepress.com/neil_foster/78/>.

Neil Foster, 'Religious Freedom in Australia' (paper presented at the Asia Pacific JRCLS Conference 2015, 29 May – 31 May 2015).

Maggie Gaelleger, 'Banned in Boston', *The Weekly Standard* (Online), 15 May 2006, <http://www.weeklystandard.com/banned-in-boston/article/13329>.

Gospel Society and Culture, *Religion and Anti-Vilification Laws* (2016), <http://www.gsandc.org.au/wp-content/uploads/2016/09/Religion-and-Anti-Vilification-Laws.pdf>.

Robert Hiini, 'Anti-Discrimination Commissioner Notifies Archbishop of Possible Breach of the Law', *The Catholic Weekly* (Online), 13 November 2015, <https://www.catholicweekly.com.au/anti-discrimination-commissioner-reportedly-finds-archbishop-julian-porteous-in-possible-breach-of-act/>.

Theo Hobson, 'A Pink Reformation' *The Guardian* (Online), 5 Feb 2007, <https://www.theguardian.com/commentisfree/2007/feb/05/apinkreformation>.

Yuval Levin, 'The Perils of Religious Liberty', *First Things Journal* (Online), February 2015, <https://www.firstthings.com/article/2016/02/the-perils-of-religious-liberty>.

Patrick McGreevy, 'State Senator Drops Proposal that Angered Religious

Universities In California', 1 September 2016, *LA Times* (Online), <http://www.latimes.com/politics/essential/la-pol-sac-essential-politics-updates-senator-drops-proposal-that-had-angered-1470853912-htmlstory.html>.

National Multicultural Advisory Council, Parliament of Australia, *Australian Multiculturalism for a New Century: Towards Inclusiveness* (1999).

Denis Shanahan, 'Anti-Discrimination Test Over Catholic Church's Marriage Booklet', *The Australian* (Online), 30 September 2015, <http://www.theaustralian.com.au/national-affairs/antidiscrimination-test-over-catholic-churchs-marriage-booklet/news-story/ea8aaee464a1a65c32db6552117fad5f>.

Holly Scheer, 'California Bill Would Ultimately Erase Religious Schools', The Federalist (Online), 21 June 2016, <http://thefederalist.com/2016/06/21/california-bill-would-ultimately-erase-religious-schools/>.

Peter Smith, 'Bashing Bishops and Free Speech too', *Quadrant* (Online), 15 November 2015, <https://quadrant.org.au/opinion/qed/2015/11/bashing-bishops-free-speech/>.

The Vatican, Catechism of the Catholic Church (2003). <http://www.vatican.va/archive/ENG0015/_INDEX.HTM>.

Andrew T. Walker, 'SB 1146 and Institutional Religious Liberty: The Good the Bad and the Ugly' on *Religious Freedom Institute Cornerstone Blog* (14 September 2016) <http://www.religiousfreedominstitute.org/cornerstone/2016/9/14/sb-1146-and-institutional-religious-liberty-the-good-the-bad-and-the-ugly?rq=anti%20discrimination>.

3

THE RELIGIOUS 'OTHER' A CRITICAL EXAMINATION OF THE BAHÁ'I MARGINALISATION IN IRAN

GIL MARVEL P. TABUCANON

ABSTRACT

Otherness is the outcome of a discursive process which divides the world into the binary camps of 'us', which sees itself as conforming to the norm and therefore possessing a valued identity, and 'them' that deviates from the norm and are therefore unworthy of belonging. This paper looks into aspects of othering, in particular religious othering, and uses as case study the experiences of the Bahá'í community in Iran. It interrogates the role of identity, the difficulty in understanding a post-Islamic claim of divine revelation, security concerns and prominence of some Baha'is during the last shah's regime as possible contributing factors to Bahá'í othering in Iran. Since much of othering springs from ignorance if not fear of the unknown, this paper argues on the need to strengthen law to protect vulnerable others, as well as promote avenues, channels and spaces for intergroup dialogue and connections, to be able to understand, and possibly respect and appreciate the other.

INTRODUCTION

A perspective on othering

Who are others? In particular, who are our religious others? Swiss professor Jean-Francois Staszak, argues that otherness is due less to differences, and more to the perspective and discourse of the person perceiving the other.[1] Otherness is the outcome of a discursive, if reductionist, process which divides the world into the binary camps of 'us', which sees itself as conforming to the norm and therefore possessing a valued identity, and 'them' that deviates from the norm and are therefore unworthy of belonging. Otherness suggests difference, but one where difference of the other is not just recognised but rather devalued and faulted, thereby laying the ground for discrimination. Greek and Italian are different, but the acknowledged difference is founded on equal notions of nationality and uniqueness; whereas, the imbalance inherent in the Greek and barbarian binary implies otherness, wherein goodness is attributed to the former and the categories of being primitive, cruel and brutish consigned to the latter. Biological male and female categorisation is based on difference, whereas gender stratification is otherness, prompting Simone de Beauvoir to declare 'one is not born, but rather becomes a woman'.[2] It is the dominant point of view as well as discourse that relegates woman to the status of second sex.

Religious othering

Othering is also present in the context of religion, as the Bahá'í experience in Iran demonstrates, which I note with some irony, considering cosmopolitan brotherhood is a recurring theme among the world's faiths. Abrahamic religions upheld universalist views that humanity is a single creation of God. St. Paul declares 'God...[who]

---

1   Jean-François Staszak, 'Other/Otherness', in Rob Kitchin and Nigel Thrift (eds), *International Encyclopedia of Human Geography* (Elsevier Science, 2009) vol. 8, 43.

2   Simone de Beauvoir, *The Second Sex* (Vintage Books, 1973) 301.

made the world and all things therein'[3] also 'made of one blood all nations of men for to dwell on all the face of the earth'.[4] The *Qur'an* upholds humanity's cosmopolitan origins, which nonetheless was not maintained: 'Once all men were but a single community; then they disagreed'.[5] The Bahá'í principle of unity calls for a paradigm shift for people to expand their loyalty beyond the borders of their respective countries towards humanity: 'It is not for him to pride himself who loveth his own country, but rather for him who loveth the whole world,' for the 'earth is but one country, and mankind its citizens.'[6] French monk Emeric Cruce argues for the 'connection that is and must be between men', and asserts that 'hostilities are only political', saying: 'Why should I a Frenchman, wish harm to an Englishman, a Spaniard, or a Hindoo? I cannot wish it when I consider that they are men like me, that I am subject like them to error and sin and that all nations are bound together by a natural and consequently indestructible tie'.[7] Religious teachings uphold humanity's universal inclusiveness. Jesus expressly taught loving one's neighbour, where neighbours include those belonging to other tribes or out-groups.[8]

In spite this, some of the most sustained, even brutal, expressions of othering are committed in the name of religion – what with religiously-motivated genocides, inquisitions and burnings at the stake of heretics and suspected witches. Stack argues religion is a 'fundamental marker of individual and group identity', even as it caters towards the need for authenticity and belonging and as such resonates deeply in the individual's most basic values and

---

3   Acts 17:20
4   Acts 17:26
5   Qur'an, 10:19
6   Bahá'u'lláh, *Gleanings From the Writings of Bahá'u'lláh* (US Bahá'í Publishing Trust, 1990) 250.
7   Emeric Cruce, *The New Cyneas* (Thomas Balch, ed and trans, Allen, Lane and Scott, 1909) 85, 86.
8   See Parable of the Good Samaritan, Luke 10:25–37

life choices.[9] Humans need to identify and connect with what they believe in as real and transcendent, and religion provides this in an absolute way. Religion is a source of 'that deep *affective* motivation' to do good.[10] Muhammad Yunnus' work in microfinancing women's projects in Bangladesh, Vandana Shiva's environmental activism and Thich Nhat Hanh's engaged peacemaking, are informed by their respective Muslim, Hindu and Buddhist faiths.[11] Yet, the same affective energy utilised for humanitarian undertaking, may also be used to punish, even force apostates and deviants to get back to the fold. The devotional zest used in outwardly spreading one's faith may also be turned inward to protect one's group from other people seen as threatening or diluting the community's doctrinal purity and integrity.

BAHÁ'I HISTORICAL PERSPECTIVE

The Bahá'í movement started in Iran in 1844 and, at present, the Bahá'í community comprises the largest non-Muslim religious minority in Iran.[12] The community grew steadily from inception and by the late nineteenth century there were an estimated 100,000 Bahá'ís which 'represented 1-2 per cent of Iran's population of between 5 and 8 million at the time'.[13] Today, an estimated 300,000

---

9   John Stack Jr, 'Religious Challenge to International Relations Theory' in Patrick James (ed), *Religion, Identity and Global Governance: Ideas, Evidence and Practice* (University of Toronto Press, 2011) 28.

10   Patrick James, 'Religion, Identity and Global Governance: Setting the Agenda' in Patrick James (ed), *Religion, Identity and Global Governance: Ideas, Evidence and Practice* (University of Toronto Press, 2011) 5.

11   Joanne Benham Rennick, 'Is Religion a Force for Good? Reformulating the Discourse on Religion and International Development' 34(2) *Canadian Journal of Development Studies* 179.

12   Dominic Brookshaw and Seena Fazel, 'Introduction', in Dominic Brookshaw and Seena Fazel (eds), *The Bahá'ís of Iran: Socio-Historical Studies* (London & New York: Routledge, 2008) 2.

13   Peter Smith, 'A Note on Bábi and Bahá'í Numbers in Iran' (1984) 17 *Iranian Studies* 295. The later part of the twentieth century saw a decline in the proportion of the Bahá'í population in relation to Iran's. This became particularly apparent after the 1979 Iranian Revolution as the 'birth rate among Bahá'ís was below the

remain in Iran comprising 'around 0.5 per cent of the population'.[14]
The othering of Bahá'ís began when its precursor, the Báb (meaning
Gate), founder of the Bábi movement, declared a new 'revelation'
(*zuhur*) and a 'new prophetic cycle independent from Islam'.[15] For this
claim, the Báb was charged with 'incorrigible heresy' (*irtidad-i-fitri*)
and was executed in 1850.[16] Bahá'u'lláh (meaning Glory of God),
founder of the Bahá'í Faith, was himself imprisoned in Tehran for
upholding the Báb's claim, then exiled to Baghdad, Constantinople
and ultimately Akka (now, Acre, Israel) where he died in 1892.[17]
The Bahá'í World Centre currently sits on Mount Carmel in Haifa,
Israel. Ironically, and as will be explained later, Bahá'u'lláh's forced
exile into the Holy Land, and the Bahá'ís' long historical association
with Israel, having established their international headquarters close
to Bahá'u'lláh's shrine in that country, has made the Bahá'í minority
community in Iran guilty by association, with some in Iran calling
the Bahá'ís spies for Israel.[18]

The Bahá'í religious minority, according to Cole, would 'on the
surface' appear to have been 'well placed to benefit' from the rise
of the modern Iranian nationalism, citing the following reasons: (1)
It has the 'advantage of being indigenous' being one of the 'only
four extant religions that arose on Iranian soil', the other three being
Zoroastrian, Ahl-I Haqq and the Bábi religions; (2) Bahá'í scriptures
are, for the most part, written in Persian, the 'vehicle of modern
Iranian nationalism.'; and (3) the Bahá'í world view has a 'generally

---

average and many Bahá'ís emigrated to the West to escape persecution'. Today,
an estimated 300,000 remain in Iran comprising 'around 0.5 per cent of the population' (Dominic Brookshaw and Seena Fazel, Ibid 2).

14   Dominic Brookshaw and Seena Fazel, above n 12.

15   Abbas Amanat, 'The Historical Roots of the Persecution of Bábis and Bahá'ís in
      Iran', in Dominic Brookshaw and Seena Fazel (eds), *The Bahá'ís of Iran: Socio-His-
      torical Studies* (London & New York: Routledge, 2008) 170.

16   Ibid.

17   Hasan M. Balyuzi, *Bahá u'lláh, King of Glory* (George Ronald, 1980) 106, 197,
      255, 420.

18   Michael Karlberg, 'Constructive Resilience: The Bahá'í Response to Oppres-
      sion' (2010) 35(2) *Peace and Change* 227.

modernist orientation'.[19] The Bahá'í message has a particular appeal to those seeking a 'cosmopolitan outlook on life' and 'peaceful relations between the different faiths'.[20] Its acceptance of the validity of past religions and emphasis on the equality of all humans resonated among Iranians seeking a liberal religious outlook.

While most early Iranian Bahá'ís came from a Shi'a background, a significant number of Iranian Jews and Zoroastrians converted. Dhalla estimated that by 1920 around 4,000 Zoroastrians in Iran had converted to the Bahá'í faith.[21] The conversion mostly occurred in the big cities of Tehran, Yazd, Kirman and Kashan and the majority of these converts were either 'merchants or young, better-educated individuals working in Zoroastrian-owned businesses'.[22] Iranian Jews also converted in large numbers. In 'Gulpayegān, where there was a particularly educated Jewish community, about 75% of the Jews became Bahá'ís'.[23] Similar processes of conversion, 'though not in such proportions, also occurred in other major cities of Iran such as

---

19   Juan R. I. Cole, 'The Bahá'í Minority and Nationalism in Contemporary Iran', in Maya Shatzmiller (ed) Studies in Nationalism and Ethnic Conflict (McGill-Queen's University Press, 2005) 127.

20   Walter Fischel, 'The Bahá'í Movement and Persian Jewry' (1934) 7 *Jewish Review* 47.

21   Maneckji Dhalla, The Saga of a Soul: An Autobiography of Shams-ul-Ulama Dastur Dr. Maneckji Nusserwanji Dhalla (H J Rustomji trans, Karachi: Gool & Behram Sohrab 1975).

22   Fereydun Vahman, 'Conversion of Zoroastrians to the Bahá'í Faith', in Dominic Brookshaw and Seena Fazel (eds), *The Bahá'ís of Iran: Socio-Historical Studies* (London & New York: Routledge, 2008) 33.

23   Moshe Sharon, 'Jewish Conversion to the Bahá'í Faith' (2011) Chair in Bahá'í Studies Publications, The Hebrew University of Jerusalem. A possible, albeit not the only, reason for Jewish and Zoroastrian affinity with the Bahá'í community is the that both Jews and Zoroastrians in Iran are themselves traditionally persecuted and considered *najis* or religiously unclean (see Fereydun Vahman, above n 22, 37). Among the earliest Jewish converts to the Bábi and Bahá'í movements were prominent physicians, such as Hakim Masih who in '1861 openly confessed his Bábi beliefs' after coming into contact with 'Bábi and later Bahá'í leader Mullah Sadiq Muqaddas Khurasani while attending to the latter's sick child (Ibn-I Asdaq) in a Tehran prison'. See Mehrdad Amanat, 'Messianic Expectations and Evolving Identities, The Conversion of Iranian Jews to the Bahá'í Faith', in Dominic Brookshaw and Seena Fazel (eds), *The Bahá'ís of Iran: Socio-Historical Studies* (London & New York: Routledge, 2008) 15.

Kashān, Tehrān, Kirmanshāh, Yazd, and Shīrāz'.[24] Within two years, from 1877-79, with the help of two prominent physicians of Jewish descent, namely Aqa Jan and Rahim Khan, who were among the earliest Bahá'í converts in Hamadan, some 'fifty Jews' converted to the 'nascent' Bahá'í community in Hamadan.[25] The only major town where the Jews did not adopt the Bahá'í faith was Iṣfahān because of the strong opposition of the Shi'a clergy and population, and the relentless 'persecution of the Bahá'ís in this city'.[26]

The notion of persecution, as othering's extreme expression, is nonetheless, not monolithic. It does not always come from the dominant majority but may emanate from members of another minority. Jewish leaders threatened with the dramatic increase in the number of converted Iranian Jews complained in 1877 to the governor and accused one of the converts, namely Hajji Yari, of offending the Jews by 'openly criticising their beliefs and customs as superstitions'.[27] Rabbis saw their roles as 'protectors of Jewish traditions' hence would not tolerate a break from customs and 'repeatedly defined Bahá'ís as being outside the acceptable boundaries of Judaism'.[28] When Aqa Jan died in 1880, the rabbis denied him burial in the Jewish cemetery, only to be 'dissuaded by the wealthy (a'yan) among the Bahá'ís'.[29] When Mulla Musa, the first Jewish convert in Kashan, defied Jewish law by 'opening his shop on the Sabbath', Jewish leaders demanded punishment including the death sentence in 'accordance with the law of the Torah'. Released from prison on condition that he would leave Kashan, Mulla Musa moved to Lahijan where he was murdered in 1905. He is considered to be the 'first Jewish convert' to pay with his

---

24   Moshe Sharon, above n 23.
25   Mehrdad Amanat, above n 23, 16.
26   Moshe Sharon, above n 23.
27   Mehrdad Amanat, above n 23, 18.
28   Ibid 19.
29   Ibid 20.

life for 'openly advocating his beliefs'.[30]

While minority to minority othering may occur as demonstrated by the Jewish-Bahá'í incidents, nonetheless, it is in the majority-minority interaction (as dominant-dominated binary) where othering takes a deeper, more glaring and sustained expression. This is so as 'dominant groups', with their social, numerical or political advantage, are in a 'position to impose their categories', their norms, values and worldviews on the dominated side of the binary.[31] Hiding behind absolutist tenets and dogmas, the religious identity of the dominant group becomes a camouflage for justifying marginalization, stigmatizing deviation and exonerating acts of persecution.

Identity

At the core of othering is the issue of identity, in particular cultural identity, which dominant groups use to distance themselves from the identity of other groups who have marked disagreement or differences with mainstream beliefs. Identity refers to how a group defines itself in relation to its members, and how individual members imagine themselves in relation to its group, religion or culture. A shared identity unifies, even strengthens a group by way of a common history and ancestry. Nonetheless, the dominant group's definition of its own identity may serve as basis not just for differentiation but for othering of numerically or politically inferior groups within the community. As previously said, othering divides humanity into two: one with the dominant group seeing itself as conforming to the norm, and the other group as deviating from mainstream standards and are therefore unworthy of belonging. The othering, devaluing and faulting of another's identity, if unchecked, then become a fertile ground for marginalization and discrimination.

---

30   Ibid.
31   Staszak, above n 1.

Post-Islamic Revelation

In the context of Iranian society, at issue is the legitimacy, freedom and even right to exist of revealed religions after Islam. The Bahá'í claim to be members of a new religion (with a new prophet claiming revelation from God) directly challenges orthodox Islamic belief on the finality of Muhammad's prophethood, one of his titles being the seal of the prophets.[32] The Bahá'í self-definition as a new religion post-Islam is problematic, particularly in a society and state like Iran where its worldview rests on absolutism – among which is the absolute finality of Muhammad's prophethood, and who is considered by Muslims as the final channel of divine revelation.

The claim to divine revelation post Islam is not unique to the Bahá'ís. Ghulām Ahmad, founder of the Ahmadiyya movement, claimed to have received revelations from God in 1882, although the group was only formally established in March 1889 with the performance of the first allegiance ceremony in Ludhiana (Punjab), in Northern India.[33] Ghulām's declaration as *mujaddid* (renewer) and *muhaddath* (someone spoken to by God), received little attention at first because 'claims of this kind had been common phenomena since the very beginning of Islam'.[34] It was his claim in 1888 as the return of the Messiah and Mahdi which stirred indignation, in particular from the orthodox Muslim community of Pakistan.[35] Similarly subjected to othering, the Ahmadis became targets of religious violence in Pakistan in 1953 and 1974. This othering was done in the name of *tehrik-i-khatam-i-nabuwwat* (movement for the protection of the finality of prophethood) whereby Pakistani religious and political leaders demanded Ahmadis to be 'declared as a non-Muslim minority' on account of their 'heretical views'. They were then removed from

---

32   Uzma Jamil, Minorities and "Islamic" States: Explaining Bahá'í and Ahmadi
      Marginalization in Iran and Pakistan (MA Thesis, McGill University, 2002) 1.
33   Andrea Lathan, 'The Relativity of Categorizing in the Context of the Ahmadi-
      yya' (2008) 48 *Die Welt des Islams* 375.
34   Ibid 376.
35   Ibid. See also Jamil, n 32, 5.

'key military and bureaucratic posts' for their alleged 'disloyalty towards the state of Pakistan'.[36] Exclusionary labelling, that is, from one of us to not-us, and removal of status signifiers (whether of employment, education or official rank), is classic othering, as one group strengthens its identity by denigrating the other through denial of real or symbolic privileges.

The Báb also made a claim in 1844 as the Mahdi,[37] and Qaim,[38] which similarly drew criticism from the orthodox Muslim community of Iran.[39] While the Ahmadiyya and Bábi (and later, Bahá'í) movements accept the prophethood of Muhammad and the *Qur'an's* authority, yet, they do not deny the possibility of divine revelation, and the emergence of revealed religions after Islam. In the case of the Ahmadiyya, facing mounting criticism, Ghulām referred to the existence of two types of prophets: the law-bearing, which brings a 'new law to humankind', and the non-law bearing – and shadow – prophet, the so-called *zilli nabi*, which 'guide the believers' back to the 'right faith' but 'without bringing anything substantially new'.[40] The Ahmadis claim that, unlike Muhammad, their founder is 'a prophet without law and without a book'.[41] As

---

36   Ali Usman Qasmi, *The Ahmadis and the Politics of Religious Exclusion in Pakistan* (Anthem Press, 2015) 1.

37   Mahdi, literally "The Guided One". See William Hatcher and Douglas Martin, *The Bahá'í Faith: The Emerging Global Religion* (Bahá'í Publishing, 2002) 5. The Mahdi, also known as the Imam Mahdi, the Hidden Imam or the Twelfth Imam, forms a very important part in the beliefs of the Twelver Shi'is, and his person is connected with the doctrine of occultation. According to Momen, the doctrine of occultation, in its 'simplest form', declares that Muhammad ibn Hasan, the Twelfth Imam (a successor to Muhamad and member of this family) 'did not die' but has been 'concealed by God from the eyes of men. That his life has been 'miraculously prolonged until the day when he will manifest himself again by God's permission'. The Mahdi will 'lead the forces of righteousness' against the 'forces of evil in one final apocalyptic battle', and his return is believed to occur 'shortly before the final Day of Judgement'. The Mahdi will 'rule for a number of years' and 'after him will come the return of Christ, the Imam Husayn'. See Moojan Momen, *An Introduction to Shi'i Islam: The History and Doctrines of Twelver Shi'ism* (George Ronald, 1985) 165-166.

38   Qaim, literally "He Who Will Arise", i.e. from the family of Muhammad. Ibid.

39   Jamil, above n 32, 5.

40   Lathan, above n 33, 376.

41   Antonio Gualtieri, *Conscience and Coercion: Ahmadi Muslims and Orthodoxy in Paki-*

Ghulām himself clarified, the Qur'anic statement *Khatam an-Nabiyyin*, usually translated a Seal of the Prophets, denotes 'only law-bearing prophets', of whom Muhammad was the last, but 'not the "shadowy" prophets'.[42] The latter continue to appear 'whenever the Muslim community is seen to deviate from true Islam'.[43]

By contrast, Bahá'ís claim the Báb and Bahá'u'lláh not only brought a new set of laws, but that the laws are of a progressive nature which contribute to humanity's carrying 'forward an ever-advancing civilization',[44] such as that on the equality of men and women.[45] Unlike the Ahmadiyya which regard themselves a Sunni sect, Bahá'í consider themselves members of a new religion. Recognizing its roots from Islam, the Bahá'í movement nonetheless sees itself as independent from Islam, a fact which may have further removed Bahá'í from Islamic identity. For while the Ahmadis continue to consider themselves Muslims, Bahá'ís do not. Bahá'u'lláh abrogated a number of Muslim laws and practices, among which: instead of five daily prayers in Muslim practice, Bahá'ís may choose one of the three obligatory prayers;[46] and, while praying, instead of facing towards the Kaaba in Mecca (an act symbolizing the unity of Muslims worldwide), Bahá'ís face, while saying their obligatory prayer, towards Bahá'u'lláh's resting place in Bahjí, near Acre, Israel.[47] Further, Bahá'í practice also allowed women living in predominantly Muslim countries not to cover their faces, or wear a veil, a fact which easily sets Bahá'í women apart from their Muslim counterparts. Physical demarcations aside, Bahá'í othering, in Iran,

---

stan (Guernica Editions, 1991) 26.

42   Lathan, above n 33.

43   Ibid.

44   Bahá'u'lláh, *Gleanings From the Writings of Bahá'u'lláh* (Bahá'í Publishing Trust, 1990) 215.

45   Bahá'u'lláh, *Compilation of Compilations* (Bahá'í Publications Australia, 1991) 355: 'Praised be God, the Pen of the Most High hath lifted distinctions from between His servants and handmaidens, and, through His consummate favours and all-encompassing mercy, hath conferred upon all a station and rank of the same plane.'

46   Bahá'u'lláh, *The Kitáb-i-Aqdas* (Bahá'í Publications Australia, 1993) 126.

47   Ibid 145.

at least, may have other triggers and causes. Chehabi identifies three possible causes of anti-Bahá'í sentiments in Iran, which will be briefly discussed below: (1) challenging a key tenet of Islam that Muhammad was the last of the prophets; (2) allegedly causing division in the nation and conspiracy theories, and (3) prominence during the Shah's regime.[48]

Challenging a key tenet of Islam

The Bahá'í theology, seen from an Islamic viewpoint, appears to challenge a key doctrine of Islam which considers Muhammad as the last of the prophets (*Khatam an-Nabiyyin*, literally the Seal of the Prophets. As Chehabi posits, it is 'impossible' for a Muslim to recognise Bahá'u'lláh's divine mission as it is for a 'Jew to recognize Jesus Christ as the Messiah'.[49] This is so as in the Abrahamic tradition, a 'religion can make a place for preceding ones', but not for one that, 'implicitly, declares it to be obsolete'.[50] In line with this reasoning, Bahá'ís found themselves charged with heresy, apostasy or being a *muharib*, that is, a combatant 'against God and his religion'.[51] Mere admission of belief in, or in some cases refusal to publicly denounce, the new prophets is ground for being regarded a *murtadd* or apostate, putting one 'outside the pale' of Islam and thus 'subject to the legal punishment requested by *shari'a*'.[52] A modern variation of this form of religious othering may be found within Iran's laws. Its *Constitution* expressly declares the Iranian society's foundation be 'based on Islamic principles and norms'.[53] Article 13 names the 'Zoroastrian, Jewish, and Christian' faiths as the 'only recognized

---

48   Houchang E. Chehabi, 'Anatomy of Prejudice: Reflections on Secular Anti-Bahá'ísm in Iran', in Dominic Brookshaw and Seena Fazel (eds), *The Bahá'ís of Iran: Socio-Historical Studies* (London & New York: Routledge, 2008) 184-199.

49   Ibid 184.

50   Ibid.

51   Amanat, above n 23 172, 174.

52   Ibid 174.

53   Constitution of the Islamic Republic of Iran, Introduction.

religious minorities', constitutionally guaranteed to 'exercise matters of personal status and religious education' and to 'follow their own rituals'.[54] The constitutional mention of Bahá'í is conspicuously absent, notwithstanding that today the Bahá'í community is the largest non-Muslim minority in Iran. The most telling difference is perhaps that only Bahá'í is a post-Islamic revelation, while all three faiths mentioned in the *Constitution* are pre-Islamic.

The constitutional non-mention of Iran's largest non-Muslim minority, this paper argues, is significant. The withholding by Iran of constitutional recognition and protection of the minority which to it appears to challenge a key doctrine of Islam, is in fact part of a pattern of domination and attempt to coercively control a minority group whose members are seen as having deviated from the norm and are therefore unworthy of belonging. As will be seen below, government jobs and university admission are denied to applicants because they are required to state their religious affiliation on application forms, and Bahá'ís were not able to do so because Bahá'í is not among the legally recognised religions.

Disturbing national security and collaboration with foreign powers

One of the charges against the Bahá'ís is their 'political coloration', that is, of their support for and being supported by 'foreigners'.[55] The seven members of an informal group, known as the *Yaran* (literally, friends), appointed to tend to the 'spiritual and social needs' of the Bahá'í community in Iran were arrested in 2008.[56] They were charged with disturbing and conspiring against national security, spreading

---

54   Constitution of the Islamic Republic of Iran, art 13.
55   Firaydun Adamiyat, *Amir Kabir va Iran* (Bungah-i Azar, 1944) 258.
56   Bahá'í International Community, *The Bahá'í Question Revisited: Persecution and Resilience in Iran* (A report of the Bahá'í International Community, October 2016) 20. One was arrested on 5 March 2008, while the other six were arrested on 14 May 2008.

propaganda, gathering classified information, collaborating with foreign governments and espionage.[57] Particularly, they were tried for 'spying for Israel', 'blasphemy against Islam' and for 'offenses against the Islamic Republic', where the Attorney General accused them of 'gathering information, intrusive activities and subverting the foundation of people's beliefs'.[58] After three trial postponements, relatives were informed the accused would be tried as *muharib ba khuda* or 'enemies of God', with possible death sentences.[59] In August 2010, each was sentenced to twenty years imprisonment, which was reduced to ten years due to a change in the penal code.[60] The sentences were met with international protests, with at least 21 nations mentioning the situation of the Bahá'ís in Iran.[61] Many called for an 'end to religious discrimination' against the Bahá'ís and other minorities, while others expressed 'specific concerns for the detention of the seven Bahá'í leaders'.[62] Since 2005, 860 Bahá'ís have been arrested with 275 serving time in prison.[63]

The Bahá'ís' long-association with Israel was a result of a historical event which occurred long before the establishment of the state of Israel in 1948. Bahá'u'lláh, the founder of the Bahá'í Faith, as prisoner of Qajar Persia (and Ottoman Turkey) was exiled to Israel, arriving in Akka on 31 August 1868.[64] He remained there until his death on 29 May 1892, and it was also in Israel where the Bahá'í

---

57   Ibid. The seven, namely: Mahvash Sabet, Fariba Kamalabadi, Jamaloddin Khanjani, Afif Naeimi, Saeid Rezaie, Behrouz Tavakkoli, and Vahid Tizfahm were put on trial in 2010 for the following crimes: '1) forming or managing a group that aims at disturbing national security; 2) spreading propaganda against the regime of the Islamic Republic of Iran; 3) gathering classified information with the intention of disturbing national security; 4) engaging in espionage; 5) collaborating with foreign governments hostile against Iran; and 6) conspiring to commit offenses against national security.

58   Fereydun Vahman, *175 Years of Persecution: A History of the Bábis and Bahá'ís of Iran* (Oneworld Publications, 2019) 233.

59   Ibid.

60   Ibid 234.

61   Bahá'í International Community, above n 56, 75.

62   Ibid.

63   Ibid 7.

64   Shoghi Effendi, *God Passes By* (Bahá'í Publishing Trust, 2010), 288, 289, 356.

World Centre was established.[65] Ironically, the connection, in a sort of guilt by association, is now made the basis in calling Bahá'ís foreign agents or spies for Israel. Ascribing common attributes between two unwanted but otherwise disparate groups whose only connection is geographical proximity is classic othering, where devaluation is done by mere association.

This is not the first time the Baha'is have been accused of association with foreign powers. Historian Adamiyat avers that Bahá'ís were 'first supported by the Russians and later by the British'.[66] The supposed source of such attribution is a 'fictitious memoir' purportedly written by Prince Dimitri Ivanovich Dolgoruv, the Russian ambassador to Persia between 1846 and 1854, when he supposedly described how 'he created the Bábi-Bahá'í religion' to 'weaken Iran and Shi'ism'.[67] While the document was found to be a forgery, it is still 'reprinted on occasion' and is 'referred to in anti-Bahá'í polemics'.[68] The choice of supposed Bahá'í association with the Russians and the British is deliberate and calculated to evoke Iranian nationalist sentiments over Russia and Britain's role in invading Iran, deposing the former Reza Shah, and installing his twenty-one year old son, Muhammad Reza Shah during the so-called Anglo-Soviet invasion of Iran in 1941.[69] It is a common technique to associate an 'othered' minority

---

65   Ibid 350, 563.

66   Chehabi, above n 48, 187.

67   Ibid.

68   Ibid.

69   Douglas Martin, *The Persecution of the Bahá'ís of Iran, 1844-1984* (Association for Bahá'í Studies, 1984) 21: 'The British and Russian governments saw Iran as a vital «back door» route through which British supplies could reach the battered Soviet forces. When Reza Shah refused to cooperate in this plan and when his wellknown Nazi sympathies appeared to pose a threat to British control over the Near East, the two nations acted swiftly to resolve the problem. Russian troops entered Azerbaijan from the north to seize the vital rail communications, while their British allies moved into southern Iran, deposed Reza Shah, and sent him into exile. In his place, the British installed his twenty-one year old son, Muhammad Reza Shah, who was expected by all concerned to serve as a compliant puppet.' Ibid. Baha'i scholar Moojan Momen has combed the available British records and found no evidence of a Baha'i-British conspiracy. See Moojan Momen, *The Babi and Baha'i Religions, 1844-1944: Some Contemporary Western Accounts* (George

group with another hated community, entity or derogatory concept, and lump the negative qualities of the hated entity onto the othered minority.

Not so subtle are the name-callings resorted to by Iran's religious leaders in a number of *fatwas* or official decrees. In these decrees, the Bahá'í faith is called an 'incorrigible heresy', a 'perverse' and 'misguided sect', and its members are called 'apostates', 'blasphemous', 'enemies of Islam', 'ritually unclean', so that 'association with them must be avoided' because they are 'even more unclean than dogs'.[70] Coming from an ordinary man on the street, the epithets may not amount to much. But these statements are part of official discourse among highest level ayatollahs, who are high-ranking Shi'ah clerics, and considered experts in Islamic studies.

Foucault sees knowledge propagated through discourse and power as intimately related.[71] Knowledge and power are in fact two sides of the same coin, for what ordinary people naturally assume as 'objective knowledge' is nothing more or less, than the 'version of events' expressed by those authorised to exercise power.[72] Thus, political or social authorities' version or interpretation of events is then impressed with the imprimatur of truth.[73] Derogation and name-calling are well-known techniques of subjugation, commonly-found within domestic violence or religious persecution scenarios. These techniques are used by persons or groups who try to dominate others by belittling their self-worth, thereby relegating them to the margins of society. By calling Bahá'ís apostates, the name-givers identify themselves as 'normal', and the other as 'heretics' and enemies of Islam.

Ronald, 1981).

70   Bahá'í International Community, above n 56 at 14. Also see Abbas Amanat, above n 15.

71   Michel Foucault, The History of Sexuality, Volume 1 (Penguin Books, 2008) 7.

72   Denise Meyerson, *Jurisprudence* (Oxford University Press, 2013) 221.

73   Ibid.

Prominence during the Shah's regime

One of the most common accusations against the Bahá'ís is their alleged prominence in high positions during the reign of the last shah, implying a monarchical favouritism over the majority citizens. The Minister of Court, Asadullah Alam, wrote in 1973, with considerable exaggeration, that the 'Bahá'ís have infiltrated all walks of public life,' and that it is thought 'half of the cabinet, is Bahá'í' causing a lot of 'dissatisfaction among that people'.[74] He also noted that 'General Ayadi' the 'Shah's personal physician', is 'known to be a Bahá'í, which hurts the Shahanshah a lot'.[75] Among the Bahá'ís in Iran, General Abd al-Karim Ayadi (also known as Dr. Abdolkarim Ayadi), was probably the best known, and one who was most written-about particularly in Iranian anti-Bahá'í polemics claiming special ties between the regime of the last shah and the Bahá'í community.[76] A diligent and capable man, Ayadi was appointed head of the Health Office of the army, putting him in-charge of 'all medicinal purchases' for both the 'army and the Organization of Social Insurance'.[77] Beyond being Shah Mohammad Reza's personal physician, Ayadi also 'functioned' as his 'private secretary, trusted emissary, and advisor on health matters'.[78] Two other Bahá'ís became high-ranking public servants during the reign of the shah: General Asad Allah Sani'i, who became Iran's Minister of War, and Colonel Vahdat-i

---

74   A. Alikhani, *Yaddast-ha-yi Alam* (New World Ltd., 1995) 166.

75   Ibid. Shahanshah was a title given to the Persian emperors, meaning King of Kings.

76   Mina Yazdani, 'Towards a History of Iran's Bahá'í Community During the Reign of Mohammad Reza Shah, 1941-1979' (2017) 2(1) *Iran Namag* 83.

77   Ibid. at 84.

78   Abbas Milani, *Eminent Persians: The Men and Women Who Made Modern Iran, 1941-1979* (Syracuse University Press, 2008) 1058.

     Ayadi caught the attention of Prince Ali-Reza, the shah's brother, who believed that he possessed great healing powers. Some have suggested that Ayadi first entered the court when he cured Crown Prince Mohammad Reza, of a serious ailment. Others think that Ayadi owed his rise to the fact that the shah's second wife, Soraya, considered him a trustworthy friend in an otherwise belligerent court. The fact that the shah was a hypochondriac added to the urgency of Ayadi's constant presence at the court. (Ibid.)

Haqq, who was appointed military attaché of the Iranian embassy in Germany.[79] Vahdat-i Haqq studied 'military engineering', learned 'foreign languages' and earned a 'high score' in a 1971 exam which contributed to his appointment.[80] The success of the Bahá'ís in high government places became a lightning rod of criticism, particularly after the 1979 Islamic revolution in Iran. The allegations were that Bahá'ís are supporters of the deposed Shah, and by analogy are complicit in the decadent Western values the Shah stood for, and are therefore by extension, representatives of the very things the Islamic revolution fought against.

Nowhere is distancing, hence othering, more pronounced than in the case of former Iranian prime minister Amir Abbas Hoveyda, who not only dissociated himself but actively initiated measures against the Bahá'í community. Hoveyda was Iran's Prime Minister from 1965-77. His grandfather and father were Bahá'ís, though the latter had 'distanced himself from the religion'.[81] Though Hoveyda himself was raised a Muslim, he was not exempt from accusations from his political enemies of being a Bahá'í.[82] Accordingly, he may have 'felt impelled' to be 'particularly severe in his treatment of Bahá'ís'.[83] During his tenure, discriminatory regulations against Bahá'ís were adopted, among them: the deletion from history books of 'all events associated with the Bahá'í Faith', the implementation of a new Civil Service Code requiring government job applicants to 'state their religion', and making it clear through attendant regulations that the only ones qualified were those belonging to the recognised religions, Bahá'í not being one of them.[84] As a consequence, 'government departments, crown corporations' and even 'private industries'

---

79   Yazdani, above n 76, 82, 84, 85. As Bahá'ís are forbidden by their faith from involvement in partisan politics, the Iranian Baha'i community revoked General Asad Allah Sani'i's administrative rights for taking up a political post.
80   Ibid 82. Bahá'ís may accept appointments in non-political posts.
81   Ibid 85.
82   Ibid.
83   Martin, above n 69, 26.
84   Ibid.

which 'relied heavily on government orders', 'discharged their Bahá'í employees'.[85]

Bahá'í disqualification did not stop in public employment, as Bahá'ís have been denied access to higher education in Iran for a number of years. Similar to the way employment disqualification was implemented, the government also established a requirement that everyone taking the national university entrance examination had to 'declare their religion'.[86] Applicants who indicated affiliation with a religion 'other than one of the four officially recognised religions in Iran', namely Islam, Christianity, Judaism and Zoroastrianism, 'were excluded' from sitting the examination.[87] This practice of educational othering has had a 'demoralizing effect on Bahá'í youth'.[88] In response, the Bahá'í community established in the late 1980s its own underground program, the Bahá'í Institute of Higher Education (BIHE) to address the higher educational needs of its youth.[89] In 1998, May 2001 and again in May 2011, government agents raided and arrested BIHE faculty and staff and confiscated its records. 36 were arrested in 1998 and 19 in 2001. Of those arrested in 2001, 17 were 'sentenced to terms of four or five years in prison for 'conspiracy against national security by establishing the illegal [BIHE]', or 'membership in the deviant Bahá'í sect' with the goal of 'taking action against the security of the country'.[90] In 2011, seven educators were arrested and sentenced to prison terms of four and five years.[91] It is difficult to understand why efforts of a community to give its young members the benefits of higher education would amount to crimes against national security. What these practices

---

85   Ibid.
86   Bahá'í International Community, above n 56, 33.
87   Ibid.
88   Ibid 34.
89   International Federation for Human Rights, *Discrimination against Religious Minorities in Iran* ((A report of the International Federation for Human Rights presented to the 63rd session of the Committee on the Elimination of Racial Discrimination, August 2003) 13.
90   Bahá'í International Community, above n 56, 34
91   Ibid.

demonstrate is official Iranian government commitment to the denial of Bahá'í opportunities for advancement, human flourishing and development, with the intention of hastening the Bahá'í community's impoverishment, in every sense of the term.[92]

OTHERING AS DEALING WITH THE UNKNOWN

Othering is really about dealing with the unknown, the remote, the wild.[93] The lack of correct knowledge about the other establishes a psychological and symbolic distance which broadly, if simplistically, represents the other either as the embodiment of ideals, windows of mystery and objects of desire or, as objects of fear and scapegoats for the dominant group's failures thereby making the other, the target of hatreds.[94] The idealisation of others gives rise to exoticism, which is a fascination with faraway peoples, places or objects,[95] while making other the object of fear conjures spectres of an uncontrollable other, with social disorder and even criminality supposedly conspired

---

92 In January 2020, a new rule requires Iran's state-issued National Identity Card - the card used to facilitate government and commercial transactions - be issued only to members of the four faiths recognised under Iran's Constitution. Previously, members of Iran's non-constitutionally recognised minority religions were given a choice to tick the 'other religions' option. The removal of 'other religions' gives minority religious members a choice of only one of two difficult options: dissimulation, that is, hiding under a pretence by lying about one's religion, an act prohibited under Baha'i law, not to mention possible criminal repercussion for perjury under Iranian laws, or sticking with the truth. The latter translates to minority religious members living in Iran as citizens in name only, but without real civil rights to, among others, conduct government transactions, obtain a bank loan, make bank deposits, purchase property or to simply get a driver's licence – these transactions being dependent upon one's having a prior National ID card. See Center for Human Rights in Iran, Unrecognized Minorities in Iran Must Now Hide Religion to Obtain Crucial Government ID, 27 January 2020, https://iranhumanrights.org/2020/01/bahais-unrecognized-minorities-in-iran-must-now-hide-religion-to-obtain-government-id/; see also Steve Jacobs, 'Iran Locks Members of Minority Baha'i faith out of Identity Documents, The Sydney Morning Herald (Sydney) 9 February 2020.

93 Ellis Cashmore, *Encyclopedia of Race and Ethnic Studies* (Routledge, 2004) 306.

94 Ibid.

95 Staszak, above n 1.

by the other and directed towards the dominant community.[96] A discursive construction and mental representation based on the latter creates a generalised if unconscious sense of defensiveness if not paranoia paving the way for a narrow and extreme form of intolerance.[97] Drakulić states:

> I understand now that nothing but 'otherness' killed Jews, and it began with naming them, by reducing them to the other. Then everything became possible. Even the worst atrocities like concentration camps or the slaughtering of civilians in Croatia or Bosnia. For Serbians, as for Germans, they are all others, not-us.[98]

What Drakulić probably meant was, that if unexamined generalisations and stereotypes which begin innocuously are left unchecked, either by law or by the rest of society, they can morph into otherness, discrimination and even persecution where the worst kinds of atrocity become possible.

FREEDOM OF RELIGION OR BELIEF AND DETERMINATION OF 'RELIGION'

Freedom of religion or belief is a fundamental human right. The *Universal Declaration of Human Rights*, under article 18, articulates such a right, which includes the freedom to have, to change, and to exercise one's religion or belief.[99] The *International Covenant*

---

96   Wui Ling Cheah, 'Migrant Workers as Citizens within the ASEAN Landscape: International Law and the Singapore Experiment' (2009) 8(1) *Chinese Journal of International Law* 211.

97   Cashmore, above n 92, 53.

98   Slavenka Drakulić, *Balkan Express: Fragments From The Other Side Of War* (Norton, 1993) 145: 'I understand now that nothing but 'otherness' killed Jews, and it began with naming them, by reducing them to the other. Then everything became possible. Even the worst atrocities like concentration camps or the slaughtering of civilians in Croatia or Bosnia. For Serbians, as for Germans, they are all others, not-us. For me, those others are refugees. For Europe, the 'other' is the lawless Balkans they pretend not to understand. For the USA its more or less a 'European problem': why should they bother with the screams of thousands of people being bombed or simply dying of hunger, when those screams can hardly be heard?'

99   *Universal Declaration of Human Rights*, GA Res 217A (III), UN GAOR, UN Doc

on Civil and Political Rights (ICCPR), a binding multilateral treaty adopted by the United Nations General Assembly under Resolution 2200A (XXI), likewise guarantees, under article 18, the right to have, or to 'adopt a religion or belief of [one's] choice', and to exercise one's religion or belief.[100] Additionally, under article 27, the *ICCPR* requires that in those states where 'ethnic, religious or linguistic minorities exist', the members of such minorities, have the right individually and collectively, to 'enjoy their own culture, [and] to profess and practise their own religion'.[101]

It is noteworthy that while Iran is a party to the *ICCPR*, but the mandate that religious minorities within each member state 'shall not be denied the right... to profess and practise their own religion' is not complied with". A fuller dissection of the reasons behind the denial of Bahá'í minority religious rights in that country is beyond the scope of this paper. However, one social reason for that failure appears to be founded in the dominant religious community in Iran to legally or culturally recognise Bahá'í as a religion. The consequence of that social fact is that, Iran, considers that it has no legal duty or constitutional obligation to treat Bahá'í as a religion. That is reiterated by the non-mention of the faith in the *national Constitution*, with Iranian religious and social leaders continuing

---

A/810 (10 December 1948). Article 18 'Everyone has the right to freedom of thought, conscience and religion; this right includes freedom to change his religion or belief, and freedom, either alone or in community with others and in public or private, to manifest his religion or belief in teaching, practice, worship and observance.'

100   *International Covenant on Civil and Political Rights*, opened for signature 19 December 1996, 999 UNTS 171 (entered into force 23 March 1976) ('ICCPR'). Article 18 (1)
Everyone shall have the right to freedom of thought, conscience and religion. This right shall include freedom to have or to adopt a religion or belief of his choice, and freedom, either individually or in community with others and in public or private, to manifest his religion or belief in worship, observance, practice and teaching.

101   Ibid art 27. Article 27,
In those States in which ethnic, religious or linguistic minorities exist, persons belonging to such minorities shall not be denied the right, in community with the other members of their group, to enjoy their own culture, to profess and practise their own religion, or to use their own language.

to label the community an incorrigible heresy, and its members apostates.

While official rhetoric suggests non-recognition, an analysis of the decisions of Iran's religious and social leaders point otherwise. Absent a *de jure* acknowledgement, the leaders' actions and policies point to a *de facto* recognition of Bahá'í as religion, evidenced by the following: (1) the systematic eradication of Bahá'í leaders, among them the Báb who was executed, Bahá'u'lláh who was banished and the Yaran who were imprisoned; (2) the deletion of Bahá'í from Iran's history books; (3) the destruction and demolition of Bahá'í holy and historical places, such as the house of the Báb in Shiraz in 1979, the gravesite of early disciple Quddus, in April 2004 and the house of Mirza Abbas Nuri, father of Bahá'u'lláh, in June 2004, and (4) the denial of opportunities for Bahá'ís to enter government service and for Bahá'í youth to enrol at universities. To the author, these indicate a thorough attempt to bring down the Bahá'í religious movement, while unwittingly and tacitly admitting the movement's existence as a rising, but feared and hated, religious group in Iran. For if Bahá'í is not officially recognised as a religion, why would Iran go to such lengths to erase its holy shrines and eradicate its leaders – markers which have great significance for Bahá'í believers? After a 'careful investigation into the meaning of the term heretic', Sebastian Castellio, a French proponent for religious toleration writes, 'I can discover no more than this, that we regard those as heretics with whom we disagree'.[102] Many of the great faiths were also labelled heretical sects in the early eras of their history.

This raises the question: who determines what is or what is not a religion? International law does not categorically define what religion is, and instead uses the term in its declarations and conventions with a tacit assumption that it is universally understood. While this may not pose a problem in places which uphold religious toleration

---

102   Perez Zagorin, *How the Idea of Religious Toleration Came to the West* (Princeton

and diversity, in absolutist countries like Iran, the case is different. Without a working definition, it is easy for countries such as Iran to hide their acts of othering behind the pretext of not recognising as legitimate the existence of a post-Islamic religion like Bahá'í. A close reading of the *ICCPR* indicates religious members or adherents themselves are allowed to determine whether or not they belong to a religion. The *ICCPR* categorically states freedom of religion includes the 'freedom to have or to adopt a religion or belief *of his choice*' (emphasis added),[103] that is, without requiring an imprimatur from the dominant religion. As long as a religious group operates within the law, and has not done anything harmful to society, its believers are the best determinants of their faith as religion. As the Bahá'í experience in Iran suggests, allowing a dominant religious group to determine the legitimacy or existence of minority religions may run counter to the interests of the religious other.

AVENUES FOR INTERGROUP DIALOGUE

A way to mitigate distancing is to promote opportunities for intergroup dialogue and interaction, through a common project. The aim is to give groups a chance to get to know one another through collaboration. Article 100 of the *Constitution of Iran* establishes councils to 'advance social, economic, developmental, public health, cultural, and educational programs as well as other welfare-related matters' through the 'collaboration of the people'.[104] Elected by the 'people of that locality', councils are formed at village, district, city, municipal and provincial levels.[105] This in theory offers spaces and channels for intergroup collaboration, dialogue and connections. In practice, minority candidates are 'always vetted', and even those who supported existing constitutional provisions for the 'use of

---

University Press, 2003).

103   *International Covenant on Civil and Political Rights*, above n 99, art 18.
104   Constitution of the Islamic Republic of Iran, art 100.
105   Ibid.

minority languages have been 'harshly rejected'.[106] Assuming, arguendo, members of religious minorities, such as Bahá'í, are elected, Article 105 mandates 'decisions of the councils may not contradict the Islamic criteria and the laws of the country'.[107] The conformity requirement to Islamic criteria leaves little room indeed, if at all, for councils to entertain contrary ideas.

Not all religious minorities are denied participation in Iran's public life. Article 64 of the *Constitution* grants parliamentary representation for Iranian Jews, Christians and Zoroastrians, with the Bahá'í community, again, left out. [108] Still, minority *representation* need not be confused with minority *influence*.[109] While the recognised religious minorities have parliamentary *representation*, work needs to be done on representation in other areas of governance. Representation in 'other branches' of the government, such as the judiciary and other ministries, would give minorities a greater influence in Iran's public life.[110]

Social justice, fairness and respect for human dignity and rights, in any country will be diminished if minority voices continue to be muted. States, according to the Lund Recommendations on the Effective Participation of National Minorities, should 'establish advisory or consultative bodies within institutional frameworks' to 'serve as channels for dialogue between governmental authorities

---

106 Nazila Ghanea-Hercock, *Ethnic and Religious Groups in the Islamic Republic of Iran: Policy Suggestions for the Integration of Minorities through Participation in Public Life* (A paper submitted to the U.N. Commission on Human Rights, Sub-Commission on Promotion and Protection of Human Rights Working Group on Minorities, 9th session, 12-16 May 2003) 24.

107 Constitution of the Islamic Republic of Iran, art 105.

108 Constitution of the Islamic Republic of Iran, art 64. 'There shall be 270 representatives in the Islamic Consultative Assembly.... The Zoroastrians and the Jews each elect one representative; the Assyrian and Chaldean Christians elect one representative together; the Armenian Christians of the North and the South each elect one representative. The law determines voting districts and the number of the representatives.'

109 Ghanea-Hercock, above n 105.

110 Ibid.

and national minorities'.[111] To do this, structural discrimination and officially sanctioned minority discrimination within the law itself needed to be addressed and corrected. Effective communication channels and a broad feedback system from all segments of society are required to stem an intellectual in-breeding and social solipsism that may make a society unmindful, and therefore unheeding, to possible areas of advancement and improvement. Numerical inferiority, and divergence of world view, cannot justify any kind of officially sanctioned marginalisation and silencing. On the contrary, an openness to accommodate and listen to differences makes for a more aware, enriched and cohesive society.

IMPLICATIONS FOR AUSTRALIA

The experience of the Bahá'ís in Iran carries with it implications worth noting for Australia, on areas involving legal definition of religion and recourse to law in Australia that would reduce racial and ethnic discrimination against religious minorities.

Legal definition

An advantage of Australia relative to religious freedom and recognition of its religious minorities, is that its highest court was able to come up with a broad and inclusive definition of religion as a legal category. This in itself is a good start, because it means that no dominant ethnic or religious group can decide whether a minority group is or is not a religion. Though Chief Justice Latham, had suggested in 1943 that it would be 'difficult, if not impossible, to devise a definition of religion' which would 'satisfy the adherents' of 'all the many and various religions which exist, or have existed in

---

111　Organization for Security and Co-operation in Europe, *The Lund Recommendations on the Effective Participation of National Minorities in Public Life & Explanatory Note* (A report to the OSCE Office of the High Commissioner of National Minorities, September 1999) 9.

the world',[112] his successors in the High Court of Australia eventually adopted a two-fold definition of religion for the purpose of the law:

> We would therefore hold that, for the purposes of the law, the criteria of religion are twofold: first, belief in a supernatural Being, Thing or Principle; and second, the acceptance of canons of conduct in order to give effect to that belief, though canons of conduct which offend against the ordinary laws are outside the area of any immunity, privilege or right conferred on the grounds of religion.[113]

This definition is inclusive and accommodates a broad range of theistic and non-theistic faiths including Bahá'í. As the High Court stated, to 'restrict the definition of religion to theistic religions' is to 'exclude Theravada Buddhism, an acknowledged religion, and perhaps other acknowledged religions'.[114] The High Court thus acknowledged that religion may also be couched in non-theistic terms, so long as there is belief in ultimate concerns and principles. Religious ideas, the High Court added, should address the 'fundamental questions' of human existence which is similar to Paul Tillich's view that the essence of religion is to address the 'ultimate concerns'. Tillich saw religion as dealing with the concepts that are of the 'greatest depth and utmost importance' to human beings.[115] Religion caters to an individual's most basic values, and addresses one's need for authenticity and belonging.[116] As a cultural phenomenon, Stack has said that religion also serves as a 'fundamental marker of individual and group identity.'[117] The importance of religion and its protection under the law cannot be overestimated. Yet, it should also not be

---

112   *Adelaide Company of Jehovah's Witnesses Inc v Commonwealth* (1943) 67 CLR 116, 123.

113   *Church of the New Faith v Commissioner of Pay-Roll Tax* (Vic) (1983) 154 CLR 120, 136. This case came about when the Church of the New Faith (the Church of Scientology) applied for an exemption from having to pay pay-roll tax on the basis that it was a 'religious institution' for the purposes of section IO(b) of the Pay-roll Tax Act 1971 (Vic.). The High Court determined the Church was a 'religion', and that no 'reasonable man' or majority view test can be used to determine a religion.

114   Ibid.

115   Ibid.

116   See Stack, above n 9.

117   Ibid.

forgotten that freedom of religion has its limits, and carries with it responsibilities, as no religion may just simply dominate or claim dominance to the exclusion of other faiths. Learning from the Bahá'í experience in Iran, religious freedom must be balanced with respect for the existence and dignity of other persons or groups who may have different ideological, religious or spiritual viewpoints.

Discrimination springing from religious othering

An inclusive – as opposed to othering – orientation within either the law or society such as that demonstrated by Australia reinforces and helps to counter-check dominant others and prevents a society from swinging to ideological extremes. As an immigrant to Australia, the writer's Australian experience in liberal multiculturalism has provided an eye-opening vision of tolerance and acceptance despite occasional incidents of racial and religious discrimination. But there are no guarantees that Australia's largely tolerant accommodation of religious diversity will continue. Australia is not insulated from the worldwide rise of fundamentalist and extremist ideas. Those are facilitated by increased migration and borderless communication. We must be vigilant to preserve our current religious freedoms in Australia and to close gaps within our existing laws.

A case in point is the *Racial Discrimination Act 1975* (Cth) which does 'not specifically prohibit discrimination' on the ground of religious identity or belief, unless the concerned religious group can establish a common 'ethnic origin'.[118] Thus far only two religious groups have been identified as having common ethnic origins, namely the Jewish and Sikh people. On 14 December 1979, the Court of Appeal of New Zealand held in *King-Ansell v Police* that Jewish people form a group with common ethnic origins within the

---

118 Australian Human Rights Commission, Religious Freedom Review (An Aus-
     tralian Human Rights Commission Submission to the Expert Panel, February
     2018) 23.

meaning of the *Race Relations Act 1971* (NZ). The decision was based on the Jews' 'historically determined social identity', as Jewishness is ethnic and religious.[119] Similarly, on 24 March 1983, the House of Lords of the United Kingdom considered Sikhs an ethnic group for the purpose of the *Race Relations Act 1976* (UK), because of their shared history, common cultural tradition and the fact that they are a minority within a larger community.[120]

As there is yet no jurisprudence concerning other religious minorities being considered ethnic groups, complaints involving racial discrimination committed against them will theoretically not prosper, unless the elements of race and ethnicity are proven. This is an area of religious freedom and protection in Australia which would need additional attention, even inclusive reform. While the *Constitution of Australia* under s 116 forbids the Commonwealth from making any law which would prohibit the free exercise of religion, such a provision is not an absolute individual right to freedom of religion and is subject to 'limitations which it is the function and the duty of the courts to expound'.[121] Minority religious groups, as the experience of the Bahá'ís in Iran, and the Ahmadiyya in Pakistan demonstrate, due to their numerical inferiority and different world views compared with the dominant and mainstream groups are highly susceptible and vulnerable to discrimination and abuse. Such minorities, need legal protection whether they live in Iran, Pakistan or in a Western multicultural nation such as Australia.

CONCLUSION

Freedom of religion or belief is a fundamental human right, and from it flows other rights such as the freedom of speech and assembly. Freedom of conscience, toleration and religious pluralism provide the

---

119   *King-Ansell v Police* [1979] 2 NZLR 531, 543.
120   *Mandla v Dowell-Lee* [1982] UKHL 7
121   *Adelaide Company of Jehovah's Witnesses Inc v Commonwealth* (1943) 67 CLR 116.

critical foundation for freedom of speech and freedom of the press. Law plays an important role in establishing a culture of inclusivity. A society's determination to include everyone is deeply connected with issues of religious liberty as the Iranian experience suggests. For when the law is weak or silent, othering can be translated into discrimination and even persecution.[122]

My first recommendation, thus, is to strengthen law both locally and internationally, to mandate protection for vulnerable others. And secondly, promote avenues, channels and spaces for intergroup dialogue and connections, so that all majorities and minorities can understand and appreciate the other.

Who are others? Are the differences between us and people of other faiths a matter of essence or a passing accident? Huserl regards the other as the 'unthought' and the 'implicit.' For Marcuse, the other consists of the 'virtual' or 'unfulfilled possibilities.'[123] For Levinas, alterity is a relational concept, echoing Martin Buber's 'I and Thou' which addresses the phenomenon of the other as a potential partner in dialogue.[124] In a final analysis, it is through laws designed to implement policies which actively include others that minority religious believers are best safeguarded. Open and sincere dialogue also enables those who participate to get to know the skin, personal beliefs and religious worldviews of others without judging them.

BIBLIOGRAPHY

Articles

Wui Ling Cheah, 'Migrant Workers as Citizens within the ASEAN Landscape: International Law and the Singapore Experiment' (2009) 8(1) *Chinese Journal of International Law* 211.

---

122   The International Covenant on Civil and Political Rights, under Article 18 mandates freedom of religion or belief. Iran is a signatory and has ratified ICCPR, and entered into force on 23 March 1976.
123   Cashmore, above n 92.
124   Ibid.

Walter Fischel, 'The Bahá'í Movement and Persian Jewry' (1934) 7 *Jewish Review* 47.

Michael Karlberg, 'Constructive Resilience: The Bahá'í Response to Oppression' (2010) 35(2) *Peace and Change* 227.

Andrea Lathan, 'The Relativity of Categorizing in the Context of the Ahmadiyya' (2008) 48 *Die Welt des Islams* 375.

Joanne Benham Rennick, 'Is Religion a Force for Good? Reformulating the Discourse on Religion and International Development' 34(2) *Canadian Journal of Development Studies* 179.

Peter Smith, 'A Note on Bábi and Bahá'í Numbers in Iran' (1984) 17 *Iranian Studies* 295.

Mina Yazdani, 'Towards a History of Iran's Bahá'í Community During the Reign of Mohammad Reza Shah, 1941-1979' (2017) 2(1) *Iran Namag* 83.

Book Chapters

Abbas Amanat, 'The Historical Roots of the Persecution of Bábis and Bahá'ís in Iran', in Dominic Brookshaw and Seena Fazel (eds), *The Bahá'ís of Iran: Socio-Historical Studies* (London & New York: Routledge, 2008).

Dominic Brookshaw and Seena Fazel, 'Introduction', in Dominic Brookshaw and Seena Fazel (eds), *The Bahá'ís of Iran: Socio-Historical Studies* (London & New York: Routledge, 2008).

Houchang E. Chehabi, 'Anatomy of Prejudice: Reflections on Secular Anti-Bahá'ísm in Iran', in Dominic Brookshaw and Seena Fazel (eds), *The Bahá'ís of Iran: Socio-Historical Studies* (London & New York: Routledge, 2008).

Juan R. I. Cole, 'The Bahá'í Minority and Nationalism in Contemporary Iran', in Maya Shatzmiller (ed) Studies in Nationalism and Ethnic Conflict (McGill-Queen's University Press, 2005).

Patrick James, 'Religion, Identity and Global Governance: Setting the Agenda' in Patrick James (ed), *Religion, Identity and Global Governance: Ideas, Evidence and Practice* (University of Toronto Press, 2011).

John Stack Jr, 'Religious Challenge to International Relations Theory' in Patrick James (ed), *Religion, Identity and Global Governance: Ideas,*

Evidence and Practice (University of Toronto Press, 2011).

Jean-François Staszak, 'Other/Otherness', in Rob Kitchin and Nigel Thrift (eds), *International Encyclopedia of Human Geography* (Elsevier Science, 2009) vol. 8.

Fereydun Vahman, 'Conversion of Zoroastrians to the Bahá'í Faith', in Dominic Brookshaw and Seena Fazel (eds), *The Bahá'ís of Iran: Socio-Historical Studies* (London & New York: Routledge, 2008).

Books

Firaydun Adamiyat, *Amir Kabir va Iran* (Bungah-i Azar, 1944).

A. Alikhani, *Yaddast-ha-yi Alam* (New World Ltd., 1995).

Bahá'í International Community, *The Bahá'í Question Revisited: Persecution and Resilience in Iran* (A report of the Bahá'í International Community, October 2016).

Bahá'u'lláh, *Compilation of Compilations* (Bahá'í Publications Australia, 1991).

Bahá'u'lláh, *Gleanings From the Writings of Bahá'u'lláh* (US Bahá'í Publishing Trust, 1990).

Bahá'u'lláh, *The Kitáb-i-Aqdas* (Bahá'í Publications Australia, 1993).

Hasan M. Balyuzi, *Bahá'u'lláh, King of Glory* (George Ronald, 1980).

Simone de Beauvoir, *The Second Sex* (Vintage Books, 1973).

Ellis Cashmore, *Encyclopedia of Race and Ethnic Studies* (Routledge, 2004).

Emeric Cruce, *The New Cyneas* (Thomas Balch, ed and trans, Allen, Lane and Scott, 1909).

Maneckji Dhalla, *The Saga of a Soul: An Autobiography of Shams-ul-Ulama Dastur Dr. Maneckji Nusserwanji Dhalla* (H J Rustomji trans, Karachi: Gool & Behram Sohrab 1975).

Slavenka Drakulić, *Balkan Express: Fragments From The Other Side Of War* (Norton, 1993).

Shoghi Effendi, *God Passes By* (Bahá'í Publishing Trust, 2010).

Michel Foucault, *The History of Sexuality, Volume 1* (Penguin Books, 2008).

Antonio Gualtieri, *Conscience and Coercion: Ahmadi Muslims and Orthodoxy in Pakistan* (Guernica Editions, 1991).

William Hatcher and Douglas Martin, *The Bahá'í Faith: The Emerging Global Religion* (Bahá'í Publishing, 2002).

Uzma Jamil, *Minorities and "Islamic" States: Explaining Bahá'í and Ahmadi Marginalization in Iran and Pakistan* (MA Thesis, McGill University, 2002).

Douglas Martin, *The Persecution of the Bahá'ís of Iran, 1844-1984* (Association for Bahá'í Studies, 1984).

Denise Meyerson, *Jurisprudence* (Oxford University Press, 2013).

Abbas Milani, *Eminent Persians: The Men and Women Who Made Modern Iran, 1941-1979* (Syracuse University Press, 2008).

Moojan Momen, *An Introduction to Shi'i Islam: The History and Doctrines of Twelver Shi'ism* (George Ronald, 1985).

Moojan Momen, *The Babi and Baha'i Religions, 1844-1944 : Some Contemporary Western Accounts* (George Ronald, 1981).

Ali Usman Qasmi, *The Ahmadis and the Politics of Religious Exclusion in Pakistan* (Anthem Press, 2015).

Moshe Sharon, *Jewish Conversion to the Bahá'í Faith* (Chair in Bahá'í Studies Publications, The Hebrew University of Jerusalem 2011).

Fereydun Vahman, *175 Years of Persecution: A History of the Bábis and Bahá'ís of Iran* (Oneworld Publications, 2019).

Perez Zagorin, *How the Idea of Religious Toleration Came to the West* (Princeton University Press, 2003).

Cases

Australia

Adelaide Company of Jehovah's Witnesses Inc v Commonwealth (1943) 67 CLR 116.

Church of the New Faith v Commissioner of Pay-Roll Tax (Vic) (1983) 154 CLR 120.

New Zealand

King-Ansell v Police [1979] 2 NZLR 531.

United Kingdom

Mandla v Dowell-Lee [1982] UKHL 7.

Legislation

Constitution of the Islamic Republic of Iran.

Newspaper articles

Steve Jacobs, 'Iran Locks Members of Minority Baha'i faith out of Identity Documents, *Sydney Morning Herald* (9 February 2020).

Government Documents and Reports

Australian Human Rights Commission, Religious Freedom Review (An Australian Human Rights Commission Submission to the Expert Panel, February 2018) 23.

International Federation for Human Rights, *Discrimination against Religious Minorities in Iran* ((A report of the International Federation for Human Rights presented to the 63rd session of the Committee on the Elimination of Racial Discrimination, August 2003).

Nazila Ghanea-Hercock, *Ethnic and Religious Groups in the Islamic Republic of Iran: Policy Suggestions for the Integration of Minorities through Participation in Public Life* (A paper submitted to the U.N. Commission on Human Rights, Sub-Commission on Promotion and Protection of Human Rights Working Group on Minorities, 9th session, 12-16 May 2003).

Organization for Security and Co-operation in Europe, *The Lund Recommendations on the Effective Participation of National Minorities in Public Life & Explanatory Note* (A report to the OSCE Office of the High Commissioner of National Minorities, September 1999).

Treaties and Declarations

International Covenant on Civil and Political Rights, opened for signature 19 December 1996, 999 UNTS 171 (entered into force 23 March 1976).

Universal Declaration of Human Rights, GA Res 217A (III), UN GAOR, UN Doc A/810 (10 December 1948).

4

GENDER IDENTITY LAWS AND BASIC FREEDOMS

NEIL FOSTER*

ABSTRACT

Many Australian laws are designed to protect freedoms recognised as part of our common law and Western heritage - freedom from physical attack, freedom of movement, freedom of speech, freedom of association and freedom of religion. In recent years our society has also recognised the need to provide freedom against unjust discrimination. While there is widespread support for such laws aimed at decisions made on irrelevant grounds based on race, sex, age and disability, there is more controversy over laws which forbid discrimination, and "vilification", based on gender identity: a person's internal conviction that they do not in reality belong to the sex in which they were born. This paper addresses the nature of such laws and the complexities that arise when these laws may clash with the legal protection of other freedoms.

* BA/LLB (UNSW), BTh (ACT), DipATh (Moore), LLM (Newc); Newcastle Law School, University of Newcastle, NSW. The views presented here are of course my own and not necessarily those of my institution.

INTRODUCTION

From a theological perspective, both believers and unbelievers, as human beings made in the image of God, enjoy the protection of our legal order, and it is appropriate to say, in referring to those protections, that we enjoy "legal rights". These rights, or freedoms, ought to be respected by other people in the community. One set of rights that has become a topic of controversy are rights related to "gender identity". Do citizens have the untrammelled right to decide what gender they identify with, and to ask that other citizens also support this decision?

We start the discussion by describing some of the basic freedoms we enjoy, and how the Australia legal system protects them.

BASIC FREEDOMS AND THEIR LEGAL SOURCE

One of the most obvious freedoms is freedom from physical harm. In general, I have a right that others in the community do not do me harm by committing physical violence against me. For those within the Christian tradition, this is also a fundamental Biblical value, based on the inestimable value of human persons made in the image of God, spelled out in Genesis 9:5-6:

> 5 And for your lifeblood I will surely demand an accounting. I will demand an accounting from every animal. And from each human being, too, I will demand an accounting for the life of another human being.

> 6 Whoever sheds human blood, by humans shall their blood be shed; for in the image of God has God made mankind.

The legal system protects our freedom from physical bodily harm in two main ways: through the criminal law, which forbids crimes such as "assault" (which laws are enforced by the police, and prosecuted in the criminal courts), and through the civil law, which provides, among other things, a tort action for "battery" (which action is taken in a civil court and can result in an award of damages.)

The common law of crime and torts can to some extent be characterised as "common law human rights". Under the law of torts, for example, the common law protects (among other rights):

- A right not to have one's body interfered with (actions for battery, assault);

- A right of free movement (through the action for "false imprisonment");

- A right of enjoyment of personal property (actions for "conversion" and "detinue" and "trespass to goods");

- A right of enjoyment of real estate (actions for "trespass to land" and "nuisance");

- A right to not have one's reputation falsely degraded (the action for defamation).

These rights are further protected, and other rights granted, by Acts of Parliament and regulations. In addition, in recent years we have seen that international treaties on human rights have clarified that protection from harm in these areas should be provided by national governments. Both at common law and under international treaties we have also seen recognition of "freedom of speech" and "freedom of religion". We may note as significant examples articles 18 and 19 of the *International Covenant on Civil and Political Rights* (ICCPR):

Article 18

1. Everyone shall have the right to **freedom of thought, conscience and religion**. This right shall include freedom to have or to adopt a religion or belief of his choice, and freedom, either individually or in community with others and in public or private, to manifest his religion or belief in worship, observance, practice and teaching.

2. No one shall be subject to coercion which would impair his freedom to have or to adopt a religion or belief of his choice.

3. Freedom to manifest one's religion or beliefs may be subject only

to such limitations as are prescribed by law and are necessary to protect public safety, order, health, or morals or the fundamental rights and freedoms of others.

4. The States Parties to the present Covenant undertake to have respect for the liberty of parents and, when applicable, legal guardians to ensure the religious and moral education of their children in conformity with their own convictions.

Article 19

1. Everyone shall have the right to **hold opinions without interference**.

2. Everyone shall have the **right to freedom of expression**; this right shall include freedom to seek, receive and impart information and ideas of all kinds, regardless of frontiers, either orally, in writing or in print, in the form of art, or through any other media of his choice.

3. The exercise of the rights provided for in paragraph 2 of this article carries with it special duties and responsibilities. It may therefore be subject to certain restrictions, but these shall only be such as are provided by law and are necessary:

(a) For respect of the rights or reputations of others;

(b) For the protection of national security or of public order (ordre public), or of public health or morals.

These instruments, as well as the common law and statutes, recognise that there is no such thing as an "absolute right". All rights and freedoms have to be balanced on some occasions. My right to "free movement", for example, is constrained if you are standing in the doorway in front of me, and I cannot knock you over without interfering with your right to freedom from bodily injury. So all legal systems have to have rules that allow exceptions to rights in certain circumstances – for example, where a police officer is enforcing the law he or she may interfere with my right to free movement or bodily integrity by arresting me, so long as they use no more force than is reasonably necessary.

FREEDOM FROM UNJUST DISCRIMINATION

A particular type of freedom that has been recognised in recent years is a right to be free from "unjust discrimination". The word "unjust" in that phrase is significant, because we need to be precise when defining what sorts of discrimination are wrongful.

Let me briefly comment on something that is sometimes said, that "discrimination is not always wrong". This is justified by pointing out that all of us "discriminate" in the sense of choosing one thing rather than another. It used to be a compliment to pay someone to say that they had a "discriminating" taste in wine or books or paintings – they knew how to choose and what to choose.

But this is not an argument that is helpful to use any more in today's world. I agree with the logic, but the harsh reality is that the word "discrimination" is hardly ever used in a positive sense these days. If we want to communicate with our community clearly, we need to recognise that 95% or more of our neighbours think that all "discrimination" is bad, and so we need to speak carefully in this area. To say that we have a "right to discriminate" will be heard, to be blunt, as racist or hateful. In this paper I will usually use the word "discriminate" to mean "unjust discrimination".

Laws prohibiting unjust discrimination were first introduced in a broad way from the 1960's and were, at first, mainly responding to the reality of racial discrimination. People were being denied jobs, places in public transport, seats in café's, and rooms in hotels, on the basis of the colour of their skin. These were terrible injustices, and Christians recognise that this sort of behaviour is forbidden by the Bible, which tells us that all human beings are made in God's image (Gen 1:27) and we are all of the one human family (as Paul puts it in Acts 17:26). These laws forbidding racial discrimination were introduced to penalise those who unjustly discriminated by denying services or jobs to people on the basis of race.

Subsequently we had laws aimed at preventing unjust sex discrimination. In due course other grounds of discrimination were added. Not all of them were social problems of the magnitude of race and sex discrimination, but the model has been rolled out to other human characteristics. In federal law at the moment, we have separate legislation forbidding discrimination on the grounds of race, sex, disability and age.[1] Within those sometimes a number of connected but not identical grounds are included - the sex discrimination legislation today encompasses unjust decisions made not just on the basis of biological sex, but also on the basis of "relationship status" (whether or not someone is legally married), pregnancy, sexual orientation, and gender identity, to which we will turn in more detail shortly. (There are also a large number of other "prohibited grounds" of discrimination under state laws, but space prevents us from exploring these more closely.)

All these discrimination laws, at least initially, were based on the premise that we should not allow *irrelevant* criteria to be invoked in certain decisions such as employment or provision of services. The fact is that they all recognise that in some cases these criteria are actually *relevant* for decision-making and should not be unlawful. There are few examples in the race area, but the most obvious one is that under NSW law someone casting a play or film is entitled to employ someone of a particular race if that is important to convey the story. The life of Martin Luther King Jr can be portrayed by an African-American actor.[2] Similarly, the *Sex Discrimination Act 1984* (Cth) ("SDA") contains provisions spelling out that it will not amount to sex discrimination in circumstances where the sex of a person being offered a job is relevant to the duties of the job. This would include where the job involved fitting clothes for one sex or

---

1   The Federal *Racial Discrimination Act* 1975, *Sex Discrimination Act* 1984, *Disability Discrimination Act* 1992 and *Age Discrimination Act* 2004.

2   See s 14(a) of the *Anti-Discrimination Act* 1977 (NSW). Somewhat oddly the Commonwealth *Racial Discrimination Act* 1975 does not contain such an exemption, though I am not aware of any claims that have been made in this sort of area.

being in a bathroom designated for persons of one sex.[3]

The questions arising then in any discrimination claim will include whether a decision was made on the basis of a "prohibited ground" (such as race, sex, or some other recognised category), in some "protected sphere of life" (such as employment or education or provision of services) and then if so, was that ground actually relevant to decision-making (and is that recognised in some provision of the legislation?)

GENDER IDENTITY DISCRIMINATION

We come then to the focus of this paper, the prohibition on "gender identity" discrimination ("GID" for short.) This is implemented in the Commonwealth SDA under s 5B, where discrimination on the grounds of gender identity is defined:

SEX DISCRIMINATION ACT 1984 - SECT 5B

Discrimination on the ground of gender identity

(1)   For the purposes of this Act, a person (the discriminator) discriminates against another person (the aggrieved person) on the ground of the aggrieved person's gender identity if, by reason of:

(a) the aggrieved person's gender identity; or

(b) a characteristic that appertains generally to persons who have the same gender identity as the aggrieved person; or

(c) a characteristic that is generally imputed to persons who have the same gender identity as the aggrieved person;

the discriminator treats the aggrieved person less favourably than, in circumstances that are the same or are not materially different, the discriminator treats or would treat a person who has a different gender identity.

(2)   For the purposes of this Act, a person (the discriminator) discriminates against another person (the aggrieved person) on the

---

3   See s 30 of the *Sex Discrimination Act* 1984 (Cth), for these and other examples.

ground of the aggrieved person's gender identity if the discriminator imposes, or proposes to impose, a condition, requirement or practice that has, or is likely to have, the effect of disadvantaging persons who have the same gender identity as the aggrieved person.

(3) This section has effect subject to sections 7B and 7D.

What does "gender identity" mean? Under s 4(1) of the SDA it is defined as follows:

> *"gender identity"* means the gender-related identity, appearance or mannerisms or other gender-related characteristics of a person (whether by way of medical intervention or not), with or without regard to the person's designated sex at birth.

Interestingly, these provisions of the Commonwealth SDA are relatively recent, having been added to the Act only in 2013.[4] But something similar was already in place in state law.

Under NSW law, the *Anti-Discrimination Act* 1977 ("ADA"), there is a prohibition which seems to operate in the same area, but which is described as discrimination on "transgender grounds" under s 38B. It is sufficiently different from the Commonwealth law to need to be set out in full here:

> **38B   WHAT   CONSTITUTES   DISCRIMINATION   ON TRANSGENDER GROUNDS**
>
> (1) **A person** ("the perpetrator") **discriminates against another person** ("the aggrieved person") **on transgender grounds if the perpetrator--**
>
> (a) **on the ground of the aggrieved person being transgender** or a relative or associate of the aggrieved person being transgender, **treats the aggrieved person less favourably than in the same circumstances** (or in circumstances which are not materially different) **the perpetrator treats or would treat a person who he or she did not think was a transgender person** or who does not have such a relative or associate who he or she did not think was a

---

4   See the *Sex Discrimination Amendment (Sexual Orientation, Gender Identity and Intersex Status) Act* 2013 (Cth).

transgender person, or

(b) requires the aggrieved person to comply with a requirement or condition with which a substantially higher proportion of persons who are not transgender persons, or who do not have a relative or associate who is a transgender person, comply or are able to comply, being a requirement which is not reasonable having regard to the circumstances of the case and with which the aggrieved person does not or is not able to comply, or

(c) treats the aggrieved person, being a **recognised transgender person**, as being of the person's former sex or requires the aggrieved person, being a recognised transgender person, to comply with a requirement or condition with which a substantially higher proportion of persons of the person's former sex comply or are able to comply, being a requirement or condition which is not reasonable having regard to the circumstances of the case and with which the aggrieved person does not or is not able to comply.

(2) For the purposes of subsection (1) (a), something is done on the ground of a person being transgender if it is done on the ground of the person being transgender, a characteristic that appertains generally to transgender persons or a characteristic that is generally imputed to transgender persons. (emphasis added)

The legislation, in s 38A, provides a definition of what it is to be "transgender".

A reference in this Part to a person being transgender or a transgender person is a reference to a person, whether or not the person is a recognised transgender person--

(a) who identifies as a member of the opposite sex by living, or seeking to live, as a member of the opposite sex, or

(b) who has identified as a member of the opposite sex by living as a member of the opposite sex, or

(c) who, being of indeterminate sex, identifies as a member of a particular sex by living as a member of that sex,

and includes a reference to the person being thought of as a transgender person, whether the person is, or was, in fact a transgender person

There is also a definition in s 4(1) ADA of the term "recognised transgender person" ("RTP"):

> **"recognised transgender person"** means a person the record of whose sex is altered under Part 5A of the Births, Deaths and Marriages Registration Act 1995 or under the corresponding provisions of a law of another Australian jurisdiction.

It is worth noticing that under the ADA someone who has actually had the sex of their birth certificate altered (after a medical procedure of some sort), has greater rights than someone who does not. For such a person, an RTP, it will be an act of discrimination simply to "treat the aggrieved person…as being of the person's former sex", under s 38B(1)(c). But for someone who has not had a formal "sex change", but simply "identifies" as a member of the opposite sex, treating them as belonging to their biological sex will not automatically be discriminatory.[5]

What is the effect of these provisions?

OFFICIAL GUIDANCE

We may be tempted to seek guidance from public service summaries of the law. But the gap between "guidance" provided by the public service, and what the law actually says, in this area, has recently been highlighted in the United Kingdom. There a recording of "training" given by a transgender lobby group to school teachers, revealed assertions about the law which just could not be supported by what the law actually says.[6]

---

5   There are some helpful comments in *Lawarik v Chief Executive Officer, Corrections Health Service* [2003] NSWADT 16, one of the few decided cases on the provision, on what it means to "identify" as a person of the opposite sex, at paras [41]-[54]. The Tribunal says that it requires some sort of ongoing commitment to the new identity, rather than just occasional "cross-dressing".

6   See "Transgender indoctrination at CofE primary school", 28 May 2019 <https://christianconcern.com/general/transgender-indoctrination-at-cofe-primary-school/>.

What is the situation in Australia? The current guidance given to schools by the NSW Education Department, for example, urges schools generally to accept the "gender of choice" indicated by a student, but does not in terms assert that a school would be breaking the law if it does not do this. The web-page (updated as at 26 March 2019) is headed "Legal Issues Bulletin 55 – Transgender students in schools", but carefully leaves assertions about the law to simply repeating in an appendix the broad terms of the relevant anti-discrimination legislation.[7] Against this uncertainty, it is important to be as clear as possible on what the law *actually* says.

What do these provisions set out above mean? While it is sometimes assumed that they require treatment of "pre-operative" transgender persons (that is, those who have not yet been through surgical procedures) as if they were for all purposes members of their preferred sex, this is by no means obvious, and in fact seems wrong.

It is arguable, rather, that a prohibition on discrimination against transgender persons simply means that they must not be denied services others would be provided in "neutral" areas such as service in a café or employment in a job, where their status would be irrelevant. But it seems that the law does **not** currently require a biological male (who has not undergone medical and surgical reconstruction) to be allowed to wear a girls' school uniform, or to be allowed access to female bathrooms, or to be called by a female pronoun, or to compete in a women's sporting event, or to be housed in a women's prison.[8]

In other words, while the law forbids detrimental treatment of persons in a protected category on "irrelevant" grounds, it seems likely that it does not prevent the application of criteria in decision-making which

---

7   See "Bulletin 55 – Transgender students in schools", <https://education. nsw.gov.au/about-us/rights-and-accountability/legal-issues-bulletins/bulle-tin-55-transgender-students-in-schools>.

8   For a helpful review of the area see Patrick Parkinson, "Is Gender Identity Discrimination a Religious Freedom Issue?" (September 6, 2019), available at SSRN: <https://ssrn.com/abstract=3449085>.

are *relevant* to the decision. It is *relevant* to ask, when considering when someone should be allowed to use a women's bathroom or change-room, whether that person is a biological female. For all the recent history of bathroom construction, they have been constructed on assumptions about the biology of the users.

It is *relevant* to ask, when making decisions about the use of masculine pronouns, whether the person being referred to is a biological male. That is simply the way that the English language operates. For a speaker to use a masculine pronoun is generally for the speaker to assert that the person being referred to is a biological male.

Such questions are also *relevant* in determining who should be allowed to compete in a women's sporting event. For example, even the SDA, in s 42, contains a clear exclusion of the "gender identity" discrimination provisions (as well as the normal "sex" provisions) from decisions in relation to participants in over-12 sporting competitions "in which the strength, stamina or physique of competitors is relevant":

> **SDA   42 (1)** Nothing in Division 1 or 2 renders it unlawful to discriminate on the ground of sex, gender identity or intersex status by excluding persons from participation in any competitive sporting activity in which the strength, stamina or physique of competitors is relevant.

We also find s 38P of the ADA:

> **ADA 38P(1)** Nothing in this Part renders unlawful the exclusion of a transgender person from participation in any sporting activity for members of the sex with which the transgender person identifies.

As noted already, the NSW ADA sets out separate grounds of discrimination which are applicable to 'recognised transgender persons' in s 38B(1)(c), and they are not the same as the grounds which are expressed to apply in relation to a person who is simply described as 'transgender'. The difference between these categories of persons is that a 'recognised' transgender person will be one who has undergone a medical 'sex affirmation procedure'. It is *only* such persons for whom, under s 38B(1)(c), it is explicitly said to be discriminatory to treat them "as being of the person's former sex".

Given this, it seems fairly clear that by implication, under NSW law, treating a 'transgender' person who has **not** had the formal medical procedure, as if they belong to their biological sex, does **not** amount to unlawful (or "less favourable") treatment *per se*. A similar result seems to follow under the Commonwealth SDA.

The operation of this type of legislation was a significant issue in the only detailed consideration under discrimination law in Australia of a claim based on a "wrong pronoun", and the placement of a transgender female in a male prison, in *Tafao v State of Queensland*,[9] and the appeal from that decision.

The first decision, by a Member of the Queensland Civil and Administrative Tribunal, is not of formal precedential status,[10] but provides an important example of the reasoning that might be applied in similar cases. The prisoner, Leilani Tafao, was a biological male person who had had some medical treatment to transition to female but was still able to function as a male.[11] The prisoner's relevant identity documents noted the prisoner as male. An internal "Custodial Operation Practice Directive" ("COPD") noted as follows:

> Staff will address transgender prisoners:
>
> – With the same respect given to all other prisoners.
>
> – By either the name that they are currently registered as having (refer *Births, Deaths and Marriages Registration Act* 2003) or the name on a Warrant committing the prisoner to a Corrective Services facility or requiring a prisoner to be produced to the General Manager of a Corrective Services facility.
>
> All records must reflect the prisoner's registered name and gender to

---

9   [2018] QCAT 409.

10   Decisions of Tribunals, as opposed to decisions of "superior courts", are not regarded as formally establishing a binding precedent for future decision-makers, although of course in practice an earlier decision may be influential on a later one.

11   *Tafao v State of Queensland* [7].

ensure the accuracy and consistency of the prisoner's identification.

While in the prison the prisoner was referred to by male pronouns, and at one stage was directed in relation to their behaviour towards other prisoners, not to behave in an "overtly sexualised" way. They complained of "gender identity" discrimination under the Queensland *Anti-Discrimination Act* 1991 ("Qld ADA").

On the complaint that the wrong pronoun was used, Member Fitzpatrick ruled that a "desire to be addressed by reference to the gender with which one identifies" was indeed a characteristic associated with the prohibited attribute of "gender identity" under s 7(m) of the Act.[12] Hence the prisoner had experienced "less favourable treatment" by being addressed by male pronouns, as a "cisgender" male prisoner[13] would have been addressed by his preferred pronouns.[14]

But the next question was whether this "less favourable treatment" was "on the basis of" the prohibited attribute of gender identity. Here the Member ruled that the real reason for the practice of using male pronouns was the COPD, the administrative guideline laid down by the Government, and hence she ruled that there had been no discrimination on "gender identity" grounds.[15]

With respect, there was arguably another avenue to this same outcome, which may be relevant in other cases when no administrative guidelines are laid down. When asking the question, "was the male pronoun used *on the basis of* the attribute of gender identity?", another answer was possible. In the Dictionary to the Qld ADA, in the Schedule to that Act, "gender identity" is defined as follows:

    "gender identity", in relation to a person, means that the person—

---

12   Ibid, [68].
13   A person who identifies themselves in a way which is consistent with their biological sex.
14   *Tafao v State of Queensland* [83].
15   Ibid [86].

(a) identifies, or has identified, as a member of the opposite sex by living or seeking to live as a member of that sex; or

(b) is of indeterminate sex and seeks to live as a member of a particular sex.

But none of those matters were what led to the prisoner's being addressed by male pronouns. It was not as if the form of address was some sort of arbitrary "punishment" for the prisoner's "identification" with the opposite sex. No; the authorities were entitled to say, we simply used male pronouns because the prisoner was a biological male.

In any event, the direct discrimination claim based on pronoun use failed. So also did the direct discrimination claim based on a directive not to engage in overtly sexualised behaviour, which the Member found had been reasonably imposed in the interests of the safety of the prisoner and the good order of the prison, and would have also been imposed on a "cisgender" male prisoner who behaved similarly.[16]

There were also "indirect discrimination" claims based on the alleged imposition of conditions on the prisoner. One such alleged condition was that the prisoner "be a male". The Member rejected this claim:

> [175]... [I]t is a nonsense to construe a requirement in the given scenarios that the applicant be a man, when the applicant is a man. The submissions of the applicant make the claim that because the applicant identifies as female and seeks to live as a female, she is therefore a female. I reject that submission. **I do not think an injunction against discrimination on the basis of the attribute of gender identity is a requirement to adopt the applicant's perception of reality for all purposes.** The applicant has the male gender because of her biological sex. (emphasis added)

Other "indirect discrimination" claims were also rejected. Later the

---

16   Ibid [162].

Member commented:

> [193]I accept that the use of male personal pronouns caused the applicant distress. However, in weighing that against what I find to be the genuinely held reasons for doing so, and the broader implications for the safe operation of the prison, I find that it was reasonable to address the applicant by reference to her gender, not gender identity.[17]

On appeal, in *Tafao v State of Queensland*,[18] the decision of Member Fitzgerald was overturned and the State (and other respondents) found to have been guilty of unlawful indirect discrimination due to the use of male pronouns. The Appeal Tribunal upheld the Member's decision that the use of a male pronoun in referring to the prisoner was "based on" the prison authorities' understanding of the administrative requirements of the COPD, and not on any intent to discriminate.[19] The Tribunal also upheld the Member's decision that there had been no "direct discrimination", although they differed from the Member in why that was so.[20]

However, the Appeal Tribunal overturned the Member's finding on indirect discrimination. With respect, the reasoning here is somewhat hard to follow. The Member had said that there was no condition imposed on the prisoner "to be a man", as the prisoner claimed. But the Tribunal decided that they would reframe the alleged condition as "to identify as a man".[21] Once this condition was reframed, they considered that the Member had not considered all the relevant factors in coming to the view that imposing a condition of this sort was "reasonable". The Tribunal noted that referring to the prisoner by

---

17   Note that contrary to some other popular usage, the Member here was using "gender" to refer to "biological sex"- she explains the reasons for this usage in the case at [73].

18   [2020] QCATA 76 (22 May 2020).

19   Ibid [79]-[82].

20   For the Appeal Panel, this could not be framed as a case of "direct discrimination" because "All biologically male prisoners were called by male pronouns"- see [64]. Hence there was no discrimination against the applicant on the basis of gender identity.

21   *Tafao v State of Queensland* [2020] QCATA 76 [139].

their preferred pronoun would not have had any cost implications,[22] and that the prison could have adopted another approach, of simply using the prisoner's given name rather than pronouns, which would have been less distressing to the prisoner.[23] They concluded, "after a fine balancing act", that the actions of the prison authorities were "not reasonable".[24]

However, limits on the application of the Qld ADA to prisons meant that monetary compensation could not be ordered unless "bad faith" was established, which the Tribunal held had not been made out.[25] The final order was for an apology to be made.

While this decision suggests that it *could* be indirect discrimination to refuse to use a preferred pronoun, the final outcome very much depended on the specific facts. So far there seems to have been no superior court ruling on the meaning of the relevant legislation, and some aspects of the Appeal Tribunal ruling here are open to criticism.

While it still seems likely that the prohibition on "transgender discrimination" in most of Australia does not usually demand the use of a person's preferred pronouns in the absence of surgical treatment, there is a law which *may* go so far. This is the Tasmanian *Anti-Discrimination Act* 1998 ("Tas ADA") which (since amendments to the Act which came into force on 8 May 2019) now includes definitions as follows in s 3:

> **gender expression** means any personal physical expression, appearance (whether by way of medical intervention or not), speech, mannerisms, behavioural patterns, names and personal references that manifest or express gender or gender identity;
>
> **gender identity** means the gender-related identity, appearance or mannerisms or other gender-related characteristics of an individual

---

22   Ibid [149].
23   Ibid [150].
24   Ibid [152].
25   Ibid [172].

including *gender expression* (whether by way of medical intervention or not), **with or without regard** to the individual's designated sex at birth, and may include being transgender or transsexual; **(emphasis** added)

Discrimination is prohibited in s 16(ea) on "gender identity" grounds. Unlike other discrimination laws around Australia on this topic, the Tasmanian Act contains no general defence for religious groups, or for religious schools.

Let us briefly consider the situation in Tasmania should, say, a theological college run by a church with a strong belief that biological sex defines a person's "gender identity", be approached by a transgender person who was born female but now identifies as male (but has not had any medical treatment to achieve that outcome). The college decides that it will not make male bathrooms available, nor address the student by a male pronoun.

Under Tas ADA s 14(2) we read:

(2) Direct discrimination takes place if a person treats another person on the basis of any prescribed attribute, imputed prescribed attribute or a characteristic imputed to that attribute less favourably than a person without that attribute or characteristic.

On the pronoun issue, the question is: has the college treated the student "less favourably"? If the logic of the first instance *Tafao* case noted above were followed, a tribunal might find, yes, other students are referred to by their "preferred" pronouns, but this student is not. However, the same issue then arises: is this treatment "on the basis of any prescribed attribute"? Perhaps not. The choice of pronoun has arguably not been made on the basis of the person's "gender identity" in the sense defined by the Act. It has been made on the basis of the facts of biology and the college's commitment to a religious worldview. In the college's eyes, these are *relevant* factors for this decision. (The appeal decision in *Tafao* would also suggest that this was not "direct" discrimination).

It has to be conceded that the convoluted form of the definitions in the Tasmanian Act makes the outcome unclear. What is the import of the "with or without" phrase that is used? (A similar phrase is used in the Commonwealth SDA, where it is equally enigmatic.) Does it mean that the decision-maker can choose whether they do, or do not, take into account the biological sex at birth? Reading the definition into s 14 Tas ADA, to replace the phrase "gender identity" with these words (and then adding the extra words from the phrase "gender expression") seems almost impossible.

Similar difficulties will surround a decision about bathrooms, but again, the college may argue that male bathrooms have always been reserved for biological males, and this is a highly relevant and rational criterion to use.

It seems that the meaning of the "ordinary" form of transgender discrimination law is not to automatically require, to quote the first-instance decision in *Tafao* noted above, the adoption of the "applicant's perception of reality for all purposes". The law requires that transgender persons not be treated detrimentally on irrelevant grounds, but there are a number of situations where biological sex is relevant.

As noted below, even if this decision might be argued to be unlawful in Tasmania, it is more than likely that the Tasmanian law is inoperative when it clashes with protections provided by Commonwealth law.

GID LAWS AND CLASHES WITH OTHER FREEDOMS

Let me sum up some of the problems in this area. It is worth noting first, why these problems arise in the area of "gender identity" discrimination and not in some of the other areas. In brief, the earlier forms of discrimination law were broadly consistent with Biblical values. As we have seen, the Bible does not support treating people badly on the grounds of race. In most areas of life, it is also a Biblical value that men and women receive equal treatment. Where there is a Biblical case for differential treatment, is in the area of church leadership (where a number of Christians would see women not being encouraged to lead as priests or pastors) and family leadership. The latter is not an area (yet!) where discrimination law usually operates, and the former (insofar as it sees, for example, the Roman Catholic church not appoint women priests) has usually been seen to be a matter for the religions concerned, with people free to leave a religious group if they disagree with its stance on women's leadership.

Similarly, most believers have no problems with saying that there should be no irrelevant differential treatment of disabled people or the young or the elderly. But when we come to the more recent grounds, there is a serious clash with traditional religious values, and judgements about what is "relevant".

Examples can be given from the Christian perspective. A ban on "sexual orientation" discrimination focusses on persons who regularly engage in homosexual activity. Yet such activity is said to be contrary to God's will as revealed in the Bible.[26] It is a "sin"- a word which does not mean "the worst of all possible behaviour", but simply means for a Christian, "rebellion against God". Lists of sins in the Bible also include envy, murder, strife, deceit, malice, gossiping, slander, insolence, arrogance, boastfulness, and disobeying one's parents.[27] Any one of these activities is a sin and, unforgiven, will incur God's judgment. Homosexual activity is one example of rebellion against God.

No consistent Christian will want to treat people badly because of this sin alone (as such a person will acknowledge that we are *all* sinners). But that the activity is contrary to God's will means that Christians cannot offer affirmation and support of a decision to engage in this activity and will want to retain the right to explain what

---

26   To focus simply on the New Testament, see Romans 1:26-27; 1 Corinthians
      6:9-10; 1 Timothy 1:10.
27   Romans 1:29-30.

the Bible says on the matter. Similarly, the best view of the Bible's teaching on human nature seems to lead to the conclusion that there are (absent some medical problem experienced in a fallen world) only two sexes, male and female, and that a person's sex cannot be changed.[28] This view is at odds with the view that "gender" or "sex" can be altered, the assumption behind much discourse around "transgender" matters. Again, this does not require that someone who wants to, or has, "transitioned" should be treated badly where it is not relevant. But it will mean that some Christians will not be able to affirm the reality of a transition, and even in what seems like the trivial issue of a pronoun, may not wish to be forced to affirm what they see to be a lie.

(a) Clash with Freedom of Speech

So, there can be a clash between the right to freedom of speech, and the claim that to articulate God's judgment on sin in these areas amounts to doing harm to same sex attracted or transgender persons. Here one of the key issues is whether the law should forbid harm, not in the sense of bodily injury or theft of chattels or trespass to land, but in the sense of causing "offence" or "humiliation". Do I have a right not to be told that someone else disapproves of my sexual preference or gender transition? Is a sense of being denigrated a sufficient "harm" for the law to protect me against it, even at the expense of someone else's free speech?

The issue has come to the fore with two cases that have arisen in the UK. One is the case of Dr David Mackereth, a Christian doctor who was denied a contract with a government health service because he said that he could not, in all conscience, use a client's "preferred pronoun" if that did not represent biological reality.[29]

---

28 See Genesis 1:27, "male and female".
29 For more details see my blog post "Fired for using the wrong pronouns",Oct 6, 2019, <https://lawandreligionaustralia.blog/2019/10/06/fired-for-using-the-

The Department's response alleged that allowing Dr Mackereth to work in these circumstances would have been to potentially "cause offence" to clients who were transgender (even those who had not undergone all the medical procedures necessary for issue of a "gender recognition certificate" under UK law.)

Dr Mackereth sued on the basis of religious discrimination, but the Tribunal found that his religious belief ("that every person is created by God as either male or female. A person cannot change their sex/gender at will") was one which was "incompatible with human dignity and [in] conflict with the fundamental rights of others, specifically here, transgender individuals." As a result, he could not maintain his claim of discrimination.

A similar, more recent, case involved a person who was not religious at all, Ms Maya Forstater, who held on general grounds of science the view that "sex is biological and immutable" and claimed that she had been denied a job she expected to get because of this view.[30] Her claim was again rejected on the basis that this view was "incompatible with human dignity and [the] fundamental rights of others", and hence not a protected "belief" for the purposes of a claim of "belief"-based discrimination under the UK *Equality Act 2010*.

Each of these cases was a decision of a low-level Tribunal in the UK and may be over-turned on appeal. But that they have reached the stage they have illustrates that the challenges in articulating the Bible's view of sexual morality in a society which is starting to deem any expressed opposition to homosexuality or "gender transition" as the equivalent of "hate speech".

In contrast to the above decisions, a more recent Tribunal decision in the UK rejects the view that Biblical teaching on these matters

---

wrong-pronouns/>.

30   See the summary of the case in my blog post, "Losing a job for believing that biological sex is immutable", Dec 20, 2019, <https://lawandreligionaustralia. blog/2019/12/20/losing-a-job-for-believing-that-biological-sex-is-immutable/>.

is not a "protected belief". In *Mrs K Higgs v Farmor's School*[31] a teaching assistant at a school had been disciplined for comments on transgender issues from a Christian perspective expressed on a private Facebook page. There are a number of criticisms that can be made of the decision, but one positive aspect is that the Tribunal held that Mrs Higgs' views were a legitimate expression of her faith and should have been weighed up with other interests at stake in the case:

> [42] The belief that sex and gender are "set at birth" may be upsetting to certain people, but if freedom of speech and the rights within articles 9 and 10 of the Convention only extended to expressions of belief that could upset no-one they would be worthless. Essentially, to find as the tribunals did in the cases to which we were referred would amount to a declaration that it is "open season" on people that hold and express the beliefs in question – that they do not deserve protection. That seemed to us to be a strange and somewhat disturbing conclusion.

In Australia so far, we have not seen many similar decisions. The case of *Tafao* discussed above demonstrates that there are some circumstances where use of a "wrong pronoun" might amount to unlawful indirect discrimination, but there are doubts as to whether the appeal decision was correct. But it is important for those who wish to defend free religious speech to continue to resist the pressure that will be mounting for the law to change to recognise such a prohibition.

(b) Clash with Freedom of Religion

Just as there can be a clash between "gender identity" rights and freedom of speech, there can be a possible clash with religious freedom. A church wants to employ a youth worker who is a young woman, to provide a model of godly behaviour for the girls in their youth group. Someone applies for the job who was in fact born a

---

31   [2020] UKET 1401264/2019 (6 October 2020).

male, though they have undergone medical transition procedures. Can the church choose not to employ this person on the grounds of their "gender identity"?

Under most Australian laws at the moment, they can lawfully decline to employ the person, so long as they can show that this decision is in accordance with their religious beliefs. Under the Commonwealth SDA, while s 5B read with s 14 prohibits gender identity being used as a ground to decline employment generally, s 37 allows religious bodies to act in accordance with their religious beliefs.

Religious bodies

SDA s 37 (1) Nothing in Division 1 or 2 affects: ....

(c) the selection or appointment of persons to perform duties or functions for the purposes of or in connection with, or otherwise to participate in, any religious observance or practice; or

(d) any other act or practice of a body established for religious purposes, being an act or practice that conforms to the doctrines, tenets or beliefs of that religion or is necessary to avoid injury to the religious susceptibilities of adherents of that religion.[32]

It seems likely that either under para (1)(c) (viewing youth groups as a "religious... practice") or generally under para (1)(d), a church could make the case that it views sex as immutable and hence that appointment of a transgender youth worker would be contrary to their "doctrines, tenets or belief" or would cause "injury to the religious susceptibilities" of their members.

Most other Australian discrimination laws contain similar "exemptions" or "balancing clauses" to allow an appropriate balancing of different rights and interests here, at least for churches and other groups.[33] One exception is Tasmania, which does not have

---

32   SDA s 38 provides similar protections to educational institutions run on faith-based lines.

33   For my comments on why "balancing clauses" is a better description than "exemptions", see Neil J Foster, "Freedom of Religion and Balancing Clauses in Discrimination Legislation" *Oxford Journal of Law and Religion* Vol 5 (2016)

a general provision protecting religious bodies. In a paper on the issues I have argued that in these circumstances the Tasmanian law which might result in a church being sued for not employing a youth worker for religious reasons, would be contrary to the protection provided by the Commonwealth law noted above, and hence by virtue of s 109 of the Constitution would be rendered inoperative to the extent of the clash.[34]

It is worth noting that this issue, of balancing religious freedom with "gender identity" rights, is one of those which will be considered in an important inquiry being undertaken by the Australian Law Reform Commission.[35] This inquiry was due to report on 12 Dec 2020, but COVID and other matters probably mean that this deadline will not be met. It has not gone very far, because just as it was getting close to releasing its "Discussion Paper" in August 2019, the Government changed the terms of reference to say that it should not inquire into matters covered by the Religious Discrimination Bill (which has not yet been introduced into Federal Parliament). I understand that the ALRC has put this "on hold" until the final form of that legislation is established. In the meantime, there was an interesting paper presented by the President of the ALRC, Justice Sarah Derrington, at the Freedom for Faith conference in 2019, which will give some preliminary ideas about how the Commission will approach the matter.[36]

---

pp 385 – 430. For a more detailed list of religious balancing clauses see Neil J Foster, "Protecting Religious Freedom in Australia Through Legislative Balancing Clauses" *Occasional papers on Law and Religion* (2017) at: <http://works.bepress.com/neil_foster/111/>.

34   See Foster (2017), above n 34, 23-26. In that paper I refer to the fact that the 2nd edition of a major textbook on discrimination law seems to support my view. Note now that the 3rd edition maintains their support for this view of the law- see Rees, Rice and Allen *Australian Anti-Discrimination Law* (3rd ed; Federation, 2018) at para [2.14.24].

35   See the home page for the inquiry, "Review into the Framework of Religious Exemptions in Anti-discrimination Legislation" at <https://www.alrc.gov.au/inquiry/review-into-the-framework-of-religious-exemptions-in-anti-discrimination-legislation/>.

36   For the paper and linked video, see <https://www.alrc.gov.au/news/of-shields-

CONCLUSION

Christians believe that the legal system, viewed as a whole, is a good gift from God.[37] But there are some situations where the law may require them to behave in a way which God has said is wrong, or to not to do something which God says they should do. Until recently those situations have not been very common in Western democracies, which have had a moral framework substantially derived from a Christian world-view. But the more our society moves away from that shared moral framework, the more we will see such issues arise. It is good to see the recognition noted in the *Higgs* case above that views derived from Biblical teachings, such as that sex and gender are not open to change, are, if increasingly not shared by others, at least worthy of protection as genuine religious positions. The challenge for legislators and courts is to give appropriate recognition to religious beliefs in fairly balancing the other interests that are now seen to arise.

BIBLIOGRAPHY

Articles

Neil Foster, "Freedom of Religion and Balancing Clauses in Discrimination Legislation" (2016) 5 *Oxford Journal of Law and Religion* 385 – 430

Patrick Parkinson, "Is Gender Identity Discrimination a Religious Freedom Issue?", (6 September 2019) available at SSRN: <https://ssrn.com/abstract=3449085>.

Books

Neil Rees, Simon Rice, and Dominique Allen, *Australian Anti-Discrimination Law* (3rd ed; Federation, 2018).

---

and-swords/>.

37   See Romans 13.

Cases

Australia

Lawarik v Chief Executive Officer, Corrections Health Service [2003] NSWADT 16.

Tafao v State of Queensland [2018] QCAT 409.

Tafao v State of Queensland [2020] QCATA 76.

United Kingdom

Mrs K Higgs v Farmor's School [2020] UKET 1401264/2019 (6 October 2020).

Legislation

Commonwealth

Age Discrimination Act 2004 (Cth).

Disability Discrimination Act 1992 (Cth).

Racial Discrimination Act 1975 (Cth).

Sex Discrimination Act 1984 (Cth).

Sex Discrimination Amendment (Sexual Orientation, Gender Identity and Intersex Status) Act 2013 (Cth).

New South Wales

Anti-Discrimination Act 1977 (NSW).

Queensland

Anti-Discrimination Act 1991 (Qld).

Tasmania

Anti-Discrimination Act 1998 (Tas).

Treaties

International Covenant on Civil and Political Rights, opened for signature 16 December 1966, 999 UNTS 171 (entered into force 23 March 1976).

Websites

Australian Law Reform Commission "Review into the Framework of Religious Exemptions in Anti-discrimination Legislation" (last updated 2 March 2020) at <https://www.alrc.gov.au/inquiry/review-into-the-framework-of-religious-exemptions-in-anti-discrimination-legislation/>.

Christian Concern (UK), Transgender indoctrination at C of E primary school (28 May 2019) <https://christianconcern.com/general/transgender-indoctrination-at-cofe-primary-school/>.

Neil Foster, "Protecting Religious Freedom in Australia Through Legislative Balancing Clauses" *Occasional papers on Law and Religion* (2017) <http://works.bepress.com/neil_foster/111/>.

Neil Foster, "Fired for using the wrong pronouns" (Blog Post, 6 October 2019) <https://lawandreligionaustralia.blog/2019/10/06/fired-for-using-the-wrong-pronouns/>.

Neil Foster, "Losing a job for believing that biological sex is immutable" (Blog Post, 20 December 2019) <https://lawandreligionaustralia.blog/2019/12/20/losing-a-job-for-believing-that-biological-sex-is-immutable/>.

NSW Education Department "Legal Issues Bulletin 55 – Transgender students in schools" (26 March 2019) <https://education.nsw.gov.au/about-us/rights-and-accountability/legal-issues-bulletins/bulletin-55-transgender-students-in-schools>.

Other

The Hon Sarah Derrington, "Of Shields and Swords – let the jousting begin!" (4 September 2019) <https://www.alrc.gov.au/news/of-shields-and-swords/>.

5

FREEDOM OF RELIGION AND FREEDOM OF SPEECH

THE UNITED STATES, AUSTRALIA AND SINGAPORE COMPARED*

A. KEITH THOMPSON

ABSTRACT

In this article I note the logical connection of freedom of religion and freedom of speech but suggest that their separation in modern human rights instruments has weakened both. I suggest that is partly the consequence of John Rawls' concept of public reason. I then compare the way freedom of conscience and speech are protected in Australia, the United States and Singapore and counter-intuitively, observe that the protection that exists in all three countries is identical for all practical purposes and falls below the standard expressed in the *ICCPR*. In Australia, that is because speech that merely offends can be disciplined in domestic law. In Singapore, that is because the narrow interpretation of practice favours the interests of the state over those of the individual. And in the US, that is because the Supreme Court has returned to its 19th century view that government can restrain religious practice so long as it does so by law that has general application. Even though all three countries have practical reasons not to protect freedom of religion to *ICCPR* standards, I suggest they should do so to encourage the human rights project in other countries.

INTRODUCTION

Freedom of Religion (more correctly, freedom of conscience, belief and religion under the *International Covenant on Civil and Political Rights 1966 (ICCPR)*), and Freedom of Speech have been logically tied together since human beings were sentient creatures. The two rights are inseparably connected by logic, since one cannot speak freely unless one has the freedom of conscience to think out something to say.[1] For this reason, the two rights were combined in the First Amendment to the *US Constitution* in 1789 and that joinder has cemented the connection ever since even though the extrapolation of the two rights has seen them separated in modern human rights instruments. That latter-day separation in the interests of more complete expression however, seems to have disconnected the two rights in the minds of modern philosophers, legislators and judges. There are also questions as to whether the expressions of these freedoms in modern international human rights instruments have binding force especially in the United States, Australia and Singapore since none of these countries has implemented the freedom of conscience and religion norm in their domestic law despite late and seemingly reluctant ratification of the *ICCPR* convention by the first two countries. In Singapore where a fierce commitment to sovereignty is at least part of the reason for non-ratification, there are

---

*An earlier version of this paper was published in the conference proceedings of the 6th Annual International Conference on Law, Regulations and Public Policy (Singapore 2017).

1   Brett Scharffs says that freedom of conscience and religion are the tap root of all human rights. He also suggests that "without freedom of religion and belief, the entire human rights project may collapse" ("Why Religious Freedom? Why the Religious Committed, the Religiously Indifferent and Those Hostile to Religion Should Care", <https://ssrn.com/abstract=2911086>, 1-2).

deeper questions. Does the *ICCPR* convention provide an objective and determinate standard that is binding upon countries which have not indicated any intention or wish to be subject its norms?

I begin this paper in Part I, by setting out the logical connection between the two rights as simply as I can before briefly discussing the philosophical separation of the two in US jurisprudence and in the political philosophy of John Rawls since 1991. In that discussion, I will suggest that it is John Rawls' version of the notion of 'public reason'[2] which has powered the rise of 'political correctness' (PC) at the expense of both freedom of speech and religion, despite Rawls' denials of inconsistency. I will then explain how the imposition of public reason onto the human rights expressed in the *US Constitution* by the US Supreme Court is inconsistent with the doctrine of parliamentary sovereignty inherited by both Australia and Singapore before outlining the current debate in Australia concerning both freedom of speech and freedom of religion.

In Part II, I move to Australia. While s 18C of the *Racial Discrimination Act 1975* (Cth) was the pivot around which the Australian debate swirled until the postal plebiscite on same-sex marriage, that debate brought the relatively unprotected nature of religious freedom into more general public awareness. I will therefore position my discussion of religious freedom in Australia in the context of that country's long term struggle to protect and balance *UDHR* human rights against more recent anti-discrimination norms. While contemporary arguments about racism, immigration and same sex marriage may seem intellectually discrete and separate, they are unwillingly joined together at the intersection between freedom of conscience and speech. My purpose in identifying that connection,

---

2   Scharffs also observes that Rawls was not the first to use the idea of 'public rea-
     son'. Immanuel Kant and Thomas Hobbes used it before him. Scharffs observes
     that for Hobbes, public reason and individual conscience were always at odds
     since the sovereign denied freedom of conscience as the price of his protection
     from nasty and brutish state of nature (ibid 16-17).

is to enable the consideration of how human rights are best balanced when they compete despite the PC demands of a particular moment.

In Part III, I explain how freedom of conscience and speech have been balanced in past US and Australian jurisprudence, and I measure that against the international standards that are now set out in the *ICCPR*. As a part of that discussion I engage the limited Singaporean freedom of religion jurisprudence and ultimately conclude that there is not a great deal of difference in practice – the jurisprudence of all three countries falls short of the *ICCPR* standard though there was a thirty year period between 1960 and 1990 when the US came close to meeting that standard even though it never became binding. The unnecessarily narrow approach to the free exercise of religion in Australia is identified as a primary reason why s 116 has been described as a dead letter in commentary. I suggest that all three governments should explore ways to upgrade their protection of freedom of conscience and speech so that it coincides with the standards set in the *ICCPR* and so that the self-evident human rights of their citizens are recognised and respected in practice. In part III, I suggest that is because all three nations are morally and perhaps even legally bound to the norms set out in the *ICCPR* despite assertions that they are immune from those norms to the extent they have avoided ratification or domestic implementation.

I conclude that because the protection afforded to freedom of conscience and speech in the US, Australia and Singapore falls below the bar set by the *ICCPR*, all three countries have work to do to enhance human freedom. As a teacher of Australian constitutional law, it is simple for this author to observe that Australia could achieve this goal by passing domestic legislation using its federal external affairs power. Singapore could begin by ratifying the *ICCPR* and then taking steps to implement it in domestic law. The US ratified the *ICCPR* in 1992 with reservations and could pass domestic law to implement it except that the Supreme Court does not currently agree that the *Constitution* can be interpreted consistent with the *ICCPR*. There is the possibility that the Supreme Court's view may change if future Presidents appoint judges who see the Free Exercise Clause differently than their post 1990 predecessors.

PART I – FREEDOM OF CONSCIENCE AND FREEDOM OF SPEECH ARE INSEPARABLY CONNECTED

My first observation is that the freedoms recognised in international human rights instruments since the *Universal Declaration of Human Rights (UDHR)* in 1948 do not stand alone. They are a 'compound in one'. They stand or fall together. Though it is trite, a single matchstick can be easily broken, but a collection of matchsticks is harder to break. Freedom of Conscience, Speech and Association stand together or they fall. The stronger they are, the stronger the individual rights and freedoms of the citizens of the country concerned. That these rights are compound rights, is demonstrated by their logical connection. Freedom of conscience logically precedes freedom of speech because one cannot speak freely unless one can first think freely. But equally, freedom of conscience is meaningless unless the things an individual thinks about, can be freely expressed. While some human laws have been designed to regulate human thought (as with tests for public office), human conscience is generally unregulated as international human rights norms mandate. But international human rights norms also say that the expression that flows from freedom of conscience (the forum externum) should only be regulated to the extent it interferes with public safety, health or morals.[3]

---

3   Article 9 of the *European Convention on Human Rights* (1950) does not anticipate any limitations on the forum internum in Article 9(1). Article 9(2) says the forum externum shall be subject only to such limitations as are prescribed by law and are necessary in a democratic society in the interests of public safety, for the protection of public order, health or morals, or for the protection of the rights and freedoms of others.

Article 18(3) of the *International Covenant on Civil and Political Rights* (1966) follows the *European Convention* and states that freedom to manifest one's religion should be subject only to such limitations as are prescribed by law and are necessary to protect public safety, order, health, or morals or the fundamental rights and freedoms of others.

Just as freedom of conscience is antecedent to freedom of speech, so freedom of conscience and speech are logically antecedent to freedom of association. That is, freedom of association is meaningless unless someone can think and speak freely so as to communicate in association with others. Again, freedom of conscience, speech and association are a compound. To the extent one is diluted, so are all the others.

When this compound or indivisible nature of the human rights and freedoms that theorists have traditionally named as the first freedoms is misunderstood,[4] we pass laws abridging one or other of these freedoms without counting the combined cost, and freedom as a whole suffers a slow "death by a thousand cuts".[5]

This understanding of freedom as a compound of sub-freedoms - conscience including religion, plus speech and association - was elementary for the American framers. It is a part of the reason why they lumped freedom of religion and speech together in their First Amendment. John Rawls, the famous late 20th century American political philosopher, accepted that these freedoms were foundational in US jurisprudence when he published *A Theory of Justice* in 1971.[6] But something had changed in his understanding when he wrote *Political Liberalism* in 1993[7] and "The Idea of Public Reason Revisited" in 1999.[8] In *A Theory of Justice* in 1971, he wrote that because people in his 'original position' "do not know ... what

---

4   Martha Nussbaum has said that democracies need to be vigilant in teaching their citizenry the interrelationship of fundamental human rights lest they be unwittingly whittled away (*Liberty of Conscience*, Basic Books, New York (2008), 359-360). In that connection, she has recalled Thomas Jefferson's statement
     The Tree of Liberty must be refreshed from time to time by the blood of patriots and martyrs. It is its natural manure (Thomas Jefferson to William Stephens Smith, Paris, 13 November 1787).
     Human rights are a comparatively recent human discovery and have come as the legacy of thousands of years of bloodshed.
5   *International Finance Trust Company v New South Wales Crime Commission* (2009) 261 ALR 220 per Heydon J 238 [57].
6   John Rawls, *A Theory of Justice* (Harvard University Press, 1971).
7   John Rawls, *Political Liberalism* (Columbia University Press, 1993).
8   John Rawls, 'The Idea of Public Reason Revisited' in John Rawls, *The Law of Peoples* (Harvard University Press, 1999).

their religious or moral convictions are ... [t]he question they are to decide is which principle they should adopt to regulate the liberties of citizens in regard to their fundamental religious, moral and philosophical interests."[9] He concluded quite simply that

> equal liberty of conscience is the only principle that the persons in the original position can acknowledge. They cannot take their chances with their liberty by permitting the dominant religious or moral doctrine to persecute or to suppress others if it wishes.[10]

For Rawls in 1971, equal liberty of conscience was not absolute. As in the *ICCPR*, it "is limited...by the common interest in public order and security"[11] since from the original position, each would recognise "that the disruption of [public order and security] is a danger for the liberty of all".[12] But in *Political Liberalism* in 1993, Rawls' position on equal liberty of conscience had shifted. In my 2015 article in *The University of Notre Dame Law Review* (*UNDALR*),[13] I explained Rawls' 'idea of public reason' this way:

> "In a nearly just society there is a public acceptance of the same principles of justice".[14] But there does not need to be complete agreement. There can even be "considerable differences in citizen's conceptions of justice provided that these conceptions all lead to similar political judgments".[15] "[D]ifferent premises can yield the same conclusion"[16] and therefore groups with different perspectives can accept the same judgment in a dispute though for different reasons. However, "there comes a point beyond which the requisite agreement in judgment breaks down and society splits... on fundamental questions".[17] Responsible citizens will not then

---

9   Rawls, above n 6, 181.
10   Ibid.
11   Ibid 186.
12   Ibid 187.
13   "Should 'public reason' developed under US establishment clause jurisprudence apply to Australia?", (2015) 17 *UNDALR*, Article 6, 107-134 <http:// researchonline.nd.edu.au/undalr/vol17/iss1/6/>.
14   Rawls, above n 6, 340.
15   Ibid.
16   Ibid.
17   Ibid.

do as they please. While they may act conscientiously and disobey law, yet they will be held responsible for what they do.[18] Citizens responding to such differences should sacrifice their comprehensive doctrines in the interests of preserving the overlapping consensus necessary to preserve society when viewed from the original position. To use Rawls' own words:

> Citizens realize that they cannot reach agreement or even approach mutual understanding on the basis of their irreconcilable comprehensive doctrines. In view of this, they need to consider what kinds of reasons they may reasonably give one another when fundamental political questions are at stake. I propose that in Public Reason comprehensive doctrines of truth or right be replaced by an idea of the politically reasonable addressed to citizens as citizens.[19]

By the late 1990s, equal liberty of conscience in Rawls' thought was not compromised by the sacrifice of one's comprehensive beliefs if they lay outside political consensus because everyone was making the same sacrifice and that sacrifice was part of a citizen's "duty of civility".[20]

In my 2015 *UNDALR* article, I explained that Rawls did not believe he was sacrificing any part of equal liberty of conscience when he asserted the need for his idea of public reason to trump it in the interests of overlapping consensus in liberal democracies. But I suggest that a life spent marinating in US Establishment Clause jurisprudence and particularly the compromises of the free exercise of religion which were embedded in the 1991 decision in *Employment Division v Smith*,[21] blinded him as to how his idea of public reason undermined liberty of conscience as understood in international human rights instruments. Rawls' belief that religious ideas should not be used in the public square unless they could be explained in

---

18   Ibid 341.
19   Rawls, (n 8), 131-32.
20   Ibid 135-136, 138.
21   *Employment Division v Smith* 494 US 872 (1990).

proper political terms, misunderstood the idea of freedom of religion prized by the US framers and expressed more fully in the *ICCPR*. In the First Amendment and in the *ICCPR*, religious believers could speak about anything they chose in the public square unless, in the *ICCPR*'s modern expression, those words would endanger "public safety, order, health, or morals or the fundamental rights and freedoms of others".

Outside of the US, the idea that religion and the state must be completely insulated from one another in the interests of freedom of conscience and religion is foreign. Europe is full of countries with established state churches where freedom of religion is accepted and protected. In Australia where there can be no national church,[22] the federal government does not offend 'the establishment clause' by spending 35% of its educational budget in the support of private schools many of which are sponsored by churches.[23] Nor can the High Court of Australia strike down legislation on constitutional grounds because it offends human rights because there is no constitutional Bill of Rights in Australia. Additionally, in Australia, under the doctrine of parliamentary sovereignty, the Parliament can abolish any common law right it wishes to abolish, so long as it does so in sufficiently clear and unambiguous words.[24] But the absence of constitutional protection for human rights in Australia does not mean that those rights do not exist. Political accountability to the public is not something that just happens three yearly at the ballot box; it is vigorous and is part of the reason why Australia had five different Prime Ministers between 2012 and 2018. However, to date the Australian federal government has not seen fit to pass domestic human rights legislation implementing the commitments

---

22   *Attorney-General (Vic); Ex rel Black v Commonwealth ('DOGS case')* (1981) 146 CLR 559.

23   Ibid.

24   See for example *Electrolux Home Products Pty Ltd v Australian Workers' Union* (2004) 221 CLR 309 per Gleeson CJ and *K-Generation Pty Ltd v Liquor Licensing Court* (2009) 237 CLR 501 per French CJ.

it made when it ratified the *ICCPR* in 1980[25] and which it has the constitutional power to pass.[26]

In Singapore, freedom of religion is protected by the *Constitution* but it is interpreted narrowly when the resulting jurisprudence is considered against the expression of religious freedom in the *ICCPR*.[27]

However, the fact that Rawlsian public reason has not led, and should not lead to the invalidation of laws in Australia because a trace of religious influence can be detected in their text,[28] does not mean that Rawlsian ideology is without influence in Australia. As I noted in my article in the *UNDALR* cited above, journalists and other opinion leaders regularly repeat Rawls' idea that religious

---

25   Article 2 of the *ICCPR* sets out the commitments made by ratifying states. Australia's agreement to be bound by Article 2 was made subject to her constitutional processes and the agreement of the Australian states and territories. The full text of the reservation is set out at <http://www.austlii.edu.au/au/other/dfat/treaties/1980/23.html>.

26   See for example *Koowarta v Bjelke-Petersen* (1982) 153 CLR 168, *Victoria v Commonwealth (Industrial Relations Act Case)* (1996) 187 CLR 416 and *Toben v Jones* (2003) 199 ALR 1.

27   Article 15 provides:
  (1)   Every person has the right to profess and practice his religion and to propagate it.
  (2)   No person shall be compelled to pay any tax the proceeds of which are specifically allocated in whole or in part for the purposes of a religion other than his own.
  (3)   Every religious group has the right –
    (a)   to manage its own religious affairs;
    (b)   to establish and maintain institutions for religious or charitable purposes; and
    (c)   to acquire and own property and hold and administer it in accordance with law.
  (4)   This Article does not authorize any act contrary to any general law relating to public order, public health or morality.
  See below nn 44-56 and supporting text for discussion of the narrow interpretation of this Article in Singapore.

28   The state of the law in these two Westminster democracies stand in contrast to the position in the United States where even the results of public referenda have been struck down on that basis. See *Perry v Schwarzenegger* Case No. C 09-2292 VRW (US District Court for the Northern District of California, 4 August 2010) where District Court Chief Justice Vaughan Walker struck down a constitutional ballot proposition (Proposition 8) which had amended the *California State Constitution* because it had no rational basis even though it was the will of the majority of the voters in that state.

expression and belief has no place in the public square and that it should not justify government law or policy.[29] And the Rawlsian idea that speech should be voluntarily managed in the interests of overlapping consensus in the public square, is increasingly evident in new anti-discrimination laws despite *ICCPR* freedom of speech, free exercise of religion under s 116 of the *Constitution* and the freedom of political communication recognised by the High Court as an implied right under the *Australian Constitution* since 1992.[30] There are many examples of challenges to freedom of conscience and expression in Australia that could be discussed to show the reach of the Rawlsian ideology popularly known as PC,[31] but for the sake of brevity, I shall only canvass the current debate concerning s 18C of the *Racial Discrimination Act 1975* (Cth) and the future of religious freedom in Australia subsequent to the same-sex marriage plebiscite. I have chosen that debate as my focus in Part II, not because it most clearly focuses the conscience and religious aspects of the friction, but because it is a federal law and so applies in every state.

---

29   Above n 13, nn 3-7. Well known Australia media personality Andrew Denton has reaffirmed this proposition recently with his insistence that the churches should step aside from the public debate concerning euthanasia law reform (*The Australian*, August 10, 2016). For details of the address behind this report see <https://dwdnsw.org.au/wp-content/uploads/2016/08/NATIONAL-PRESS-CLUB-speech-by-denton-100816.pdf>.

30   The High Court of Australia first recognized an implied freedom of political communication arising under ss 7 and 24 of the *Constitution* in two cases in 1992 - *Nationwide News Pty Ltd v Wills* (1992) 177 CLR 1 and *Australian Capital Television Pty Ltd v Commonwealth* (1992) 177 CLR 106. That implied right has been developed since including in *Lange v Australian Broadcasting Corporation* (1997) 189 CLR 520, *Coleman v Power* (2004) 220 CLR 1 and most recently in *McCloy v NSW* (2015) 325 ALR 15.

31   For example, the proposed 'prosecution' of Catholic Archbishop Julian Porteous under Tasmanian anti-discrimination laws despite constitutional protection of freedom of religion in that state because he distributed a booklet to Catholics concerning traditional marriage that offended transgender Greens political activist, Martine Delaney; the settled 'prosecution' of two pastors who had offended Muslims attending their seminars about Islam (*Catch the Fires Ministry Inc v Islamic Council of Victoria* [2006] VSCA 284); and the successful appeal by a gay outreach group seeking to prevent youth suicide when they were denied the use of a Convention Centre run by the Brethren Church (*Christian Youth Camps Limited & Ors v Cobaw Community Health Services Limited & Ors* [2014] VSCA 75 (16 April 2014).

PART II – SHOULD WE LIMIT SPEECH THAT IS MERELY OFFENSIVE?

In the international context, the expression of religious belief can only be limited if the limitation is prescribed by law and it is "necessary to protect public safety, order, health, or morals or the fundamental rights and freedoms of others."[32] Of course religious expression is not the only speech that may be limited. But speech generally, is subject to an equivalent limitation under Article 19(3) of the *ICCPR*.[33] To accord with these *ICCPR* specifications, limitations on freedom of speech, including religious speech, passed by the legislatures of countries which have ratified the *ICCPR* and are striving to conform their law to these principles, must be passed in valid national or state law and they must be "necessary to protect public safety, order, health, or morals or the fundamental rights and freedoms of others."[34]

The requirement in the *ICCPR* that limitations on freedom of speech including religious speech, be created by valid national or state law, denies '*ICCPR* legitimacy' to arbitrary or capricious exercises of discretion by law enforcement officers or other public officials which do not carry the stamp of formal legislative authority. The point is that any limitations on freedom of speech including

---

32   *ICCPR* Article 18(3).
33   The full text of Article 19 setting out the right to freedom of expression under the *ICCPR* reads:
> 1. Everyone shall have the right to hold opinions without interference.
> 2. Everyone shall have the right to freedom of expression; this right shall include freedom to seek, receive and impart information and ideas of all kinds, regardless of frontiers, either orally, in writing or in print, in the form of art, or through any other media of his choice.
> 3. The exercise of the rights provided for in paragraph 2 of this article carries with it special duties and responsibilities. It may therefore be subject to certain restrictions, but these shall only be such as are provided by law and are necessary: (a) For respect of the rights or reputations of others;
> (b) For the protection of national security or of public order (ordre public), or of public health or morals.
Article 20(1) prohibits war propaganda and Article 20(2) requires the prohibition by law of expression that would incite discrimination, hostility or violence on the grounds of race.
34   *ICCPR*, Article 18(3).

religious speech, must be created as formal law or they do not meet the *ICCPR* standard.

In western countries like the United States, Australia and Singapore, the requirement that formal law be passed before freedom of expression including freedom of religious expression can be limited, ought to be elementary. But compliance with the second limb of the *ICCPR* limitation requirement, is anything but elementary. For if the word 'necessary' is interpreted subjectively to mean that a law can be passed because the legislature believes, hopes, or wants to decide as a matter of policy that such a law is necessary, the protection intended is denuded of practical effect. The limitations expressed in Articles 18(3) and 19(3) of the *ICCPR* rely on a strongly objective interpretation to achieve their protective purpose. This strongly objective interpretation of the necessity requirement in the *ICCPR* is controversial in countries that accept the principle of parliamentary sovereignty rather than the older American developed idea that courts can strike down any law that does not accord with fundamental principles including those set out in constitutional instruments and supra-national human rights covenants.[35]

This strongly objective interpretation of the necessity requirement, is also controversial in Europe where the European Court of Human Rights accords the legislatures of member states a 'margin of appreciation' in setting laws for their own countries since the Court is said not to know what is necessary in the member states.[36] Still, the European Court of Human Rights does make some decisions against member states despite protestations of necessity and reference to the margin of appreciation doctrine, if the Court considers that such laws could not have been passed by any reasonable legislature.[37]

---

35   Martin Krygier, "The Rule of Law: Pasts, Presents, and Two Possible Futures", *Annual Review of Law and Social Science*, 12 (2016) 199, 207.

36   See for example *Handyside v United Kingdom* 5493/72; (1976) 1 EHRR 737; [1976] ECHR 5.

37   For example, *Kokkinakis v Greece* 14307/88; [1991] 17 EHRR 397; [1993] ECHR 20.

The point flowing from this brief discussion of a vexed topic, is that sovereign legislatures do not always pass objectively reasonable laws especially when they are confronted with crises like the war on terror.[38] The point is good for all countries regardless of the extent of their rule of law compliance tradition. Respect for the rule of law and objectively adjudged human rights, is only as good as the last law that a legislature has passed. Human fallibility and caprice is not a uniquely individual human trait. It can be manifested by groups of human individuals including legislatures.

So how should the *ICCPR* limitations on freedom of expression including religious expression be interpreted in practice? I submit that a strongly objective interpretation of the *ICCPR* limitation principles was intended, remains appropriate and is essential if human rights are to survive. The post WWII context of the *UDHR* and the *ICCPR* demonstrates the intention that strongly objective interpretation was intended. That is because the *UDHR* and the follow-on covenants are widely accepted as flowing from the excesses of the Axis regimes and particularly the Nazi regime during that World War. Anything less than strong objectivity would thus subvert the intention of those who framed the *UDHR* and the *ICCPR*. Thus, I further submit that objective interpretation of those covenants is an integral part of their whole meaning.

It is now appropriate to situate the current debate about whether s 18C of the *Racial Discrimination Act 1975* (Cth) in Australia, is consistent with the level of freedom of speech established in international law by Articles 18 and 19 of the *ICCPR*. While a full bench of the Federal Court of Australia in *Toben v Jones* in 2003[39] affirmed that s 18C was a valid law under the *Australian Constitution*, those judges did not address the *ICCPR* question, and even if they had done, any observations they made would have been obiter dicta and not binding since the Australian federal government has

---

38   See for example Krygier, (n 35), 208.
39   *Toben v Jones* (2003) 199 ALR 1.

not made the *ICCPR* part of Australian domestic law despite their promises to do so. The reason s 18C was valid under the *Australian Constitution* was because the full Federal Court considered it was consistent with the provisions of the *International Convention on the Elimination of All Forms of Racial Discrimination 1966* (the Race Convention) which Australia had sought to implement in domestic law.[40] My following suggestion is that if Australia were to keep its commitment to similarly implement the provisions of the *ICCPR* in domestic law and to interpret those provisions in the strong objective manner I have outlined above, then s 18C would be invalid from the date of that implementing legislation.

Why would s 18C be inconsistent with the *ICCPR* if the *ICCPR* were implemented in domestic law? Because it cannot be said that a law which outlaws speech that merely offends on grounds of race is necessary to implement the provisions of the Race Convention in a manner that is consistent with Freedom of Speech under the *ICCPR*. I suggest that although the full Federal Court found that s 18C was reasonably adapted to the purpose of implementing the Race Convention as the only applicable international instrument then binding in Australian domestic law,[41] that finding would not be available if the *ICCPR* was also a part of Australian domestic law and was interpreted objectively. That is because the balance that the *ICCPR* requires be struck in favour of freedom of speech before it can be limited, is a manifestly higher standard that the full

---

40   I observe that there are compelling arguments that this interpretation is incon-sistent with the implied freedom of political communication developed in High Court jurisprudence since 1992 (see for example Joshua Forrester, Lorraine Finlay and Augusto Zimmerman, *No Offence Intended: Why 18C is wrong*, Connor Court Publishing, 2016). While fascinating, that debate is beyond the scope of the current paper that is focused on international law with regard to freedom of speech including freedom of religious speech.

41   *Toben v Jones* (2003) 199 ALR 1, 35 [144] per Allsop J. Note that Carr J found that it [wa]s for the legislature to choose the means by which it carrie[d] into or g[a]ve effect to a treaty" (ibid 10 [20] citing the *Industrial Relations Act Case* (1986), 487) and Kiefel J simply concurred with Carr J on the constitutional issues arising.

Federal Court observed in respect of the implied freedom of political communication under the *Australian Constitution*. That is not to say that the full Federal Court in *Toben v Jones* incorrectly interpreted the nature of the implied freedom of political communication under the *Australian Constitution*,[42] but a different balance would have to be struck if the *ICCPR* had a place in Australian domestic law as the federal government has promised.[43]

So what has this got to do with Singapore? Like Australia and the US, Singapore is subject to international law whether it accepts it as binding and follows its imprimatur in domestic law or not. To the extent that Singaporean freedom of religion and speech jurisprudence is inconsistent with the *ICCPR*, it should be reformed as an example to other Asian nations and in the interests of consistent international freedom. However, because Singapore has a completely different religious and security climate than Australia, the balancing would not be the same. To interpret freedom of speech under the *Singaporean Constitution* in a manner consistent with the *ICCPR*, the Singaporean courts would have to determine whether any limitations on freedom of speech including religious speech, had been validly passed as laws by the legislature including whether they were objectively "necessary to protect public safety, order, health, or morals or the fundamental rights and freedoms of others."[44] But to determine whether these observations are fair and accurate enough, it

---

42   See the discussion at n 40 above.

43   The High Court of Australia has recently developed a structured proportionality approach when deciding whether statutes offend the implied freedom of political communication they identified in the *Australian Constitution* after 1992 (*McCloy v New South Wales* (2015) 257 CLR 178). This may represent the advent of a new way of balancing interests when human rights and anti-discrimination norms are found in conflict in future Australian jurisprudence. But the structured approach in *McCloy* is an example of the High Court's measured used of the European idea of proportionality in its reasoning since the complete European idea is inconsistent with the idea of parliamentary sovereignty which is foundational in Australian jurisprudence. See also Paul Babie, "National Security and the Free Exercise of Section 116: Time for a Judicial Interpretive Update" (2017) 45 *Federal Law Review* 351).

44   *ICCPR* Article 18(3).

is necessary to engage with the relevant Singaporean jurisprudence.

In *Chan Hiang Leng Colin v PP* in 1994[45] Yong CJ rejected the submission that there had to be a 'clear and present danger'[46] to public order before freedom of religion could be restricted. That assessment is not consistent with the *ICCPR*. His honour preferred Malaysian precedents to find instead that "religious beliefs and practices which tend to run counter to [the security of the country] had to be restrained."[47] He did not accept that any balancing of individual freedom of religion was required although it is arguable that he chose scales which set the balance in favour of state interests rather than the individual as the *ICCPR* requires.[48]

Five years later in *Nappali v ITE*,[49] Yong CJ further ruled that the *Singaporean Constitution* was "primarily to be interpreted within its own four walls and not in the light of analogies drawn from other countries such as Great Britain, the United States or Australia".[50] However to achieve a uniquely Singaporean result which arguably ignored the *Constitution's* requirement that there be "no discrimination against any citizens of Singapore on the grounds only of religion" and that "[n]o person sh[ould] be required to receive instruction or to take part in any ceremony or act of worship or a religion other than his own",[51] he invoked Australian and United States jurisprudence but arguably misinterpreted same. For example, from Australia he quoted the *Kruger*[52] and *Hozack*[53] cases in support of his propositions that "the plaintiffs had to demonstrate that the

45   *Chan Hiang Leng Colin v PP* [1994] SGHC 207; [1994] 3 SLR (R) 209.
46   Chan Hiang Leng Colin's counsel cited a Malaysian case (*Tan Boon Liat v Menteri Hal Ehwal Dalam Negeri, Malaysia* [1976] 2 MLJ 83 (High Court)) as his authority for this interpretation of the limitation in the Singaporean Constitution.
47   *Chan Hiang Leng Colin v PP* [1994] 3 SLR (R) 209, 235 [64].
48   Ibid 233, [58-59]. No evidence was called suggesting Chan Hiang Leng Colin's expression posed any direct threat to national security.
49   *Nappalli Peter Williams v Institute of Technical Education* [1999] 2 SLR 569.
50   Ibid 574 [19].
51   Ibid [20] quoting Article 16 of the Constitution.
52   *Kruger & Ors v Commonwealth of Australia (Stolen Generations Case)* (1997) 190 CLR 1.
53   *Hozack v Church of Jesus Christ of Latter-day Saints* (1997) 79 FCR 441.

policy complained of breached...art 16"[54] and that the defendant had acted "in good faith in dealing with the appellant's conduct". But the Chief Justice's analysis ignored the High Court's affirmation in *Kruger* that it would have heard the argument that the Northern Territory's government had interfered with the plaintiffs' freedom of religion if the plaintiffs had called evidence on that subject, and he ignored the fact that Madgwick J in *Hozack* found that the employing church had not acted in good faith in that case since its temple worthiness requirement did not apply to two employees who were not members of the defendant church. And his honour was similarly selective in his choice of quotations from the *Barnette* case in the United States. In respect of that case, his honour quoted Justice Jackson only to observe that "a person gets from a symbol the meaning that he puts into it, and what is one man's comfort and inspiration is another man's jest and scorn".[55] But he conveniently ignored Justice Jackson's most famous affirmation of freedom of conscience and religion in that case when he said:

> If there is any fixed star in our constitutional constellation, it is that not official, high or petty, can prescribe what shall be orthodox in politics, nationalism, religion, or other matters of opinion or force citizens to confess by word or act their faith therein. If there are any circumstances which permit an exception, they not now occur to us.[56]

This narrow interpretation of the ambit of religious freedom under the *Singaporean Constitution* is not just a quirk of Chief Justice Yong's approach in the 1990s. It has effectively been reaffirmed by the current High Court in *Vijaya Kumar's* case in 2015 since Tay Yong Kwang J found that the possibility of a law and order interruption, still trumped a Hindu community's wish to add traditional music to their 'Thaipusam Procession' after 42 years of

---

54   *Nappalli Peter Williams v Institute of Technical Education* [1999] 2 SLR 569, 575 [23-24].

55   Ibid 576 [27] quoting Justice Jackson from *West Virginia State Board of Education v Barnette et al* (1943) 319 US 624, 632.

56   *West Virginia State Board of Education v Barnette et al* (1943) 319 US 624, 642.

running the procession in peaceful silence.[57]

However, Yong CJ's narrow interpretation of Article 15 of the *Singaporean Constitution* is consistent with what the Australian High Court has said about s 116 of the *Australian Constitution*. It is also arguably consistent with what the US Courts have been saying about the free exercise of religion under the First Amendment since the decision in *Employment Division v Smith* in 1991. In Part III, I shall therefore discuss that overall consistency against my suggestion that the *ICCPR* requires a broader objective approach and the more general jurisprudential idea that human rights guarantees should be interpreted generously so that minority interests are not sacrificed on the altar of inchoate majoritarian security demands.

PART III – BALANCING IN A MANNER CONSISTENT WITH THE RULE OF LAW

The first time the US Supreme Court adjudicated the meaning of the Free Exercise clause in their First Amendment was in *Reynolds v US* in 1879.[58] In that case, the Court held that while the polygamist being prosecuted was entitled to freedom of belief and opinion under the clause, the First Amendment did not prevent the federal government from passing laws that criminalised his religious practice. That narrow view was varied beginning with the Warren Court in the 1960s until 1990. During that period, the Supreme Court held that the State could not interfere with religious practice unless it had a compelling reason to do so and there was no less intrusive way to achieve its otherwise legitimate goals.[59] But in its decision in

---

57   *Vijaya Kumar s/o Rajendran et all v Attorney-General* [2015] SGHC 244.
58   *Reynolds v US* 98 US (8 Otto) 145 (1878).
59   For example, see *Sherbert v Werner* 374 US 398 (1963) where the Supreme Court overturned a State law which denied unemployment benefits denied to a Seventh Day Adventist woman who would not work on Saturdays, and *Wisconsin v Yoder* 406 US 205 (1972) where the Supreme Court held that the State's interest in educating Amish children was outweighed by their parents' religious wish to continue their education after the 8th grade outside the state school system.

Employment Division v Smith in 1990,[60] the Court returned most of the way to the *Reynolds* decision in 1879 when it found once again that the application of a neutral law of general applicability did not offend the Free Exercise clause. Religious speech gets more space than religious manifestation in the US since US jurisprudence arguably protects freedom of speech more than any other country in the world. However, even freedom of speech is under threat from the logic that was used by US federal District Court Judge Vaughan Walker in his decision in the *Schwartzenegger* decision referred to above in Part I.[61]

In Australia, there was no 'Warren court' period where the High Court was generous towards the free exercise of religion. Indeed, there have only been two cases where the free exercise of religion clause was considered closely by the Court,[62] and in one, it was interpreted so narrowly that a conscientious objector still had to do his military service. Some commentators have described the High Court's treatment of the conscientious objector's argument as dismissive.[63] Certainly 70 years later in the *Church of the New Faith* case,[64] the High Court's treatment seemed more respectful towards freedom of religion since religion itself was given a broad ecumenical definition. In that case, the Church of Scientology was

---

60　　*Employment Division v Smith* 494 US 872 (1990) where the State of Oregon was allowed to deny unemployment benefits to an employee dismissed for smoking peyote in Native American Church services because the law was not targeted at that religious observance.

61　　See n 28 and related text.

62　　In *Krygger v Williams* (1912) 15 CLR 366 the High Court denied that an adherent of the Jehovah's Witness faith was denied free exercise of religion by being compelled to undergo compulsory military training; and in *Adelaide Company of Jehovah's Witnesses Inc v Commonwealth (Jehovah's Witnesses Case)* (1943) 67 CLR 116, the High Court denied that regulations passed to disestablish the Jehovah's Witness church in South Australia interfered with the free exercise of religion though the regulations were struck down on other grounds.

63　　Blackshield and Williams (*Australian Constitutional Law & Theory*, Federation Press, 6th ed., 2014, 1174) say that Griffith CJ and Barton J "impatiently dismissed the suggestion that s 116 was infringed" in the appeal in *Krygger* (above n 62) and that their "grudging approach in *Krygger* was reinforced in the *Adelaide Company of Jehovah's Witnesses* case in 1943 (ibid).

64　　*Church of The New Faith v Commissioner of Pay-Roll Tax (Vic)* (1983) 154 CLR 120.

as entitled to the same exemption from Victorian state payroll taxes as any other church that believed in a supreme being or principle and adhered to a code of conduct as part of its religious practice. But the breadth of the Court's definition of religion did not signal a marked change since the concession that some civil liberty flowed from s 116 in the *Stolen Generations* case was as crowded with qualifications as ever.[65] In the *Stolen Generations* case, the High Court held that the Northern Territory laws in question did not offend s 116 because they had not been passed with the intention of prohibiting the free exercise of religion and, in any event there had not been sufficient evidence at the trial to prove such interference anyway.

To summarise – despite the pretense that the US and Australia respect the rule of law where the free exercise of religion is concerned, the evidence suggests otherwise if Article 18 of the *ICCPR* is accepted as the gold standard. Though two Australian High Court judges have confirmed that grants of human liberty are to be interpreted generously[66] so that the free exercise clause in s 116 of the *Australian Constitution* could have been read consistently with Article 18 and without implied limitations, to date the High Court has always found implied limits on the free exercise of religion even though those limits do not appear in the text of the *Constitution*.

Arguably, the US Supreme Court settled in a similar place when they found that a neutral law of general applicability did not offend their Free Exercise clause in *Employment Division v Smith* in 1990. That means that Chief Justice Yong's decision in *Chan Hiang Leng Colin v PP* in 1994 was consistent with the enduring jurisprudence of freedom of religion in Australia and in the US. It also means that all three sets of jurisprudence are inconsistent with the standard of freedom of religion set out in Article 18 of the *ICCPR*.

---

65   *Kruger v Commonwealth (Stolen Generations Case)* (1997) 190 CLR 1.
66   Barwick CJ and Murphy J in *DOGS case* (1981) 146 CLR 559 (per Barwick CJ at 577, and per Murphy J at 622 and 632-634).

In the words of Chief Justice Yong, the discord concerns how religious manifestation and expression can be legitimately restrained. His finding again was that "religious beliefs and practices which tend to run counter to [the security of the country] had to be restrained."[67] The US Supreme Court has found that the government may restrain religious practice by any neutral law that did not single out the religious practice in question for attention.

Paraphrasing the language of Justice Rich of the Australian High Court in 1943, the Australian position remains that religious practice can be lawfully restrained to prevent the "cloak[ing of]...subversive opinions or practices and operations dangerous to the common weal".[68] In contrast, Article 18 of the *ICCPR* says that the freedom to manifest religion including in speech, may only be limited by law when that law is objectively "necessary to protect public safety, order, health, or morals or the fundamental rights and freedoms of others."[69] The difference is the *ICCPR's* necessity requirement. Even if one argues that 'necessity' does not need to be interpreted objectively, it has to mean more than that the government just has to be reasonable when it interferes with religious freedom.

In Singapore beliefs and practices may be restrained by law whether that restraint is necessary or not. Though the Appellant's 'clear and present danger to national security' submission in *Chan Hiang Leng Colin v PP* may have suggested a bar higher than the necessity standard in the *ICCPR*, the Court's finding that religious practice or expression which runs counter to an undefined requirement of national security, falls below the standard expressed in the *ICCPR* and undermines freedom generally. The same conclusion follows an analysis of the US and Australian jurisprudence. In the US, the idea that a neutral law that is generally applicable trumps any

---

67   Above n 47.
68   *Adelaide Company of Jehovah's Witnesses Inc v Commonwealth (Jehovah's Witnesses Case)* (1943) 67 CLR 116, 149-150.
69   Article 18(3).

manifestation of religious liberty, neuters the *ICCPR* standard on two counts. First, it does not limit state intrusion into religious practice or expression to matters of "public safety, order, health, or morals or the fundamental rights and freedoms of others"; and secondly, it does not impose the necessity requirement under Article 18(3) of the *ICCPR*. The only legislation that is forbidden to the state in the US under the Supreme Court's interpretation of the Free Exercise clause in *Employment Division v Smith,* is legislation that directly targets religious practice. It is difficult to accept that the US framers would have considered that finding protected the church from the state at all as seems to have been the original intent.

In Australia, Rich J's statement that "opinions or practices subversive of the common weal" may be legitimately restrained, may be worse because it is so pregnant with subjectivity and because it anticipates the regulation of mere opinion which is non-derogable under all of the international human rights instruments. The additional subjectivity problem in Rich J's formulation, is that it denies the existence of a fixed religious freedom standard in Australian constitutional law. The purpose of the *ICCPR's* necessity limitation standard on the other hand, is to insist that freedom of conscience, belief and religion are foundational and may not be challenged on the basis that they are "subversive of the common weal" without formal proof. Rich J's analysis and the apparent unwillingness of the High Court to accept that s 116 at least implied a fixed religious freedom standard, is a part of the reason why Keith Mason has suggested that the section has become "a dead letter"[70] reflecting the views of Murphy J in the *DOGS* case,[71] though for different reasons.

But what of the argument that nations which have not ratified or domesticated the norms of international law do not become subject to them? Does this contractual idea that obligation requires privity,

---

70   Keith Mason, *Constancy and Change: Moral and Religious Values in the Australian Legal System,* Federation Press, 1990, 118.

71   *DOGS case* (1981) 146 CLR 559, 631 [38].

apply in international law, or as in tort law, can obligation end-run an intention to create legal relations? There are of course arguments that run both ways in answer to this question and some of the answers appear to reflect the agenda of the responder. That is, those who wish to assert the independence of their state, will assert that sovereignty is trumps while those who aspire to an enforceable world order will assert the contrary. The United States' Supreme Court for example, ruled in 1957 that the *Constitution* superceded even international treaties which it had ratified.[72] But US commentators since have been divided on whether the consequential US reservations practice enhances the human rights project domestically or internationally.[73] Singapore has avoided that contest by declining to ratify the *ICCPR* at all and officially takes the view that her signature of the *UDHR* and ratification of the *International Covenant on Cultural Economic and Social Rights* is enough to prove that she is both committed to the rule of law and the human rights project generally.[74] But other Singaporean views suggest that human rights are a continuing manifestation of western imperialism and do not resonate with Asian

---

72   *Reid v Covert* 354 US 1 (1957).

73   For example, Kristina Ash ("U.S.Reservations to the International Covenant on Civil and Political Rights: Credibility Maximization and Global Influence", *Northwestern Journal of International Rights*, Volume 3, Issue 1, Article 7 (Spring 2005)), Jack Goldsmith ("The Unexceptional U.S. Human Rights RUDs", *University of St. Thomas Law Journal*, Volume 3, Issue 2, Article 8 (Fall 2005), and Madeleine Morris ("Few Reservations about Reservations", *Chicago Journal of International Law*, Volume 1, Issue 2, 341 (Fall 2000) have all argued that genuine reservations enhance U.S. credibility in international human rights discourse because the U.S. has such a committed record to domestic and international human rights. But Kenneth Ross, the Director of Human Rights Watch, is diametrically opposed and characterizes U.S. international treaty ratification as a charade because its ratification method is designed "to preclude the treaty from having any domestic effect" reflecting fear and arrogance—fear that international standards might constrain the unfettered latitude of the global superpower, and arrogance in the convictions that that United States, with its long and proud record of domestic rights protections, has nothing to learn on this subject from the rest of the world ("The Charade of US Ratification of International Human Rights Treaties", *Chicago Journal of International Law*, Volume 1, Issue 2, 341 (Fall 2000), 347).

74   See for example, the 2001 statement by Zainul Abidin Rasheed, Senior Parliamentary Secretary for Foreign Affairs at the World Conference Against Racism, Racial Discrimination, Xenophobia and Related Intolerance in Durban South Africa (<http://www.un.org/WCAR/statements/singE.htm>).

values.[75] Regardless of which view is taken of Singapore's continued avoidance of ratification of the *ICCPR*, there is no doubt that the twin covenants were designed and intended to take the principles of the *UDHR* (including the freedom of conscience, belief and religion there expressed) to full international law status regardless of whether those covenants were ratified by every nation and rendered legally enforceable by a supranational judicial body in a utopian future. The fact that both covenants have been formally ratified and even domesticated in the vast majority of nations, morally undermines denials of their customary international law status regardless of their origin even without international enforcement.[76]

CONCLUSION

And so I conclude that the protection intended for the free exercise of religion in the *ICCPR*, does not yet exist in the United States, Australia or Singapore. While all three countries provide a measure of protection for the free exercise of religion under their

---

75   See generally *Asian Discourses of Rule of Law*, Randall Peerenboom (Routledge Taylor Francis Group, London 2004), but more particularly Li-ann Thio's chapter where she discusses whether the emphasis on communitarian values and government collective goals, reduce human rights to state grants rather than inalienable entitlements and whether emphasis on Singaporean values repudiates the common law's protective philosophy towards human dignity or enables it. Note also the Think Centre's 2011 view that Singapore has obligations to more fully implement human rights under the *UDHR* notwithstanding its status as a 'mere declaration' in some eyes (Hongbin Sheng, "Does Singapore abide by any international laws such as Universal Declaration of Human Rights?" <https://www.quora.com/Does-Singapore-abide-by-any-international-laws-such-as-Universal-Declaration-of-Human-Rights>) since Singapore has been a member of the United Nations since 1965 and the *UDHR* "is accepted globally as customary international law" (<http://lib.ohchr.org/HRBodies/UPR/Documents/session11/SG/TC_ThinkCentre-eng.pdf>).

76   See for example, Gillian Triggs, *International Law: Contemporary Principles and Practices*, LexisNexis Butterworths, Australia, 2006, [14.4 – 14.6] where she states that "[i]n many respects, [the UDHR] has come to represent customary law" (para 14.4) and that "the International Law Association and juristic commentators... confirms that many of the provisions of the [UDHR] and the ICCPR constitute custom and are treated as such by national and international tribunals" (para 14.6). But she has also said these "general statements about the customary status of human rights provision are unsatisfactory, because it is necessary to 'prove' the customary rule in each instance" (para 14.6).

constitutions, in each case that protection allows the governments to abrogate that freedom any time they choose to do so. All of these countries theoretically have the legislative power to pass laws that provide the protection intended for the free exercise of religion under the *ICCPR*. In the US, the reason for the decision not to pass such legislation would appear to be that it seems futile after the Supreme Court struck down the last attempt to create such protection in *City of Boerne v Flores* even though Congress had unanimously passed the *Religious Freedom Restoration Act 1993*.[77] Republican President Donald Trump restoration of a conservative majority to the Supreme Court, may encourage better legislative protection of free exercise of religion in the future even if it does not lead to a significant change in US Supreme Court religious freedom jurisprudence.

In Australia, better protection of religious freedom is a matter of political willpower. Despite recommendations from the Human Rights and Equal Opportunity Commission in 1998 that such legislation is necessary,[78] members of the Commonwealth Parliament always fear that such legislation will see them lose their seats at the next election. Until the 2018 general election, that was because religious freedom legislation would protect the unpopular Muslim minority and might also protect Christian interests above those of the gay and lesbian lobby that recently achieved the legalization of same sex marriage. But the unlikely election victory of Scott Morrison suggests that a small window had opened which might allow bi-partisan cooperation in creating a truly *ICCPR*-kosher Australian religious freedom law. Whether that window has remained opened during the Australian government's management of COVID-19 crisis remains to be seen.

---

77   *City of Boerne v Flores* 521 US 507 (1997) where the *Religious Freedom Restoration Act 1993* was passed to reinstate the compelling interest test which was struck down by the Supreme Court in *Employment Division v Smith* in 1990, was itself struck down.

78   *Article 18, Freedom of religion and belief*, Human Rights and Equal Opportunity Commission, Australia, 1998.

In Singapore, the government does not want to increase free exercise protection because it does not want to protect religious extremists who potentially threaten the nation's security.

All three countries have practical reasons not to improve the protection of religious freedom in a manner that accords with *ICCPR* standards even though they have the power to pass laws that accord with the *ICCPR*, but to date, they have lacked the faith to do so. If these three western nations cannot manifest faith in *ICCPR* standards and international law in general, there seems little hope for other countries where the dictates of personal liberty make human rights protection more essential.

BIBLIOGRAPHY

Articles

Zainul Abidin, "2001 Statement at the World Conference Against Racism, Racial Discrimination, Xenophobia and Related Intolerance in Durban South Africa" (<http://www.un.org/WCAR/statements/singE.htm>).

Kristina Ash, "U.S.Reservations to the International Covenant on Civil and Political Rights: Credibility Maximization and Global Influence", *Northwestern Journal of International Rights*, Volume 3, Issue 1, Article 7 (Spring 2005).

Paul Babie, "National Security and the Free Exercise Guarantee of Section 116: Time for a Judicial Interpretive Update" (2017) 45 *Federal Law Review* 351.

Andrew Denton, "National Press Club Speech", August 10, 2016 (<https://dwdnsw.org.au/wp-content/uploads/2016/08/NATIONAL-PRESS-CLUB-speech-by-denton-100816.pdf>) reported in *The Australian* on the same date.

Jack Goldsmith, "The Unexceptional U.S. Human Rights RUDs", *University of St. Thomas Law Journal*, Volume 3, Issue 2, Article 8 (Fall 2005).

Martin Krygier, "The Rule of Law: Pasts, Presents, and Two Possible Futures", *Annual Review of Law and Social Science*, 12 (2016) 199.

Madeleine Morris, "Few Reservations about Reservations", *Chicago Journal of International Law*, Volume 1, Issue 2, 341 (Fall 2000).

Kenneth Ross, "The Charade of US Ratification of International Human Rights Treaties", *Chicago Journal of International Law*, Volume 1, Issue 2, 341 (Fall 2000).

Brett Scharffs, "Why Religious Freedom? Why the Religious Committed, the Religiously Indifferent and Those Hostile to Religion Should Care" (<https://ssrn.com/abstract=2911086>).

Hongbin Sheng, "Does Singapore abide by any international laws such as Universal Declaration of Human Rights?" < https://www.quora.com/ Does-Singapore-abide-by-any-international-laws-such-as-Universal-Declaration-of-Human-Rights>).

Li-ann Thio, "Rule of Law within a Nonliberal 'Communitarian' Democracy: The Singapore Experience" chapter 6 in *Asian Discourses of Rule of Law*, (Routledge Taylor Francis Group, 2004).

Keith Thompson, "Should 'public reason' developed under US establishment clause jurisprudence apply to Australia?", (2015) 17 *UNDALR*, Article 6, 107-134 (<http://researchonline.nd.edu.au/undalr/vol17/iss1/6/>).

Book Chapters

John Rawls, 'The Idea of Public Reason Revisited' in John Rawls, *The Law of Peoples* (Harvard University Press, 1999).

Books

Joshua Forrester, Lorraine Finlay and Augusto Zimmerman, *No Offence Intended: Why 18C is wrong*, (Connor Court Publishing, 2016).

Keith Mason, *Constancy and Change: Moral and Religious Values in the Australian Legal System,* (Federation Press, 1990).

Randall Peerenboom ed., *Asian Discourses of Rule of Law*, (Routledge Taylor Francis Group, 2004).

Martha Nussbaum, *Liberty of Conscience,* Basic Books, New York (2008).

John Rawls, *A Theory of Justice* (Harvard University Press, 1971).

John Rawls, *Political Liberalism* (Columbia University Press, 1993).

Gillian Triggs, *International Law: Contemporary Principles and Practices,* (LexisNexis Butterworths, 2006).

George Williams, Sean Brennan and Andrew Lynch, *Blackshield and Williams Australian Constitutional Law &* Theory, (Federation Press, 6th ed., 2014).

Cases

Australia

Adelaide Company of Jehovah's Witnesses Inc v Commonwealth (Jehovah's Witnesses Case) (1943) 67 CLR 116.

Attorney-General (Vic); Ex rel Black v Commonwealth ('DOGS case') (1981) 146 CLR 559.

Australian Capital Television Pty Ltd v Commonwealth (1992) 177 CLR 106.

Catch the Fires Ministry Inc v Islamic Council of Victoria [2006] VSCA 284.

Christian Youth Camps Limited & Ors v Cobaw Community Health Services Limited & Ors [2014] VSCA 75.

Church of The New Faith v Commissioner of Pay-Roll Tax (Vic) (1983) 154 CLR 120.

Coleman v Power (2004) 220 CLR 1.

Electrolux Home Products Pty Ltd v Australian Workers' Union (2004) 221 CLR 309.

Hozack v Church of Jesus Christ of Latter-day Saints (1997) 79 FCR 441.

International Finance Trust Company v New South Wales Crime Commission (2009) 261 ALR 220.

K-Generation Pty Ltd v Liquor Licensing Court (2009) 237 CLR 501.

Koowarta v Bjelke-Petersen (1982) 153 CLR 168.

Kruger & Ors v Commonwealth of Australia (Stolen Generations Case) (1997) 190 CLR 1.

Krygger v Williams (1912) 15 CLR 366.

Lange v Australian Broadcasting Corporation (1997) 189 CLR 520.

McCloy v NSW (2015) 325 ALR 15.

Nationwide News Pty Ltd v Wills (1992) 177 CLR 1.

Toben v Jones (2003) 199 ALR 1.

Victoria v Commonwealth (Industrial Relations Act Case) (1996) 187 CLR 416.

European Union

Handyside v United Kingdom 5493/72; (1976) 1 EHRR 737; [1976] ECHR 5.

Kokkinakis v Greece 14307/88; [1991] 17 EHRR 397; [1993] ECHR 20.

Malaysia

Tan Boon Liat v Menteri Hal Ehwal Dalam Negeri, Malaysia [1976] 2 MLJ 83.

Singapore

Chan Hiang Leng Colin v PP [1994] SGHC 207; [1994] 3 SLR (R) 209.

Nappalli Peter Williams v Institute of Technical Education [1999] 2 SLR 569.

Vijaya Kumar s/o Rajendran et all v Attorney-General [2015] SGHC 244.

United States

City of Boerne v Flores 521 US 507 (1997).

Employment Division v Smith 494 US 872 (1990).

Perry v Schwarzenegger Case No. C 09-2292 VRW (US District Court for the
    Northern District of California, 4 August 2010).

Reid v Covert 354 US 1 (1957).

Reynolds v US 98 US (8 Otto) 145 (1878).

Sherbert v Werner 374 US 398 (1963).

West Virginia State Board of Education v Barnette et al 319 US 624 (1943).

Wisconsin v Yoder 406 US 205 (1972).

Government Documents and Reports

Australian Department of Foreign Affairs and Trade, "Reservations and
    Declaration" in relation to Australia's ratification of the *International
    Covenant and Civil and Political Rights* on 13 November 1980 (<http://
    www.austlii.edu.au/au/other/dfat/treaties/1980/23.html>).

Human Rights and Equal Opportunity Commission, *Article 18, Freedom of religion and belief*, (Australian Human Rights and Equal Opportunity Commission, 1998).

Legislation

Australian Constitution.

Religious Freedom Restoration Act 1993 (US).

Singapore Constitution.

United States Constitution.

Newspaper articles

The Australian, August 10, 2016 (Report of National Press Club Speech by Andrew Denton about Euthanasia).

Treaties

European Convention on Human Rights (1950).

International Covenant on Civil and Political Rights (1966).

About our contributors

Neil Foster is an Associate Professor at Newcastle Law School in the University of Newcastle, Australia. He teaches, researches and publishes in the areas of torts, workplace health and safety law, and law and religion. He was previously a federal public servant and worked briefly with a Christian NGO in Pakistan. He blogs at https://lawandreligionaustralia.blog .

Jonathan Powys is an Adjunct Research Associate at the Sydney School of Law of The University of Notre Dame Australia. Born and raised in Sydney Australia, Jonathan currently practices as a Senior Lawyer in the areas of commercial and property law, and also assists a number of not-for-profit agencies.

Alana Anne Rafter is an Associate to the Hon Justice Michael Walton at the Supreme Court of New South Wales. She is also the Vice Chair of the NSW Young Lawyers Public Law and Government Committee and a Young Lawyer Representative on The Law Society of NSW Public Law Committee. Prior to her position at the Supreme Court, she worked in property law and volunteered at Legal Aid NSW.

Gil Marvel Tabucanon is an Adjunct Senior Lecturer at the Sydney School of Law of The University of Notre Dame Australia, and teaches Dispute Management and Resolution courses at Macquarie Law School, Macquarie University. He writes poetry, is listed in World's Lawyer Poets and is working on a book translating Emily Dickinson's poems into Cebuano, a language spoken in Central Philippines.

A. Keith Thompson is a Professor and Associate Dean at the Sydney School of Law of The University of Notre Dame Australia. He previously worked as International Legal Counsel for The Church of Jesus Christ of Latter-day Saints through the Pacific and African continent and as a partner in a commercial law firm in Auckland, New Zealand.

Index